TEILHARD DE CHARDIN ON LOVE

Teilhard
de Chardin
on Love

Evolving Human Relationships

Louis M. Savary and Patricia H. Berne
Foreword by Ilia Delio

Paulist Press
New York / Mahwah, NJ

Cover image by ScrappinStacy / Bigstock.com
Cover and book design by Lynn Else

Library of Congress Cataloging-in-Publication Data

Names: Savary, Louis M., author. | Berne, Patricia H., author.
Title: Teilhard de Chardin on love : evolving human relationships / Louis M. Savary and Patricia H. Berne ; foreword by Ilia Delio.
Description: New York ; Mahwah, NJ : Paulist Press, 2017. | Includes index.
Identifiers: LCCN 2016026700 (print) | LCCN 2016038607 (ebook) | ISBN 9780809153220 (pbk. : alk. paper) | ISBN 9781587686634 (Ebook)
Subjects: LCSH: Teilhard de Chardin, Pierre. | Love. | Interpersonal relations. | Love—Religious aspects—Christianity. | Interpersonal relations—Religious aspects—Christianity.
Classification: LCC B2430.T374 S275 2017 (print) | LCC B2430.T374 (ebook) | DDC 177/.7092—dc23
LC record available at https://lccn.loc.gov/2016026700

ISBN 978-0-8091-5322-0 (paperback)
ISBN 978-1-58768-663-4 (e-book)

Published by Paulist Press
997 Macarthur Boulevard
Mahwah, New Jersey 07430

www.paulistpress.com

Printed and bound in the
United States of America

The day will come when,
after harnessing space, winds, the tide and gravitation,
we shall harness for God the energies of love.
And, on that day,
for the second time in the history of the world,
man will have discovered fire.[1]

—*Pierre Teilhard de Chardin, SJ*

Contents

Foreword

IN THE MIDDLE AGES, the great scholastic theologians debated whether God's essence was being or goodness. The Dominican school, following Thomas Aquinas, argued for essential being while the Franciscan school, following Bonaventure, claimed that God was essentially good. The import of this debate was far-reaching, since understanding the nature of God influenced everything from how God acted to the role of God in creation and human destiny. One of the major questions in the thirteenth century centered on the nature of God: Did God create according to divine will or divine freedom? The Franciscan school, in particular, placed the emphasis on divine will, since in the New Testament God is revealed as good: "No one is good but God alone" (Luke 18:19). Medieval scholars defined love as the highest good, since love goes out of itself toward another for the sake of the other. Love is what God is, as we read in the New Testament: God *is* love (1 John 4:8, emphasis mine). The emphasis on love marked Franciscan theology, as well as the theology of the Victorines and Cistercians, who preceded the Franciscans and influenced them. Bernard of Clairvaux taught that love and knowledge were intertwined, *amor ipse notitia est*, and his teaching was influential on the School of Chartres, where the Canons of St. Victor developed a sophisticated understanding of cosmology, theology, and the mechanical arts along the lines of the platonic cosmos and the essential role of love.

Love fell off the radar with the rise of modern science and took a turn for the worse in the modern age. The history of modernity and the rise of modern philosophy can be interpreted as the death of love in the cosmos. Modern knowledge was based on the turn to the subject and the power of knowledge. Love turned inward and became associated with feelings and the emotional life while knowledge was expressed in the will to power. However, in the twentieth century, Pierre Teilhard de

Chardin, a Jesuit scientist, was not convinced by the modern project. As a paleontologist, he recognized a deep power of attraction within nature that imparted a dynamic impulse of transcendence to nature. This deep power of attraction, he noted, is present in the smallest of molecules but cannot be readily distinguished. Whereas the medievalists thought of love as the highest good (based on the platonic cosmology of their age), Teilhard conceived of love as the fundamental energy of attraction that bore with it a radial energy of transcending consciousness. "Love is the most universal, the most tremendous and the most mysterious of the cosmic forces,"[1] he wrote. "The *physical* structure of the universe is love."[2] Because love is the fundamental energy of life, he developed a doctrine of "love-energy" that underlined his philosophy and metaphysics of the future. Love-energy is the history of the universe, present from the Big Bang onward, though indistinguishable from molecular forces. "But even among the molecules," he wrote, "love was the building power that worked against entropy, and under its attraction the elements groped their way towards union."[3] Love draws together and unites; in uniting, it differentiates. Love is the core energy of evolution.

Taking a position highly consonant with Franciscan theology, Teilhard began to develop a philosophy of love. His ideas are closely related to the fourteenth-century Franciscan theologian, Duns Scotus, who wrote on univocity, individuation, and the primacy of Christ, all grounded in a core doctrine of love. Teilhard's ideas take their immediate impetus, however, from modern physics where relativity, mass-energy equivalence, and wave-particle duality gave him a new understanding of nature and the inherent interconnectivity of nature. Reflecting on the primacy of love-energy in evolution, he wrote that union precedes being because love is the core energy of evolution and love is intrinsically relational: "What comes first in the world for our thought is not 'being' but 'the union which produces this being.'"[4] Teilhard's philosophy of love is thoroughly consonant with our interconnected universe, as science now understands it. He emphasized union-in-love as core constitutive existence. To be is to be self-gift. Isolated existences, even on the molecular level, "give themselves up" for greater union. Hence, unitive being is relational and always toward *more being*. On the level of evolution, Teilhard claimed, life is constantly directed toward more life and ultimately toward a future fullness of life, or better yet, a future fullness of unity in love.

Foreword

The implications of Teilhard's philosophy of love are enormous for evolving life because how we understand nature, creation, humanity, and God impacts our values and choices. Lou Savary and Patricia Berne have provided a valuable contribution in this book by clearly explaining Teilhard's doctrine of love on every level of life, from God to friendship, marriage, parenting, and human community. Their book is less a scholarly exposition on a Teilhardian doctrine of love than a masterful illumination of love as the core energy of evolving life. Each chapter clearly explains Teilhard's insights and then provides practical ways of incorporating these ideas into daily life. I think Teilhard would have been very pleased with this book because he struggled throughout his life to make his ideas clear and cogent. Lou and Patricia have followed Teilhard's dream—to make known to the world the power of love.

Love is the energy that can transform the darkness of our age into the light of hope by empowering us to work toward a future fullness of life together. How we love is how we live, and who we love shapes our relationships, communities, our connection to the Earth, and the future of the Earth. We are, in the most basic sense, the sum of our loves. Teilhard's philosophy of love borne out in the evolution of God, self, and future Earth is a vital doctrine for our time. It awakens us to the essential goodness at the heart of all life and kindles within us the desire to work toward a more unified world. We are born out of love, we exist in love, and we are created for the fullness of love. It is time to change our focus from knowledge to love, letting go of the need for power and control and recognizing our intrinsic need for others. Lou and Patricia's book invites us to shift our horizon of life, for in the evening of life we will be judged on love alone.

Ilia Delio

Preface

FOR MANY YEARS, we—Louis, a theologian, and Patricia, a psychologist—have been studying the writings of the Jesuit Pierre Teilhard de Chardin (1881–1955). As we pondered the significance of his insights about evolution, science, and religion, we were amazed at how he had integrated these three important fields for our times and for the future of humanity. We have been chewing on and digesting his ideas over many decades with the intent of making them easier for others to assimilate and practice, especially for those who find his writings difficult to understand.

Few people realize how important and powerful Teilhard's ideas are for today, or the breadth of their usefulness. When clearly articulated, they provide a powerful resource to help bring about personal growth, a deepening of relationships, and world peace.

In teaching graduate courses on Teilhard's spirituality, our students struggled to grasp the value of his ideas for their personal lives. They challenged us to turn his ideas and insights into meaningful practices and attitudes for contemporary believers. That task was not easy, since many of our students—and both of us—were brought up and bred in a spirituality that separated itself from the discoveries of modern science. Most certainly in our youth, we were taught to be suspicious of the theory of evolution.

In contrast, early in the twentieth century, Teilhard, a Roman Catholic Jesuit priest, was professionally involved in both science and evolution as a geologist and paleontologist. For him, evolution has been the most dynamic process operating throughout the universe in its multibillion year history. As he saw it, evolution is the force that continues to drive forward all fields of life today, from astronomy to technology, from physiology to psychology, including morality, philosophy, religion, and theology.

For Teilhard the theologian, this evolutionary process had to have been initiated by God at the first moment of creation, at what scientists call the Big Bang. Applying his scientific perspective to theology, Teilhard realized that God had not created a cosmos that, after seven divine days, was finished, complete, fixed, and unchanging. Rather, God set in motion a universe of elementary particles that has been constantly evolving and continues to evolve and develop.

God created this evolving universe because God is Love and each of us is God's gift to the world. Our life purpose is to make a difference in transforming that world. It may take much of this book to explain those last statements.

Absorbing Teilhard's evolutionary ideas and applying them to spirituality required a revolutionary shift in our personal thinking—a genuine metanoia. Another tremendous challenge for us was finding spiritual practices to facilitate that shift in others.

Our intent in this book is to open the door specifically into Teilhard's ideas on the evolution of love and relationships. Many of his ideas may feel surprisingly new, as they did to us when we first encountered them, such as the potential of friendships and marriage to move evolution forward.

To start looking at the world from an evolutionary perspective, as Teilhard says, people need to think of love in a new way. When people hear the word *love*, most of us spontaneously evoke a variety of images—people feeling strong affection, warm attachment, familial bonding, friendship, mutual commitment, sexual desire, tenderness, or devotion.

In contrast, Teilhard always thinks of love in all its many forms primarily as energy—as the ability to do work. Love is energy because it is able to accomplish things, make a difference, transform people. Almost everyone agrees that people—and the world—have been changed by people loving and by being loved. It is the energy of love inside each of us that makes us want to make a positive difference in our world. Unless you grasp this connection between love and energy, you will miss Teilhard's most basic insights about the nature of love. For him, love is the driving force of evolution. It logically follows, then, that love must be the core of spirituality and the motive for all spiritual practices.

So, our first task in this book will be to present these Teilhardian ideas on love simply and clearly. The second is to offer throughout the book some practical suggestions for turning these ideas into spiritual practices that provide fresh perspectives on living daily life. For Teilhard, love, like thinking, continues to evolve. Love is progressing in full growth mode on Earth now. There is no stopping it, and we are called to be fully involved in fostering love's development. We are called to learn how to practice evolutionary love.

A significant part of our challenge is to bring Teilhard's ideas, many of them developed by him almost a hundred years ago, to people who are well into the twenty-first century. Teilhard died on Easter Sunday in New York City in 1955, well over half a century ago. His writings, most of which were completed during the first half of the twentieth century, do not integrate many of the advances made since then that are so familiar to us. Humanity has grown and evolved in a variety of ways since his death. It is hard for most of us to grasp what life was like for someone like Teilhard who was born in 1881 and died in 1955.

There was so much Teilhard never got to see or experience. In medicine, for example, Teilhard in his lifetime knew little or nothing of organ transplants, hip replacements, arthroscopic surgery, in vitro fertilization, CT and PET scans, laser surgery, modern pharmaceuticals, bones and organs created on a 3-D printer, or the kinds of computer-driven artificial hands, arms, and legs that are common today.

In biology, Teilhard died before the human genome was mapped—or the human biome. He never lived to see genetic engineering, cloning, test-tube babies, or science experiments carried out in a space station orbiting high above Earth.

Even in Teilhard's fields of expertise, geology and paleontology, he knew little of plate tectonics or continental drift and nothing of aeromagnetic surveying, electron microscopes, gas spectrometry, or the more recent discoveries tracing the pathways of early human migration.

In the world of energy, he never heard of solar panels, wind turbines, nuclear electrical plants, driverless cars, or artificial intelligence.

In psychology, he never heard of the human potential movement, transpersonal psychology, or a psychology of consciousness.

In communication, Teilhard could never have imagined a sky full of orbiting communication satellites. He never took a photo with a smartphone, found his way to a restaurant using a GPS system in a car, looked at a computer screen, or paid for a purchase with a computer chip imbedded in a plastic credit card. He never used a photocopy machine, let alone a 3-D printer. He never had the joy of doing research on Google, sending instant emails to friends abroad, tapping text messages on an iPhone, or maintaining a Facebook page with photos.

In travel, he never rode on a jet plane or saw a human land on the moon, looked at photos of spiral nebulae taken by the Hubble telescope in space, or dreamed of starting a human community on Mars.

He never saw a *Star Wars* movie, warmed coffee in a microwave oven, watched color television, or Skyped with someone on the other side of the planet.

Today, with our smartphones, computerized cars, and sophisticated medicines, we might tend to think we know a lot more than Teilhard ever did. He might challenge the depth of our human development by asking, "How much more does this generation know about the power of love to transform the world than the generation before it? Or the last fifty generations before it?"

I suspect an honest answer to his challenge would be, "Very little." In the quotation that began this book, Teilhard wisely observed that our generation has made great strides in mastering the forces of tides, winds, the sun, and space, but little growth in mastering the forces of love.

Teilhard might say that today we can no more grasp what forces will be released in love's potential in ages to come than the cave man sitting by his fire could grasp how this same fire would one day drive the steam engine and start the Industrial Revolution.

We might say that Teilhard did envision a far richer future potential of fire. Except the "flames" he was looking at came from the fire of love. He was always the visionary, encouraging us to explore the power of love. We hope in this book to take some practical baby steps in this exploration.

Although Teilhard in his evolutionary spirit encourages us to explore new ways of loving, he would never for a moment ask us to stop expressing those signs of love that have been essential to human life from its beginnings: showing kindness and gratitude toward one another; being slow to anger and quick to forgive; always thankful; ever patient; sharing goods generously; showing care and concern for children and the defenseless, and compassion for the sick, the lonely, and the grieving; seeking justice for the powerless, the forgotten, the outcasts, the marginalized; welcoming the traveler, the refugee, and the newcomer. These are the many basic expressions of love that richly nourish and nurture our planet every day. We cannot live without them, as we cannot live without the air we breathe. These gestures, however, only begin to tap the evolutionary power of love that is still hidden from the eyes of most of us.

If Teilhard had lived into our twenty-first century, he would delightedly have watched evolution happening in all these many scientific and technological fields. He would also have evolved in his thinking and expectations along with the rest of us. So, our challenge was to write this book in the spirit of Teilhard, as if he were alive and writing to us today aware of all the evolutionary changes that have happened since his time on Earth.

Finally, Teilhard remained a faithful and devout Catholic throughout his life. Thus, he expresses some of his evolutionary insights in Catholic theological language and imagery based on the New Testament. To use any other theological language would be unfaithful to Teilhard and to his vision. While some readers may not share his theology and imagery, they can easily adapt his powerful insights about love into their own ways of thinking.

We could not have written this book without all the helpful comments and challenges of friends, students, and colleagues over the past forty years, especially those whose lives manifested for us the kinds of love Teilhard talks about. Nor could we have written this book if it were not for the publishers, especially HarperCollins and Harcourt Brace Jovanovich, who trusted that Teilhard's works translated into English would make a powerful contribution to the growth and development of the human family. More recently, we want to acknowledge the scores of helpful suggestions of Robert Mason, Clare Crawford-Mason, and Patricia Collins, who reviewed our manuscript line by line. Thanks also go to Susie Timchek, a current theology student, who read the chapters from an academic as well as a personal perspective. As always, we thank for their guidance Paul McMahon and the other editors at Paulist Press who continue to believe in the value of spreading Teilhard's message to an ever-wider audience.

May Teilhard bring you fresh understanding of the transformative power of love that rests in your hands and heart, and may his insights enrich your perspective on the meaning of love and its pivotal place in an evolving cosmos.

Introduction

IT HAS BEEN DOUBLY challenging to assemble this book. First, it was our responsibility to our readers to take Teilhard's ideas about love scattered throughout his many books and essays, and put them into some kind of order and organization.

Second, we had to realize that if Teilhard were alive today, he would have integrated not only the theological ideas he had during his lifetime but also those insights shaped by the innovative scientific thinking that has evolved since his death in 1955. These fields include physics, astronomy, biology, medicine, technology, psychology, and other social sciences. Teilhard's thought would have been influenced also by the breakthroughs, since his death, that have occurred in communication, transportation, politics, and global awareness as well as theology. Please be forewarned, then, that "in the spirit of Teilhard," you will encounter in these pages various ideas, theories, and facts spoken or written by people who lived *after* Teilhard but whose thinking was *in his spirit*.

The book is divided into two major sections, Theory and Practice. The Theory section is sprinkled with suggestions for ways to practice Teilhard's ideas, while the Practice section is sprinkled with theoretical ideas, some from Teilhard and some from other people.

Our aim is always to make Teilhard's ideas easy to understand, without diluting their power and potential.

Chapter 1 clarifies Teilhard's unique perspective on love as the most powerful force in the world.

Chapter 2 describes *the most important relationship between a God whose name is Love and God's vision for creation in its many ongoing evolutionary processes.* We have named the fulfillment or completion of these processes "God's project."[1] It is a divine love project. Teilhard sees love's power as central not only to God's life and human life, but also to all creation. Most importantly, he sees love as providing the motivational force driving all evolutionary processes toward their fulfillment.

In chapter 3, Teilhard reveals his unique perspective on love. He views love not only emotionally, as we so often use the word in our daily conversations, but rather as "source of energy." He asserts that physicists have no exclusive claim on sources of energy. If they define energy as "the ability to do work," Teilhard says, love does more work and gets more work done on this planet than all the other physical energy sources put together. He feels we should learn to study love-energy scientifically. Unfortunately, he does not show us how to do it. He leaves such research to others.

Chapter 4 explores how love attracts and brings things together into what Teilhard calls, in French, *unions*. Since *union* in English typically calls to mind an assembly of workers fighting for their rights, we prefer to use more generic terms like *connections* or *relationships*. Connections happen at all levels of existence. Relationships happen at the atomic level, at the molecular level, at the biological level, at the animal level, and at the human level. What Teilhard realized is that each of these connections has a life of its own, with qualities, capacities, and properties of its own. Human connections, or *unions*—like marriages, friendships, and teams—can even have a personality of their own. Connections generate new life, new being, and new personality.

In chapter 5, Teilhard shows us how human relationships created by love bring out the very best in the individuals involved in a relationship. For example, it is only in relationships that individuals discover potentials and possibilities within themselves that they never realized they possessed. If it were not for their involvement in these loving connections, they would probably never have identified and developed these capacities.

With these theoretical ideas clarified, the book shifts from Theory to Practice. Teilhard wants to show how to apply his ideas about love-energy in the relationships people encounter every day—marriage, family, friendships, teams, and larger groups. He wants to *give these familiar relationships an evolutionary thrust, so that they can help further God's work.*

In chapter 6, Teilhard explores a higher spiritual path for committed partners, whether the partners are married couples or deep friendships. Paradoxically, he uses the concept of "chastity" to develop his evolutionary approach. It is paradoxical because chastity is traditionally seen as a virtue belonging primarily to consecrated religious life and the Catholic priesthood. Instead, he is applying it—in an evolutionary way—to married life. In his approach, Teilhard does not equate chastity with avoiding sex and choosing not to get married (that is, celibacy). Rather, he sees chastity as a virtue primarily of the heart or spirit—rather than of the body—since it is measured by the purity and single-mindedness of a couple's loving commitment to doing God's work in the world.

Chapter 7 develops Teilhard's idea that the more humanly mature—or ripe—a person is, the more that person can grow and evolve spiritually and the more that person can contribute to God's project.

Chapter 8 shows how spiritual maturity involves individuals integrating into their lives and personalities the best of both masculine and feminine qualities. In this way, they enrich their consciousness and become more fully human.

Chapter 9 explores the parent-child relationship as the setting for evoking powerful evolutionary potential during a child's early days of growth and development. The parent-child relationship is one that Teilhard seldom spoke of. However, what some contemporary psychologists have discovered in this regard would have fascinated him. The quality of parent-child bonding proves to be most essential in the development of a child's ability to evolve in love-ability.

In chapter 10, Teilhard talks about the evolutionary potentials of friendships. It offers examples of friends who have made a positive difference in the world. We encourage readers to recall friendships, famous or not, that have helped the human race to mature.

Chapter 11 develops the special kind of love that happens in teams of people who are working to make the world a better place. Teilhard shows the powerful dynamics of teamwork and team spirit. He wants us to discover and participate in teams, many of them hidden or unnoticed, that are helping the world to evolve.

Chapter 12 assembles the beginnings of a theology based on a God who is not only merciful and forgiving, but a *God whose very nature is Love*. It shows how an unconditionally loving God invites us to be creative and inventive in finding ways to help complete God's project. With God and in Christ, as Teilhard might say, we are helping turn all creation into one loving union, where everyone becomes fully conscious of the greatness to which we have been called.

Chapter 13, "Omega-Love," attempts to gather some of Teilhard's ideas about what life might be like when God's project for creation has been completed and creation has reached what Teilhard called its Omega Point. In traditional theology, we would say that these are some of Teilhard's ideas about life in heaven with God and enjoying the company of all those who have lived on Earth and contributed to God's project.

By the way, although our text contains many notes, it is not necessary to check them whenever they occur. You may simply disregard them as you read, as they are almost always references to places in Teilhard's or other's writings that inspired and support our text. However, if you want to explore further a certain Teilhard idea or insight, the citations are readily available.

PART ONE
THEORY

CHAPTER 1

Teilhard's Perspective on Love

PIERRE TEILHARD DE CHARDIN asserted that love is the most powerful force in the universe. Yet he never wrote a book about love or even an essay with the word *love* in its title.[1] This is not to say that Teilhard is silent on the topic of love. In fact, it appears in many of his writings and lies at the heart of his vision for humanity.

For Teilhard, "love is the most universal, the most tremendous and the most mysterious of the cosmic forces."[2] Love is both human and divine. Divine love is the energy that brought the universe into being and binds it together. Human love is whatever energy we use to help divine love achieve its purpose.

Or, more fully, *human love is the energy that drives whatever we do to keep ourselves and our world growing together in unity and peace.* This definition of love includes everything from giving a smile to the checkout person at the supermarket, to adopting an abandoned pet, to setting up a recycling program in a neighborhood, to defending an innocent person being wrongly accused of a crime, to negotiating a peace accord between nations, or discovering a cure for cancer. Whatever helps bring about healing, wholeness, compassion, creativity, and care for our world is an act of love. It is using the energy of love to make a positive difference.

Every day, we encounter family members, friends, classmates, colleagues, salespeople, strangers, and enemies. The way we respond to each person and each event that happens to us can be important. Each encounter provides an opportunity to show love and grow in love. If Teilhard were a schoolteacher, he might say that by being born you are automatically enrolled in a lifelong course on learning how to love.

For Teilhard, love explains who God is and the reason God created the universe. The universe is God's ongoing self-revelation to us. Thanks to modern science, we are slowly learning how to read and interpret this cosmic drama and discover what God is revealing to us about God's self.

Because of this insight, Teilhard, for the first time, shows how we can begin to see more clearly the reason we human beings are on Earth. We are here as an integral part of this great journey of life. We have not been born simply to endure suffering, avoid sin, live in fear, and earn a passing grade to enter heaven. We are here to learn the many ways of loving—kindness, compassion, tenderness, forgiveness, consolation, inspiration, patience, humor, beauty, friendship, creativity, and so on. Those are the loving ways God acts toward us. We learn to use many expressions of love in order to help transform the face of the Earth in different ways.

Our local congregation has many ministries, each of which uses different ways of showing love. For example, one ministry group feeds the poor, another delivers school supplies to migrant workers' children, another counsels anxious and depressed people, another helps those who have lost jobs to prepare for new ones, another provides shelter for victims of human trafficking, and so on. These are just a few ways love is being shown.

Transforming the face of our world was God's purpose in creating it. God's love for creation explains the purpose driving an evolving universe. For Teilhard, love is the energy that integrates for us the creative work of three powerful forces: *modern science*, *evolution*, and *religion*.

Teilhard was looking for the real energy behind the forward movement of humanity and the enrichment of human life brought about through *modern science* and technology. For him, the deepest drive behind this incredible development of human welfare is not greed or might, killing or domination, fear or terror. Rather, it is the power of love living inside each of us. He believed that it was always the generative energies of love that brought about these positive transformations in health, education, art, human rights, law, scientific research, communication, transportation, and safety. That is Teilhard's big awareness.

He is informing us that the most powerful energy we hold in our hands and hearts is our ability to cherish, value, and delight in things, to be passionately concerned and involved, to be enraptured and enchanted by life, and to desire to release our creative potential to make our world a better place. For so long, people have ignored the fundamental truth that *learning to love is what our human life is all about*, because they have forgotten that love is what God is all about.

Love is also the force driving *evolution*. God's ongoing creation is an outpouring of a love that remains unconditional. Each moment, God continues to create from within this all-embracing love. God implanted a law of love in every element of nature. That seed of love germinates and blossoms at every stage of creation, from subatomic particles in a continuous evolutionary movement all the way to human beings. God's spirit continues to imbue us with attractiveness and the desire to bond with one another, to love and be loved. God's evolutionary vision of the world is that we will all one day come to love one another. In this great union of love, we will truly recognize who we were meant to be, and we will realize that love is the only way to personal and universal fulfillment.

For Teilhard, "love is a sacred reserve of energy; it is like the blood of spiritual evolution."[3] For him, the best way of describing the evolution of life on Earth "would undoubtedly be to trace the evolution of love."[4]

Love of God and love of one another lies at the core of every traditional *religion*. Love not only permeates those religions, it transcends them and binds them together. Divine love embraces everyone and everything. There is nothing outside the divine embrace.

When we look at the world through the eyes of love, it helps us to grow in consciousness and enter more fully into the wonderfully complex mystery of our lives. Love energy helps us to open our eyes and see things more clearly and positively. Teilhard invites us to view this mystery of love and life from a new perspective, from the perspective that *God is love and that we were made for love*. Love is what moves us and changes our world for the better.

Although the essential quality of love energy may be invisible and formless in itself, we can easily apprehend it by evidence of its presence and the force it exerts in and around us physically, emotionally, cognitively, and personally.

From Teilhard's perspective, then, *helping the human family move toward the next step of human evolution in love is the most urgent and challenging task of contemporary spirituality*. This is his perspective; this is our challenge.

Let's step into Teilhard's love perspective and begin to reenvision God and the world as he saw them.

God's Creative Love Energy in All of Us

First, for Teilhard, love, following John the Evangelist, is the essential nature of God, and the best name for God (see 1 John 4:8). As Teilhard envisioned it, divine love is the self-expressive creative force that gave birth to our evolving universe.[5] It is that same divine love that continuously keeps every atom of creation existing and moving forward on its grand evolutionary journey back to God.[6] From the beginning, the successful accomplishment of this grand journey of the cosmos has always been God's purpose and vision.[7]

For Teilhard as a theologian, it was for the love of all created beings that God the Father sent his Son into the world that we might learn of God's love for us and show us how to live "The Way" of love (see John 3:16–17). For him, it was Christ above all who taught us how we can work together to further the forward movement of God's vision for us.[8]

According to Teilhard, God has implanted a divine spark of love in everything created, down to every last subatomic particle and photon of light. For Teilhard, God does not intrude into our lives from the outside, but works from *within*, not by control but by stimulation and enrichment.[9] So, all existing matter, each living thing, and each human person has a divine spark of love inside us urging us to express that love by connecting with others in love.[10] That spark in each of us waits to be cultivated and developed until it matures.

This is not some new idea; it is found in the prophetic Scriptures. "I will put my law within them, and I will write it on their hearts; and I will be their God, and they shall be my people. No longer shall they teach one another, or say to each other, 'Know the LORD,' for they shall all know me, from the least of them to the greatest, says the LORD" (Jer 31:33–34).

Only as our consciousness continues to ripen and mature will we truly begin to realize what the energy of love is capable of accomplishing and how we can make a positive difference in what God is doing in the world. For Teilhard, as for Jesus, our main task of spiritual growth involves learning new ways to nurture those divine sparks of love in ourselves and in others.

Jesus came to show us that there was a new and more all-inclusive way of loving that was unconditional, what the early Christians called *agape* love. It was a kind of loving that embraced enemies as well as friends and family. God the Creator is an *agape* lover, Jesus said, so he wanted his followers to learn to love everyone the way God loves.[11] God's love is universal and all-encompassing, full of forgiveness and hope. Jesus realized that learning to love the way God loves would be a difficult task for human beings, and that most people were not ready or spiritually mature enough to love in this unconditional way. But he got the process started.

Teilhard, studying the human race over many thousands of years, realized that humanity was indeed learning to evolve in love. And once enough people began living with *agape* love, it would create a revolution like no other revolution. In time, such all-embracing love would bring about true freedom, true peace, and true harmony on Earth.

Teilhard points out that once we accept that God loves the created universe unconditionally, it suggests a "radical reinterpretation of the notion of charity (*agape*)." In the older tradition, we said, in effect, "Thou shalt love God and thou shalt love thy neighbor for the love of God." In an evolutionary perspective, we would now say, "Thou shalt love God in and through the genesis of the universe and of mankind." This new perspective provides us with "an unparalleled field of application and power to make new."[12]

Regarding human relationships, we all know stories about the power of love, how love can turn lives around. There is no area of life where the seeds of loving and caring cannot be planted. There are thousands of ways we can show love to one another.

For example, on our street there is a little girl who, on her way to her neighborhood elementary school each day, picks up the sidewalk litter that others have thoughtlessly dropped. She collects it in a bag and drops it in the school's waste receptacle, carefully washing her hands afterward. She loves our neighborhood and wants to keep it beautiful.

Another neighbor volunteers at an animal shelter; another tutors students who need extra academic help; another volunteers at the hospital's gift shop. These are three more ways of showing love.

Many famous men's lives were totally changed by connecting with the women they fell in love with and married, which enabled them to help the larger human family to grow. John Adams, one of the founders of our nation and its second president, was transformed by the deep love of his wife, Abigail. Adams helped shape the early covenants that the United States made with European nations.

Despite his other romantic liaisons, much of Franklin Delano Roosevelt's political insights and ways of helping the poor and unemployed and rebuilding American society came from his devoted wife, Eleanor.

Coretta Scott King provided the loving energy that gave Martin Luther King Jr. the strength to persevere in the civil rights movement. Using the strength they developed together, she continued on in the movement after his death.

Before Mark Twain, whose real name was Samuel Clemens, joined his beloved Olivia in marriage, he was a cynically humorous lecturer, a party-going man who delighted in singing ribald songs. After his union with Olivia, he was able to write his two greatest books on social justice, *The Adventures of Tom Sawyer* and *The Adventures of Huckleberry Finn*, both subtly powerful novels about racial inequality in the United States. Thanks to Olivia, he also developed a fondness for singing religious hymns.

F. Scott Fitzgerald drew much of his inspiration from his beloved wife, Zelda, when writing his iconic novels *The Great Gatsby* and *Tender Is the Night*, revealing the emptiness and frivolity of high society.

British literary giant and poet G. K. Chesterton left a life of drinking and carousing when he met Frances, the woman who would become his wife. Only after deeply connecting with her was he able to write his most powerful stories and poetry.

James Joyce, whose works *Ulysses* and *Finnegan's Wake* transformed the literary genre of the novel, was himself transformed by love for his wife, Nora. He turned his life around, from an aimless life of drinking and debauchery to one of dedication to his art. Their love for each other was so powerful that they never wanted to be apart. Twice when Nora had to be hospitalized, James Joyce insisted that he be allowed to sleep in her hospital room in a bed next to her. Years later, when James was hospitalized, Nora insisted she have a bed next to his. Such is the power of Attraction and Connection between men and women.

In Teilhard's thinking, love's power of transforming the lives of these famous couples through Attraction and Connection pervades all existing reality. Those forces are available to everyone. For Teilhard, the universality of Attraction and Connection are natural laws that have been affecting everything in the universe from the first moment of creation.[13]

Author Matthew Kelly describes the discovery of his ability to show unconditional love:

> Before I became a father, I thought I knew something about the love God the Father has for me. Then my son Walter was born. I found myself constantly yearning to be with him. He couldn't walk or talk. All he did was eat, and sleep, and need his diaper changed. But I loved being with him.
>
> Over the years, that hasn't changed. As my wife and I have had more children, I yearn to be with each of them in the same way. I love my children so much it's crazy, really. And before I had them I just didn't understand. But as I began to think about this great love I have for my children, the love of God took on a whole new meaning. Because if I can love my children as much as I do, and I am broken and wounded and flawed and limited, imagine how much God loves us. This thought was overwhelming to me and took my relationship with God to the next level.[14]

After each subheading throughout the book, suggestions for reflection are offered as a way of stimulating the reader to personally connect with the ideas presented.

SPIRITUAL PRACTICE: TRANSFORMED BY LOVE'S ENERGY

Teilhard wants us always to think of love as *energy*. Unless people grasp this connection between love and energy, they will miss his most basic insights about the nature of love. Love is energy because it is able to accomplish things, make a difference, and change people. Think of people you know whose lives have been changed by being loved—or showing love. How did love do its "work" in them?

Attraction: The Primal Love Force

Attraction is the most fundamental and primal expression of the love-force, and it leads to the most fundamental process: making and building Connections. As Teilhard put it, "The hidden existence and eventual release of forces of attraction between men...are as powerful in their own way as nuclear energy appears to be."[15]

Without attraction, there would be little or no union, especially what Teilhard calls center-to-center unions, or unions of hearts. Love is supremely important to Teilhard, because he realized that love, which begins with Attraction and Connection, is the energy that is most capable of fostering God's work in the world. "Mankind will only find and shape itself if men can learn to love one another in the very act of drawing closer."[16]

Teilhard's insights about Attraction and Connection hold true not only for attractions and connections among human beings, but also at every level of existence, from the subatomic level in the formation of atoms and molecules to the great attractive forces of gravity in solar systems, holding moons, planets, and stars connected in their graceful orbits. The forces of Attraction and Connection were operating for many billions of years before our solar system and Earth came into existence.[17]

Attraction and Connection, says Teilhard, are the most commonly observable events happening on Earth and in the universe. He recognized this inherent force of attraction operating everywhere and at every level in the cosmos. As Teilhard scholar Ilia Delio notes,

> He was impressed by the levels of attraction in nature whereby elements unite center to center, leading to more being and consciousness. Teilhard called this fundamental force of attraction "love energy" because it is the primordial energy of union by which new complex entities emerge. Love-energy undergirds the process of attraction between particular entities in the openness toward greater union and is present from the Big Bang onward, though indistinguishable from molecular forces.[18]

Earth did evolve and eventually produced self-reflective human beings like all of us. Those same forces of Attraction and Connection are still operating in everyone. As Teilhard says, "God is continually breathing new being into us." God does not do this by creating from nothing but by transforming what already exists....This creative transformative action of God is imperceptible to us.[19]

Among people, says Teilhard, this force of Attraction is the start of what we call "love," understood in its widest meaning.[20] Among people, the process of Connection is what we call building friendships, marriages, families, teams, and other forms of caring, interpersonal unions. This is a book about such Connections and their evolutionary potential.

Teilhard would certainly be aware that, according to Christian theology, the three persons of the Holy Trinity manifest and model for us, in divine nature, a loving interpersonal union. Inevitably, some of his insights about love and relationship stem from this Trinitarian theology. The Trinity of Divine Persons manifests "the essential capacity of God's inherent capacity to be the personal...summit of a universe which is in process of personalization."[21] For example, St. Augustine developed metaphors to describe the Trinity of Divine Persons. One relational metaphor is Father as Lover, Son as Beloved, and Holy Spirit as the Love that flows between them and outward.[22]

SPIRITUAL PRACTICE: ATTRACTION AND CONNECTION

Think of the people and kinds of work you are attracted to and to which you are connected. Can you identify how the drive of Attraction works in you? What qualities of others attract you to them? What qualities of work or hobbies attract you to them? As you name them, realize they are the way God's laws of love work in you.

The Most Urgent and Challenging Task

From Teilhard's perspective, if we are to master love's dynamics, then helping the human family move toward the next step of human evolution in love is the most urgent and challenging task of contemporary life. In his view, releasing the power of love, which is the most potent force on Earth, becomes the primary focus of spiritual practice.[23] There are some who have developed skills in using the energies of love—love of God and love of neighbor. But they are not in the majority. For the greater part of humanity, to master love's full potential may take centuries. After all, it took a million years for human beings to master the full potential of fire.

We know from archeology that pre-humans (before *homo sapiens*) had begun to use fire intentionally more than a million years ago.

That discovery was a major step in evolution, for it enabled these cave dwellers (who may have been the first species to begin developing self-reflective consciousness) to cook food, stay warm, and ward off enemies. Making fire also allowed them to be active in the cold and darker hours of the night. For hundreds of thousands of years, our prehistoric ancestors' ability to manage and use fire remained simple—warming, cooking, and lighting. Even human beings (*homo sapiens*) never really began to develop true mastery over fire until about a million years later. This occurred in the late eighteenth century with the invention of the internal combustion engine that enabled the industrial revolution.[24]

If one were to make an analogy, one might say that our ability to manage and use the forces of love today is about as sophisticated as the cave dwellers' ability to manage fire.

According to Teilhard, until we human beings begin to master the dynamics of loving, as we have mastered so many other forces of nature, like fire, winds, ocean currents, and solar power, we will not really evolve as a human species.[25]

Yet Teilhard sees love already evolving in many ways. Prophetically, he seems to see it happening before his eyes. He says that love "is so much alive that at this very moment we can directly observe it undergoing an extraordinary mutation."[26] Human beings are becoming ever-more conscious of the universal value and transformative energy of love.

In contrast to physical forms of energy that tend to wear down (according to the Second Law of Thermodynamics in physics), Teilhard calls love "a second species of energy (not electro-thermodynamic but spiritual)" that can continue to grow in its power and force.[27]

Teilhard, like St. Paul, showed a genius when it came to prophetic insights about the laws and functions of love's power in the grand evolutionary scheme. What Teilhard didn't do very thoroughly was point out how to translate those insights into everyday behaviors and spiritual practices for people today.

We do know that Teilhard believed the next evolutionary step for humanity would be built on relationships.[28] We would evolve, he suggested, not only by inventing new kinds of relationships or connections (*unions* in French) but also by reenvisioning traditional relationships such as marriages, families, friendships, partnerships, workplaces, and sports.

For example, retired couples, instead of choosing a retirement simply full of fun and games, might choose as a couple to dedicate their lives to an important human rights cause or to join a group that serves the poor or homeless. Retired players on sports teams may offer to spend time helping inner-city kids play sports or visit hospitals serving children with cancer and other diseases. Office workers can band together to run programs to raise money for special causes, like funding safe housing for rescued victims of human trafficking. Professional friends may choose to volunteer for periods of time to work in third world countries to help rebuild their educational and economic structures. Teilhard believed traditional relationships, as their purpose got reenvisioned and revivified, would generate new Complexity in their lives and stretch them to new levels of Consciousness.

What we hope to do throughout this book is to offer a kind of primer for a spirituality of relationship that translates Teilhard's insights into practical applications that have the capacity to release love's evolutionary potential.

Our challenge is to show how Teilhard, if he were alive today and knowing what we know, might turn his insights into practical suggestions to help us take the next steps in mastering the energies of love.

SPIRITUAL PRACTICE:
PRACTICE THINKING FROM WITHIN LOVE

"Think! Think with all your power, with all your love, with all your loyalty." That was the advice of Jesuit author Emile Mersch whenever we reflect on the way God works. Because God is Love, to understand Love's mysteries we must learn to practice thinking from within love. Learning to reflect from within a loving framework is essential if we hope to have our thinking illumined by faith. Unless we love and let our thoughts be guided by that love, we cannot truly penetrate the divine mysteries, for divine mysteries are, above all, mysteries of love and union. This is important advice if we hope to understand Teilhard, who always thinks with love and from within love.

CHAPTER 2

God's Love Project

God's Project and God's Plan

IN CONTEMPORARY LANGUAGE, Teilhard might say that God has an evolutionary "project" for creation that God wants to accomplish. The word *project* refers to the *final goal* or outcome that God from the beginning envisioned for evolving creation. God wants creation to become fully conscious that it is imbued with divine love and living in that love. This final outcome is what Teilhard called "the Omega Point" and St. Paul called the *Pleroma*.

God also has a divine *plan or strategy for accomplishing this project*, that is, for reaching Omega or the *Pleroma*. God's plan involves the evolutionary power of love operating in physical matter. Love is not only central to God's *plan*, love also describes the essential characteristic of the final outcome of God's plan, namely, God's project.

"Is it not in itself a consolation and a source of strength," Teilhard explains, "to know that Life has an objective; and that the objective is a summit; and that this summit, toward which all our striving must be directed, can only be attained by our drawing together, all of us, more and more closely and in every sense—individually, socially, nationally and racially?"[1] It is an "immense organism we are constructing."[2]

It is important not to confuse Teilhard's notion of "God's plan" with traditional images of "predestination," where God somehow knows and controls every choice of every human being. Rather, for Teilhard, in our highly complex and continuingly evolving universe, billions of people are constantly interacting and making different and often conflicting free choices all at the same time. The way God's plan works is by nurturing within us the love-laws of Attraction and Connection. A loving God cannot be a God who totally controls everything.

We should acknowledge that Teilhard never called this great love experiment "God's project." We invented that name. The fact is he never really gave it a name other than the Omega Point. But we can tell he was searching for an acceptable name that people could grasp. Yet he never quite settled on one. For example, in the following sentence, Teilhard used four different vague expressions to describe what we are calling "God's project" and "God's plan." They are italicized here:

> …to the preparation and service of this *great thing* whose
> emergence is foreshadowed. The *work now in progress* in
> the universe, the *mysterious final issue* in which we are col-
> laborating, is that *'greater unit'* which must take precedence
> over everything, and to which everything must be sacrificed,
> if success is to be ours.[3]

God's project, then, as well as God's plan, or strategy for completing the project, are our expressions for what Teilhard is describing when he refers to this *great thing*, this *greater unit*, this *work now in progress*, and its *mysterious final issue in which we are collaborating*.

Scripturally, this divine project and plan is what Jesus calls the "kingdom of God" and "the kingdom of heaven." When you read Jesus' parables describing the "kingdom of God" and "the kingdom of heaven," Teilhard would have you think "the divine work now in progress" or, to use our expressions, "God's plan" or "God's project." Jesus was very clear about the ongoing nature of the divine project, when he said again and again, "The kingdom of heaven is at hand" (e.g., Mark 1:15 and Matt 3:2; 4:7; 10:7). The divine plan is already at work. Teilhard always wants to emphasize that the divine project or process is an actual and practical work in evolutionary progress, rather than a mere theological concept or spiritual vision.

The universe—and our planet Earth with the people on it—are the raw materials for God's project. God wants the human family to continue to mature and evolve in its ability to love and build a peaceful and loving unity among human beings and the rest of nature.

You will notice that the Lord's Prayer is an evolutionary prayer. It teaches us to look toward the future, when it says, "Your kingdom come. Your will be done, on earth…." God's project will not succeed merely by human beings avoiding sin. Rather it will succeed only by countless positive human choices and actions that help transform the world. The divine project will reach completion only when we are achieving what God is asking us to help accomplish on Earth, both individually and collectively.

Scripturally, this is what God asks of us: "You shall love the LORD your God with all your heart, and with all your soul, and with all your might" (Deut 6:5). Notice, in this commandment, God is not asking for our praise, thanksgiving, worship, sacrifice, or hymns. God asks only for our ongoing love as God's project progresses.

How can we show this love? We know that love is manifested more clearly in deeds than in words.[4] What better way to show our love than by helping God accomplish on Earth what God wants to happen here? And to do it with all our heart, soul, and strength.[5]

Mastery is called for in every art and science. So Teilhard reminds us that we are called by God to master the art of loving. Dabbling in it will not do. For Teilhard, only our mastery of love's dynamics of Attraction and Connection will provide enough impetus to the evolutionary process to keep it moving forward toward the complete fulfillment of all things in God. Love is the only force powerful enough to transform greed into generosity, selfishness into compassion, revenge into forgiveness, cowardice into courage, or prejudice into acceptance.

For Teilhard, love in us creates "certain inward necessities," which continue to live and move "in the most spiritual recesses of our being," and which "inexorably compel us to continue our forward progress."[6] From time to time, we see these love forces at work.

A few years ago in Charleston, South Carolina, an armed white man entered a church basement where nine black parishioners were in the midst of a bible study class. He shot and killed all nine. The families of the deceased could have labeled the murders an act of racial prejudice and could have sought revenge on the killer. Instead, their love of God inspired them to offer forgiveness to the gunman, an act that took great faith and courage. They had learned what it means to love and forgive as God loves and forgives. Only the mastery of love's dynamics will enable us to bring all humanity eventually into oneness of mind and heart.[7]

SPIRITUAL PRACTICE:
A TRANSFORMING ENERGY

From your own experience, can you recall examples of love transforming greed into generosity (like the story of Zacchaeus in Luke 19:1–10), selfishness into compassion, revenge into forgiveness (like the story from Charleston, South Carolina), cowardice into courage (the story of Joseph in Matt 1:18–25) or prejudice into acceptance (the story of the Good Samaritan in Luke 10:25–37)? As you revisit events like these in your own life, you will strengthen your grasp of connecting love with *energy*, and become more in tune with Teilhard's understanding of love.

A Long-Range View

Despite some evidence to the contrary, the innate power of love of God is at present manifesting itself in thousands of different ways worldwide as it continues to grow and evolve in us.

Two recent books gave us the confidence to make this assertion. First, Paul Hawken's *Blessed Unrest: How the Largest Movement in the World Came into Being and Why No One Saw It Coming*. Hawken describes "the growth of a worldwide movement that is determined to heal the wounds of the earth with the force of passion, dedication, and collective intelligence and wisdom." Hawken has logged over two million active groups, small and large, who are dedicated to making our world a better place. This is a phenomenon that transcends religion or nationality, and is unprecedented in human history. The second book is Arjuna Ardagh's *The Translucent Revolution: How People Just Like You Are Waking Up and Changing the World*. In it, Ardagh describes a phenomenon he calls "translucence"—how people worldwide are awakening and experiencing a deeper presence and purpose, a greater sense of joy in being of service, and a newfound selflessness and compassion.[8] Teilhard would have delighted in what these authors discovered about the transforming power of love.

Eventually, as Teilhard predicts, we will master the energies of love and find our way to God. God will not abandon his work. "I have loved you with an everlasting love; therefore I have continued my faithfulness to you. Again I will build you, and you shall be built, O virgin Israel!" (Jer 31:3–4).

For Teilhard, the goal of God's project is the full completion of creation in consciousness and love, what, as we noted earlier, he called the Omega Point and St. Paul called the *Pleroma*.[9]

However, in this great evolutionary adventure, Teilhard in his writings mostly offers us "big pictures," great vistas, the long-range view of God's love project. For example, if we were a sports team, we might say that Teilhard is primarily focused on winning the world pennant. His Omega Point describes what it will be like when our human team becomes the world champions.

Before our team today could ever hope to achieve that final goal, however, our team would have to win its league's division title, and its national title. More urgently, our team would have to win tonight's first game of the season.

So, while Teilhard focuses on the long-range, evolutionary goal of the divine project, it may be safe to say that we people in the twenty-first century are still playing our first game of the season. We are still learning the rules of God's love-process, still trying to grasp God's love-strategy, still trying to master the love game's playbook.

As we keep Teilhard's long-range view before our eyes, our current daily focus must be on learning the basic skills of the game. After all, for much of Christian history, people have not even been aware that there was a need for an evolutionary spirituality or that God had an evolutionary project going on, in which we human beings were intimately involved.

For Teilhard, loving is the most important spiritual force in God's plan, and we need a new spirituality and new spiritual practices to master loving. These must be based on a clear foundation of a Creator whose love is all-embracing and unconditional.

SPIRITUAL PRACTICE: A NEED FOR SOMETHING NEW

Can you remember the first time you became aware that there was a need for a new dimension in your spirituality or that God had a project going on for which you had some responsibility? What made you aware that certain religious attitudes just didn't work any longer? Where did you look for help?

The Evolutionary Law

Everything in this book is based on Teilhard's discovery of the evolutionary law, which we summarize as the Law of Attraction-Connection-Complexity-Consciousness.[10] This is the law that God implanted in every element of creation, from subatomic particles all the way to human beings. It is a law of love.

In simple language, according to this four-stage law of evolutionary love, everything in evolution begins with Attraction.

Attraction includes all those times and circumstances that bring people together—family, workplace, school, emergencies, chance meetings, and so on. Certain qualities attract us, such as caring, concern, charm, humor, need, and so many more.

Attractions lead to *Connections* (what Teilhard called, in French, *unions*). We all enjoy many Connections through family, friendships, sports teams, partnerships, at work, school, or church, and so on. Most of this book explores these first two stages of the evolutionary law. However, it is easy to see how the next two stages fall into place.

Connections add *Complexity* to your life; new personalities and attitudes to deal with, new time constraints in your daily schedule, and so on.

In turn, the third stage of Complexity challenges you to enlarge and enrich your *Consciousness*. You must find a way to deal with and integrate in your mind and heart all the new and different needs, wishes, wants, values, and other realities that others bring into relationships. The fourth stage of Consciousness is where you do this integration.

The four stages—Attraction-Connection-Complexity-Consciousness—repeat over and over throughout your life. They describe the pathway of love and growth in your life.

Teilhard recognized that this evolutionary law has a much wider application than just among human beings. The law of "love—that is to say, the affinity of being with being—is not peculiar to man. It is a general property of all life and as such it embraces, in its varieties and degrees, all the forms successively adopted by organized matter."[11]

Because God is Love, any law God makes must be a law of love. Therefore, this four-stage evolutionary law must also be a law of love. If so, the evolutionary law of Attraction-Connection-Complexity-

Consciousness is also the law of love that must be guiding and driving the divine plan to complete God's project.

We respond to that law not only by recognizing evolution and serving it, but also by "literally—and in a higher meaning of the word—*loving* it."[12] We are called to love the evolutionary process and the universe in which it is happening.

In the four-stage evolutionary law, it would be natural to focus our attention on the two final stages, Complexity and Consciousness. However, to do so would cause us to overlook Teilhard's profound insights on love and relationships that occur during the two earlier stages, Attraction and Connection.

Every element in the universe feels the tremendous power of Attraction and Connection, from the nuclear bonding in the smallest atoms to gravity's pull on planets, stars, and moons.[13] As human beings, we feel Attraction to bond with people and pets, flowers and trees, to eat certain foods and enjoy favorite forms of entertainment, to commit ourselves to scientific research, and to join sports teams.

The process of Attraction leading to Connection is so familiar to us in ordinary life that we tend to take it for granted. These refer to our smiles, our gestures of welcoming, our expressions of gratitude, our affirmations of others, our generous acts of forgiveness, or compassion for the sick, and so many more. Yet it is in these very ordinary Connections of daily life that we begin to feel the power of love. These early stages are very important in the evolutionary success of God's project. In exploring the deeper potentials of Attraction and Connection, Teilhard offers us insights into ways to develop spiritually.

For example, Teilhard's insights introduce us to a spirituality for *relationships* that builds upon but is quite different from a spirituality for *individuals*. Until at least the last part of the twentieth century, most spiritual practices over the past four hundred years were designed for the individual, for a *me-and-God spirituality*. In the next evolutionary step, our challenge will also be to design spiritual practices for *relationships* (as new entities distinct from the individuals that make them up). We need to design practices for a *we-and-God spirituality*. This includes spiritual practices for marriages, close friendships, and teams.

For example, to support and nurture deeply loving relationships, *physical presence* of the partners is essential, as with James Joyce demanding a bed next to his hospitalized wife. When physical presence is impossible, beloveds would write letters to each other, as John and Abigail Adams did when he spent years in Europe as a United States' ambassador. Exchanging of gifts is another way of continuing to express love for a partner. Forms of spiritual connecting, soul-to-soul, is another way lovers separated have described maintaining connection.[14]

It is tempting to think that we know all there is to know about marriage, friendship, and teamwork. Let's hear what Teilhard has to share with us about spiritual growth and what he sees as our most likely next step in human evolution.

SPIRITUAL PRACTICE: SPIRITUAL GROWTH

List two or three spiritual practices that you practice or used to practice that were designed for a "me-and-God spirituality." Can you name other spiritual practices that were designed for relationships or groups? How do both types serve you in your spiritual growth?

CHAPTER 3

Love as Energy

To UNDERSTAND TEILHARD'S insights about the nature of love, we must learn to think of love in a way different from its ordinary accepted meanings. When we hear the word *love*, most of us spontaneously think of feelings of affection, warm attachment, sexual desire, tenderness, delight, or devotion. In contrast, Teilhard sees love primarily as *energy*.

Here, Teilhard is calling for a radical shift—an evolutionary shift—in our understanding of and approach to love. He wants us no longer to focus on love as a sweet sentiment or even an overpowering emotion that we feel now and then. Rather, we are to view it as a steady *powerful energy source*. He tells us to think of love as something like fire or electricity, a powerful force with tremendous potential that we can learn to manage and direct. For example, if love were electricity, each of us would be like an electrical outlet in God's house, capable of providing energy for many different needs. Likewise, we learn to provide an outlet of love energy for many different situations—for people, animals, nature, research projects, our studies, and our work.

For Teilhard, love-energy not only drives and transforms our spiritual lives, but also underlies all the forces that drive scientific advancement and evolutionary progress.[1] Until we make this revolutionary shift from seeing love as a nice feeling to thinking of it as energy, we cannot begin to understand Teilhard's approach to spirituality, science, or evolution. Unless we re-perceive love as energy, we certainly can't understand how Teilhard sees God at work in the world. "He who wishes to share in this spirit," writes Teilhard, "must die and be reborn, to himself and to others." Teilhard describes this conversion process as not only intellectual, but as a complete change in one's fundamental values and way of acting. This spiritual conversion is individual, relational, social, and religious.[2]

People do not normally think of love as a form of energy. Certainly, most scientists don't. The study of energy has been typically the domain of physics and the other sciences, not a major concern in spirituality. But if God's project is essentially an evolutionary one driven by love, then love-as-energy, in Teilhard's eyes, takes on a totally new role.[3] It becomes the central focus in spirituality as well as a major focus in science. In fact, Teilhard is claiming that the most powerful and pervasive source of energy in the world is not gravity, electromagnetism, or nuclear forces, but love.[4]

Let's take a moment to consider Teilhard's approach to love as energy.

For the physicist, *energy* is defined as "the ability to do work, to accomplish something." When scientists think "energy," they picture things like factories, engines, motors, ovens, hammers, drills, pulleys, levers, acetylene torches, air pumps, and power lines. These things do work, they accomplish results. Thus, scientists would say that physical energy does physical work, like pushing, pulling, lifting, and so on. By the same definition, chemical energy does chemical work, like forming atoms, molecules, and other chemical substances. Biological energy does biological work, such as fostering growth, nutrition, reproduction, and so on.

Teilhard insists that love clearly fulfills the physicist's definition of *work*. Love as energy is the ability to do work. Love accomplishes things and makes a difference. For example, he observed that love in its many forms is the impetus that drives all the work that is good in the world—transformational writings and poetry, technological inventions, breakthroughs in science, advances in healthcare, exploration in the arts, organizations that care for the needs of the world, commitment to service of justice and equality, dedication and courage to do the dangerous job of peacekeeping. All are ultimately driven by love, in one form or another. Some do it out of love for God, others for love of country, others for love of science, others for love of beauty, others for love of humanity, and still others for love of nature. But they all do it out of love.

Martin Luther King Jr. and Ralph Abernathy, two young Southern black ministers met in Montgomery, Alabama, in 1954 and became close friends. In the years that followed, they did many things together—

preaching, praying, lobbying, and comforting the oppressed. "Ralph became my husband's best friend," wrote Coretta King. Their union was rooted in doing things together to bring about justice and racial equality.[5]

Many scientists have done their work and research out of love for humanity and for God. Theodosius Dobzhansky, a leading biologist of the twentieth century and a devout Eastern Orthodox Christian, dedicated his life to explorations in biology.[6]

Similarly committed to the exploration of God's purpose on Earth was another Christian, Dr. Francis Collins, head of the Human Genome Project working at the cutting edge of DNA study. His book on DNA is boldly titled *The Language of God*.[7]

Dr. Kazuo Murakami is one of the world's top geneticists and a devout Buddhist. As expressed in his book *The Divine Code of Life*, he lives and works to reveal the human potential waiting in our genes.[8]

SPIRITUAL EXERCISE: GOD'S WORK

Have you read books or articles or watched television shows that were about scientists expressing their faith in God? Did you feel a connection between their scientific work and God's work in the world? How were you affected by their work and their attitude toward it? Did it change your way of practicing your faith at all? If so, how?

Love is the Driver of Evolution

Despite love-energy's ubiquitous presence, even among top scientists, science itself is still excluding love-energy from its formal study and the systematization of the world's energy resources.[9] Science lists energy sources from fossil fuels, natural gases, tides, winds, solar, nuclear, and other physical sources, but no science textbook has ever listed love as an energy source. This omission is serious, for, as Teilhard points out, love is the most powerful force in all creation. Teilhard would have been delighted to know that Russian-American sociologist and Harvard professor Pitirim Sorokin (1889–1968) did agree with him about love needing to be studied scientifically as a power for positive social transformation.[10]

Teilhard would say that love is the driver of evolution. One has only to observe this love-force, he says, to recognize it as the unmentioned undercurrent propelling most expressions of human goodness and creativity throughout history. Love of beauty has driven history's great artists of the world to create paintings, statues, poetry, literature, music, and architecture. Love of knowledge has driven history's great thinkers, philosophers, theologians, scientists, mathematicians, historians, and writers. Love of freedom for human beings has driven statesmen throughout history to create political structures that would preserve human rights for all, especially the poor, homeless, forgotten, the undocumented, the politically persecuted, and so on. Love of what was possible—the potential future—has driven researchers, inventors, discoverers, and other kinds of explorers and pioneers to envision what was still unknown and bring it into reality. Love for human life has driven doctors and surgeons to find new ways to nurture healthy living, conquer deadly diseases, develop anesthetics, and find medicines to alleviate suffering and pain. Love of family, community, and nation has motivated those who fought in wars for the freedom of their loved ones and countrymen and women.

As almost anyone can attest, love is most often the energy behind countless everyday acts of mercy, compassion, commitment, creativity, charm, patience, forgiveness, selflessness, heroism, enthusiasm for life, and the willingness (of parents especially) to endure personal inconvenience, loss, and pain for the sake of another. *Love is the energy that drives whatever we do to keep ourselves and our world growing together in peace.*

Love, by its very nature, is outgoing. Therefore, *love is relational.* When I love, it is most often expressed toward another, someone other than myself, but never forgetting to love oneself. "Love your neighbor as yourself."

SPIRITUAL EXERCISE: LOVE'S PROPULSION

Can you verify in your own life how love has propelled you or someone you know to perform an expression of human goodness that has made a difference in someone's life?

St. Paul on the Energy of Love in Relationships

In St. Paul's paean to love in chapter 13 of his First Letter to the Corinthians, he lists some of the qualities of love found in relationships. Relationships provide the ways and situations where love most often spends its energy and achieves its good results. Paul writes,

> Love is patient; love is kind; love is not envious or boastful or arrogant or rude. It does not insist on its own way; it is not irritable or resentful; it does not rejoice in wrongdoing, but rejoices in the truth. It bears all things, believes all things, hopes all things, endures all things. Love never ends. (1 Cor 13:4–8)

Summarizing his list, Paul says that the three most powerful sources of energy in the world are faith, hope, and love. But "the greatest of these is love."

Love is the greatest for two reasons. First, faith and hope are finite, but love is infinite and everlasting; "Love never ends." Second, love is the essential quality of God. For John the Evangelist, God's very name and nature is Love. God's love is outgoing, as St. Paul says, "God's love has been poured into our hearts through the Holy Spirit that has been given to us" (Rom 5:5).

Thus, since love is by nature outgoing and cannot keep from expressing itself outside itself, the creation of the universe was undoubtedly an act of divine love and, therefore, the universe itself must be a living and evolving expression of divine love. It is natural to assume, then, that Teilhard's evolutionary law—the law of Attraction-Connection-Complexity-Consciousness—is also a law of love.

SPIRITUAL EXERCISE: ALSO A LAW OF LOVE

We will discuss this insight, that the four-stage law of evolution is also a law of love, later on in the book. But for now, can you begin to see how Attraction-Connection-Complexity-Consciousness is a law governing both the development of evolution and the development of love? This connection is crucially important to Teilhard as it unites science (including evolution) and theology.

A Book about Connection

Since this book is about Teilhard's insights into love and relationships, it shines a spotlight on the second stage of Teilhard's evolutionary law, Connection (or *Union*). Later chapters will discuss many different kinds of connections—marriages, parent-child relations, friendships, sports teams, clubs with a purpose beyond their members, research teams, and so on. Each of these kinds of relationships, based on love energy, can manifest evolutionary potential. Marriages, friendships, clubs, and teams can create ways to exert an influence for human development far beyond themselves. They do it by finding new ways of applying the energy of love waiting to be released in their relationships.

Since Teilhard's dream is to integrate evolution and spirituality, he is concerned with releasing the evolutionary potential in all forms of human relationships.[11] If God created a continually evolving universe driven by love, God wants us to keep evolving in our ability to create loving relationships and to build more and more Complexity and Consciousness into them. Teilhard hopes to sketch a spirituality for doing precisely that.

For many centuries, as we have noted, Christian spirituality has emphasized that achieving individual salvation is the primary purpose of life on Earth. For example, *The Spiritual Exercises* of St. Ignatius Loyola has been one of the major forces shaping Christian spirituality for more than four hundred years. Teilhard points out that Ignatius's Principle and Foundation statement upon which his *Spiritual Exercises* are based is a clear example of traditional individualized-salvation spirituality.[12] It begins,

> Man was created to praise, reverence and serve God our Lord and by means of this to save his soul. The other things on the face of the earth are created for him, to help him in working toward the end [i.e., saving his soul] for which he was created.[13]

27

Basically, this traditional spirituality is centered on avoiding sin and living a God-focused life by obeying the Ten Commandments. In a word, traditional spirituality emphasizes individual salvation.[14]

Teilhard wants to go beyond that individual-salvation emphasis. Because of his evolutionary understanding of what God is trying to accomplish on Earth (God's project), he thinks we must have a different—and larger—primary purpose for our lives than saving our individual soul. Rather, he believes we are called to foster the human race's evolution-in-love toward God as the primary purpose of life on Earth. Teilhard sees our life purpose focused on the human race and the human race's continual improvement in learning to love, which he sees as central to God's project for us who live on Earth.

What Teilhard proposes is "no longer simply a religion of individuals and of heaven, but a religion of mankind and of the earth—that is what we are looking for at this moment."[15] We need to learn to cherish the poor and forgotten, to delight in the development of children, enjoy nature, value our natural resources, be enchanted by art and music, delight in advancements of science, take pleasure in our own minds, and reverence the wisdom of others. This is what God wants of us.

Salvation is a word that, in its Aramaic roots, means "enjoying the fullness of life."[16] God wants the fullness of life (salvation) for everyone and everything, for all of creation, not just for this or that individual. In fact, the only way an individual can enjoy the fullness of life is in relationship to others. Love is of its nature relational.

SPIRITUAL EXERCISE: SALVATION'S MEANING

Have you ever thought of *salvation* as meaning "enjoying the fullness of life"? As you think about this perspective for the meaning of the word *salvation*, how does it shift your perception of the terms "individual salvation" or "saving my soul"? Is it possible to enjoy the fullness of life all by oneself?

The Salvation of Creation

Why would Teilhard want to insist on such a radical shift in our purpose for being created—from individual to collective? We who have been brought up on a spirituality of individual salvation find the shift

Teilhard is requesting here difficult to accept. For him, the shift seems quite logical and necessary. Here's how he would like you to proceed.

Teilhard asks you to accept two things: first, the fact that we and all of Earth's creatures are on an evolutionary journey together toward God, and second, that we human beings can make a difference in helping further God's divine plan.

Once you accept these two statements as true, the primary purpose of human life on our planet shifts from "saving my soul" to "using my life, my energy, my talents, and my resources to further the evolution of humanity in love." The shift in primacy in spirituality moves from "saving my soul" to "helping God's project succeed." We might say that, by dedicating my life to helping God's project succeed, I am saving my soul. I am helping bring about the fullness of life (salvation) for everyone and everything.

This shift in life-purpose will naturally shift the emphasis in the practices of spirituality from oneself to one's relationships. According to Teilhard, evolutionary advances in God's project in our day will likely become manifest first in human relationships. The focus of spiritual practice shifts from "me" to "us." It calls for a new Principle and Foundation to human life.

An evolutionary Principle and Foundation in Teilhard's spirit might be the following:

> You were created to make a unique contribution to the great evolutionary project initiated and continually supported by God, namely, bringing all creation together into one magnificent conscious loving union.
>
> Since all other created things in the universe share with you this common eternal destiny, they are essential to and inseparable from you as you participate in the pursuit of this ongoing evolutionary process.[17]

SPIRITUAL EXERCISE: A SHIFT IN FOCUS

What kinds of changes in your thinking and behavior would you (or anyone else) have to make in order to shift from a focus exclusively on your own soul's salvation to a focus on helping everyone enjoy the fullness of life?

A Comparison

It might be helpful to compare the basic principles, assumptions, or rules of traditional spirituality with those of Teilhard's evolutionary spirituality. One might summarize four basic assumptions of traditional spirituality—for example, using Ignatius's *Spiritual Exercises*:

- Spirituality is an individual issue.
- Its goal is my personal salvation.
- My life on Earth is primarily a test to see if I qualify for salvation.
- Sins of commission are a major concern, since the sins I commit could keep me from being saved.

In an evolutionary worldview, the assumptions of spirituality would appear quite new to most of us. One might summarize them as follows:

- Spirituality is practiced primarily within relationships.
- Its long-term goal is to transform (evolve) the world into the kingdom of God (God's project).
- The purpose of life on Earth for us, individually and collectively, is to responsibly contribute to that transformation (God's project) and keep it moving forward.
- Sins of omission are the major focus. The biggest concern is *not* to miss any chance to help the human family move consciously, compassionately, creatively, cohesively, and lovingly closer together.

SPIRITUAL EXERCISE: ASSUMPTIONS IN SPIRITUALITY

How ready are you to make the shift from traditional assumptions of spirituality to the ones Teilhard's thinking suggests? Do you find areas of resistance within you to the new assumptions? Which ones in particular do you find harder to accept? Intellectually? Emotionally?

A Focus on Relationships

For Teilhard, we evolve as individuals and as a community only in relationship. The four-stage divine law—Attraction-Connection-Complexity-Consciousness—impels us to seek others whom we find *attractive* (in the broadest sense of the word *Attraction*) and to form *connections* with them. For human beings, love is most easily recognized in the forces of Attraction and Connection.

At the Attraction stage, Teilhard is not talking merely about physical attractiveness, although he wouldn't exclude "good looks" or "good health" as evolutionary forces. Rather, when he talks about Attraction, he is talking about any quality we notice in others—a sense of humor, creativity, shared interests, a love of ideas, compassion, a certain inner joy, a common challenge, shared sorrow, and a hundred other things—that would draw us into a Connection with them.[18] Some people are attracted to new ideas or insights that lead to new ways of doing things. Others are attracted to challenges like finding a cure for cancer, exploring other planets, or searching the ocean floor for new species of life. These attractions lead to Connections with others who have similar interests.

These Connections will inevitably create Complexity in our lives. To deal successfully with new complexity, we need to enlarge and expand our Consciousness. Continual growth in consciousness will eventually teach us how to come together and converge in love as the human family.[19]

Humanity as a whole shows some hopeful signs of maturing in its ability to use the energies of love wisely. However, our many nations—and, sadly, many religions—are still moving forward slowly, in low gear, toward our shared destiny. One giant step will occur when peoples and nations have learned how to live and work together justly, in peace and love.[20]

At the same time, and in stark contrast to the slowness of humanity's maturing in love, science and technology are continually using the evolutionary law and evolving forward at full speed. We have become masters at evolutionary progress in everyday matters of concern, such as communication, transportation, space travel, information storage, housing, robotics, finance, and so on.

For example, less than fifty years ago, it took weeks for a message to get from the United States to, say, India. Today, I can send e-mail messages anywhere on Earth almost instantly or even enjoy face-to-face communication via computer with someone thousands of miles away.

At the beginning of the twentieth century, to cross the country from coast to coast could take a week or more by car and a few days by train. Today, we can fly from New York to Los Angeles in five hours. In 1950, no one believed human beings could send satellites into orbit in space. Today, we are planning to start a human community on Mars.

Fifty years ago, data storage was restricted to books and movie films in large canisters. Today, on a flash drive no larger than your thumb, you can store thousands of books, hundreds of recorded songs, and a Hollywood film or two. Theoretically, in a woman's purse full of flash drives you could carry almost all the scientific and artistic data that now exists on the planet.

In stark contrast, as a human family, we are still riddled with racial, religious, and ethnic prejudice. We still harbor jealousy and envy. Acts of murder and violence still occupy much reporting space in the daily newspaper. War is a common occurrence all over the planet. Domination of others is a predominant desire among people and nations.

Certainly as a nation, we Americans are self-centered and reluctant to forgive. While we profess to hate war, we are the world's largest manufacturer of military weapons, which we sell to other nations so that they can wage war. Poverty, hunger, and disease run rampant on every continent, and many powerful people care little about relieving this suffering unless there is a chance to make a profit from it.

Greed is still a predominantly admired quality. Money is still worshipped as a god. Research shows that 1 percent of the human beings alive today own 50 percent of all the wealth on Earth. Just picture that. In a group of a hundred people, this would mean that, if there were only two dollars to share, one person would possess one of those dollars while the other ninety-nine would have to split the other dollar, getting a penny apiece. We still have such a long way to go to achieve a human community of peace, forgiveness, compassion, equality, and true mutual concern!

Our centuries of individual-focused spirituality may have had something to do with this seemingly uncaring, unloving, selfish situation. In many ways, traditional spirituality has kept us focused on our individual salvation (personally enjoying the fullness of life) and made us blind to the social structures that are keeping millions poor, sick, and hungry (those who are *not* enjoying the fullness of life).

SPIRITUAL EXERCISE:
THE PRICE OF INDIVIDUAL LIBERTY

Teilhard feels that the extreme focus on individual liberty (and individual salvation) plus the pervasiveness of "social sins" such as racial, ethnic, religious, and sexual prejudices along with the worship of power, money, and domination are the biggest hindrances to the evolution of love among the human family. Why do you think he views an extreme focus on individual liberty as a hindrance to the evolution of love?

Cohesiveness — Coming Together

We use the word *evolution* to refer to positive forward movement, and the word *devolution* to indicate regressive backward movement. For example, television as a medium of communication is "evolutionary" because it is a tool that offers opportunities to move toward higher consciousness in journalism, education, and entertainment. However, television becomes "devolutionary" and pulls us backward when it is used to promote domination, greed, endless consumption, lying, violence, revenge, killing, and sex — just for the sake of "entertainment" or simply to titillate viewers.

In the evolutionary process, growth does not always move in a forward direction, especially among human beings. In European history, for example, one thinks of the Dark Ages and the two world wars of the twentieth century. During certain periods of history, as a human race, we have grown in maturity and wisdom. During other periods, we have reverted to immature behavior and acted unwisely.

One glaring example of immature madness in the mid-twentieth century was the arms race between the United States and the Soviet Union (USSR). For over twenty years, both nations were acting like rival teenage boys, creating and stockpiling nuclear weapons at a furious pace, competing to see who could generate the more potent arsenal. Both nations ended up with enough nuclear weapons to destroy our planet a dozen times over.

The same applies to the evolutionary process; sometimes the human race goes forward and at other times it regresses. Mostly, each age is a mixture of advances and retreats. Over time, because of divine love, forward and upward progress has prevailed.

For Teilhard, the universe is being guided and driven by the evolutionary law of love through the process of Attraction-Connection-Complexity-Consciousness. If you think about that process, you will see that it is a law that *brings things together*. Because of this law, a universe in the process of evolution is at the same time a universe in the process of *involution*—not devolution but involution.

Involution is a positive evolutionary process. For Teilhard, involution brings people and organizations together to achieve positive goals; it is a process of convergence and integration. Evolution and involution are two sides of the same positive process.

- Evolution is used to describe positive and useful change over time; creation is moving forward and upward in complexity and consciousness.
- Devolution describes negative and destructive change over time, losing ground in the forward and upward thrust of evolution.
- Involution involves positive evolutionary forces bringing everyone and everything closer and closer together over time, creating ever more complex forms of union and unity with accompanying expansions in consciousness.

Everywhere, we see signs of involution, of coming together, a cohesiveness growing toward a higher or more intense complexity and connectedness. In human beings, for example, each of our Connections makes us more "involuted," that is, more interconnected and interdependent, forming closer, more complex unions.[21] The involution process has always worked in this way.

For example, at the Big Bang, the first moment of divine creation, subatomic particles were shooting out in every direction, yet the evolutionary law of love caused them to attract and join together into more compact, structured unities that we call atoms; we name these various and now quite identifiable atoms as hydrogen, helium, carbon, nitrogen, oxygen, and so on. Teilhard described this evolutionary phenomenon as "atomic involution." In turn, in the evolutionary process, the law of love drew these atoms together to form heavenly bodies. Widely scattered atoms aggregated themselves into new and very large compact unities that we call stars. Teilhard described this phenomenon as "stellar involution." In time, various atoms, through attraction and bonding, combined to form thousands of different molecules, such as water, salt, carbon dioxide, and so on. This he called "molecular involution."

Through Attraction and Connection, planets are formed— "planetary involution."

All life forms on this planet came into being through a series of "biological involutions," more complex, concentrated, and interactive, in plants, insects, and animals. Through eons of Attraction and Connection, evolution eventually reached a structural complexity of consciousness and self-reflective thought in what Teilhard calls the noosphere. The noosphere describes the incredibly complex and interwoven myriad thinking layers of mind and heart that now cover our planet.[22] For us today, the noosphere is symbolized by the Internet. Teilhard would identify this ongoing compacting and self-structuring process in the realms of data, information, knowledge, and wisdom as "noospheric involution."

Teilhard sums up the ongoing involution happening continuously at all levels of being by saying that the entire cosmos is in a process of total and continual re-involution at ever more complex and interconnected levels.[23] We can see this happening among people throughout history: individuals first came together as extended families, families came together as communities, communities came together as tribes, tribes came together as states, and states came together as nations. Currently, nations are trying to live and work together as a cooperative, compassionate planet.

While evolution and involution are happening at all levels, Teilhard says the most important transformations are currently happening in the noosphere, the mind and heart of the planet. The noosphere is where evolution is on the move. As Teilhard points out, "Love is going through a 'change of state' in the noosphere. And, if what all the great religions teach us is correct, it is in this new direction that man's collective passage to God is being mapped out."[24]

One clear sign of this planetary involution is that individuals and nations are concerned about the hunger, health, and safety of people in other nations. Two hundred years ago, few people in the United States would have been concerned with a famine in India, or the Ebola crisis in Africa, or deforestation in the Amazon. Today, we and other nations set aside large sums of money and coordinate teams of volunteers precisely to help other nations in crisis. This is a new evolutionary phenomenon for the human race.

Private individuals, couples, and organizations in the United States, at home and abroad, support worldwide programs to alleviate hunger, fund education, expand medical services, and protect the environment. A Google search for celebrities who use their fame and money for social good reveals long lists of philanthropic individuals and groups.

For example, DoSomething.org is an organization for young people concerned about social change. In 2014, it listed twenty young celebrities who were outstanding in generosity with their time and money in supporting and promoting caring causes. Because we tend to think of media stars as self-focused, many of us would be surprised at some of the young and famous people who made this list of compassionately generous people. The Do Something list included pop star Justin Bieber, basketball star Lebron James, comedian Amy Poehler, actress Beyoncé, and singer/songwriter Taylor Swift, to name just a few.

John Cena, a professional wrestler, served as the Grand Marshal for the 2014 Susan G. Komen Global Race for the Cure, and personally granted more than 400 wishes of individual children for the Make-A-Wish Foundation.

These evolutionary products of involution happening in the noosphere are what we want to explore. Specifically, we want to look at human relationships, all kinds of relationships—marriages, friendships, partnerships, parent-child bonds, teams, communities, and so on—and how they can make a difference.

From the spiritual perspective, we want to look at how these relationships can continue to evolve and foster the evolutionary process toward the fullness of life for everyone. To paraphrase the words of prize-winning geneticist Dr. Kazuo Murakami's book, we hope to awaken the genius in loving relationships and uncover their hidden potentials.

According to Teilhard, we have a long way to go before the noosphere fully "matures." However, from our perspective today, the noosphere has all the tools and technology it needs to keep us all connected with the Internet, computers, tablets, smartphones, television, radio, newspapers, magazines, and so on. These communication tools, in effect, provide what Teilhard called a comprehensive "nervous system for humanity."[25]

From another perspective, humanity's mature ability to use these tools wisely is still a long way off. Humanity's full maturation in loving and consciousness needs to happen both individually and collectively, both intellectually and affectively, before it can use these tools wisely.[26]

Don't expect this maturation process to happen in an atmosphere of "relaxation and tranquility," says Teilhard. Rather, expect an atmosphere of tension, seething excitement, and outbursts.

Whatever the nature of the world's intellectual and emotional "atmosphere," Teilhard's evolution in the noosphere will happen primarily in and through relationships. Unless we are "Attracted" to make ever new and deeper loving "Connections," there can be little or no growth in Complexity and Consciousness. So, relationships are key to spiritual growth as well as to fostering evolution.[27]

SPIRITUAL EXERCISE: MAKING THE NOOSPHERE WORK MORE WISELY

Take a moment to identify some ways that the noosphere needs maturing. It is perhaps easier to identify some destructive or devolutionary ways of large industries, such as those that violate workers' rights, pay low wages, provide minimal workplace safety, flaunt environmental protection laws, or spew poisonous chemicals into clean rivers. It is, however, probably more important to note some destructive ways of people and groups that are much smaller and closer to you. Perhaps you live in a family whose members enjoy criticizing and complaining about one another. Perhaps you work in an office where employees are dishonest, lazy, and irresponsible. Perhaps you belong to a church group whose meetings at times degenerate into gossiping and backbiting sessions. Perhaps you attend a class where students habitually cheat on exams, disrupt the class, and show little respect for the instructor. Once you identify some of these devolutionary situations, ask yourself how you might help those people and groups begin to use some noosphere tools more wisely.

Key Teilhardian Insights for Spirituality

Here, we sum up Teilhard's insights or principles that will provide the underpinning of the rest of the book:

- Love is primarily an energy source, to be used wisely, not wasted.
- Love is shown more in deeds than in words.[28]
- The Law of Attraction-Connection-Complexity-Consciousness is the law of love driving evolution forward.
- When used well, this law releases the evolutionary potential in human relationships.
- *Salvation* means "enjoying the fullness of life."
- The aim of spirituality shifts from "saving my soul" to "helping God's project succeed"—or from personal salvation to the fullness of life for everyone and everything.
- The main purpose of one's life is to not miss any chance to help make the human family move consciously, compassionately, creatively, cohesively, and lovingly closer together.
- Evolution is currently focused in the noosphere, in that layer of love and thought that encircles the planet, bringing people together in ever higher levels of complexity and consciousness.
- Evolution is most powerfully fostered in loving human relationships.

CHAPTER 4

Relationships Are Real Beings

T WO THINGS HAPPEN in any loving relationship. First, a new being—the relationship—is born with its own unique potentials and purpose. Second, the relationship—this new being—enhances and develops the individuals within it, each with their own unique potentials and purpose. Both effects, when recognized and developed, foster evolution. Each of these relationship effects is very important, so we treat each at length. First, *the relationship as a new being*.

A Relationship: A New Being

St. Thomas Aquinas was onto something important in the twelfth century when he wrote, in Latin, *Relatio realis est*. In English, this means something like "A relationship is something real." If something is real, it means that it exists and can have an effect on other things, an effect that the individual elements of the relationship by themselves might not be able to have. This is true of relationships on all levels of existence.

Among human beings, it is easy to see that a relationship has a life of its own and can have an effect on things—both on the individuals that make up the relationship and on things outside the relationship. Think of what close-knit groups of people can accomplish, for example, sports teams, research teams, ministry groups, and certain famous families like the Kennedys. Sociologists who study groups of people never tire of reminding their students that "groups are real."[1]

This uniqueness or "realness" of a relationship (or group) manifests itself and its abilities on all levels. To demonstrate that relationships—at all levels of existence—are something real and unique in themselves, consider the chemical "relationship" NaCl. NaCl is the chemical name for the relationship formed by Na (sodium) and Cl (chlorine). Sodium by itself is a harsh salt that can eat away at almost anything. Chlorine by itself is a poisonous gas. But the "relationship" NaCl is very familiar to everyone. Its ordinary name is *table salt*. Table salt (the relationship) can be used in many ways. It can season food to make it tasty. It can be used as a preservative for food that cannot be refrigerated. Primitive people used it to treat wounds and to keep wounds from getting infected.

None of these abilities or effects is the property of sodium or chlorine alone. Only the "relationship," the molecule NaCl, possesses these special properties. We call them "emergent properties" of the relationship because they arise only from the relationship itself; they do not belong to either of the individual components of the relationship.

To take another obvious example, the "relationship" H_2O, the water molecule, is also real in itself. Its elements are hydrogen and oxygen, both of which are gases. Water, as a relationship, has hundreds of emergent properties and everyday applications in its liquid and frozen forms. Neither of the elementary gases—hydrogen or oxygen—has any of those special properties of the relationship called "water."

We can experience the power of relationships also in the world of sound. If you have access to a piano keyboard, press the note C and then press the note E. Each note has its unique sound. Now, press C and E at the same time, and you hear something new—their relationship. As a second experiment, press E, then press G—two unique sounds. Now press E and G at the same time, and you hear a new sound relationship. To compare the two relationships, press C and E together, then stop and press E and G together. Notice that each relationship produces a slightly different emotional feel.

Now, to get the sense of a team relationship, press the C, E, and G keys at the same time, and notice the new sound relationship you have created. Musicians call this a triad or major chord. All three individual notes can be distinguished (just as you can distinguish, say, three players on a basketball court), yet the harmonic sound produced by the three notes played together cannot be created by any of the notes by themselves. Such chords—there are hundreds of them—form the harmonic structure behind every song played or performed.

St. Ignatius Loyola on the banks of the River Cardoner had a mystical experience of the nature of the Holy Trinity. The Trinity was revealed not in images but in vibratory sound. Ignatius experienced what sounded like a church organ playing three separate musical notes symbolizing each of the three Divine Persons. Then he heard all three notes played simultaneously in a triad or major chord symbolizing the Trinity. Each of the single tones shared the same vibratory "nature," as does each Divine Person. Yet the triad itself was richer and more complex than any single tone. It was as if the Trinity working together was capable of more than each individual Divine Person alone.

This law of relationship operates in similar ways in every domain. However, our emphasis in this book is on human relationships. As we study human relationships, we want to be aware of their "emergent properties." Some of these properties will spontaneously occur, while other properties or abilities that are still dormant need to be awakened and developed. Emergent properties of relationships will play a key role in any potential evolutionary forward movement.

SPIRITUAL PRACTICE: IDENTIFYING YOUR RELATIONSHIPS

To make this book more practical, we ask you to list two or three important relationships in your life. They can be two-person relationships, family-sized relationships, a sports team, a workplace team, a church ministry team, and so on. The idea is that when you consciously reflect on the text in light of your specific relationships, you will become more conscious of them, their roles, and their emergent properties. Then you may more easily recognize how you might help your relationships evolve as well as their emergent properties.

Three Perceptions of Human Relationships

Let's start with perceptions of the simplest relationship: two people joined in a loving, caring friendship or marriage. Choose a two-person relationship of which you are a part. How do you perceive it? Different

41

people perceive relationships in different ways. Here are three major viewpoints or perspectives, the Romantic, the Individualist, and the Third Self.

Romantic Perspective. Some people enter into relationships because they don't feel they are a whole person by themselves. Once they enter a relationship such as a marriage, they see the relationship, finally, as a whole person. Before the union, they saw themselves as something like a half-person relating to another half-person. Mathematically, we might describe this perspective as two half-persons connecting to make one whole person:

$$\tfrac{1}{2} + \tfrac{1}{2} \rightarrow 1$$

This is a typically romantic notion of relationship. Some years ago, a song called "People" was made popular by Barbara Streisand. Its lyrics tell the listener how it feels when two special people fall in love— "You were half, now you're whole." That line of the song very clearly expresses this first notion of relationship.

This two-halves-make-a-whole approach reflects a very common way of thinking about a relationship when it's a deeply loving relationship. It is something that fulfills you and makes you feel complete. This perspective offers a comforting approach to relationship that holds much truth in it, but not the whole truth. Also, it is a very ancient idea.

Thousands of years before Barbara Streisand, in one of Plato's Dialogues on Love, each participant in the discussion was asked to describe what it meant to experience love or friendship. During the course of the discussion, many different stories about the origins of love were presented. Plato, a hopeless romantic two millennia before his time, saved his favorite story for last. In his tale, God created each human soul and, as it were, tore it in half, putting one half of the soul into one human being born in one part of the world, and the other half into a second human being born in another part of the world. The task of these two separated people was to search the world in order to find their soul's mate and, in forming a relationship, to become one whole person. The mathematical description of Plato's love story is that two halves come together to form one whole.

Individualist Perspective. Currently, most psychologists and scientists—and even spiritual directors—do not accept the romantic mathematics of relationship. For them, there is no such thing as a "half-person." They would admit that an individual might be mentally underdeveloped or emotionally immature or even have psychological problems, but that doesn't make him or her "half a person." They would say, "You certainly don't need another person — someone who is your 'other half' — to make you a person."

Rather, they might say that in a healthy relationship, the two individuals would be enhanced by their connection, or union. Mathematically, we might describe a caring and/or productive relationship of two people as one that produces two people both of whom are "enhanced" and "grow" as people through the process of relating to each other. Nothing new is produced in the world by the relationship but two enhanced people. The quotation marks symbolize personal enhancement:

$$1 + 1 \rightarrow \text{``}1\text{''} + \text{``}1\text{''}$$

The past two centuries might be called the Age of Individualism. An almost total focus on the individual person, symbolized by what psychologists call ego psychology, has almost completely pervaded the fields of psychology and spirituality. We are still quite immersed in this age.

The individualist viewpoint on relationship was succinctly summed up by Gestalt psychologist Fritz Perls: "I do my thing and you do your thing. I am not in this world to live up to your expectations, and you are not in this world to live up to mine. You are you, and I am I: if by chance we find each other, it's beautiful. If not, it can't be helped."[2]

From this individualist perspective, relationships remain very important, but they are valuable primarily for the sake of self-development. People form relationships and even enter marriage, many psychologists and anthropologists assure us, primarily for their own personal development.

Our culture reinforces the individualist ideal. It tells us to enter into relationships for our own self-enhancement. And to leave any relationship or get divorced from a marriage partner if the relationship isn't benefiting me or isn't doing for me what I wanted or expected it to. When in a relationship, partners who hold this viewpoint are conditioned to ask, "What is this relationship doing for me?" and "What am I getting out of it?" They are describing the extreme individualized perspective.

Today, only a small fraction of people hold the romantic notion of relationship. Most people today hold the individualist notion. Yet the individualist notion offers a still incomplete picture of a relationship's potential.[3]

Third-Self Perspective. In the third approach, Teilhard's approach, when two people come together in a caring and productive way, not only are the two relating people enhanced and their capacities developed by their interaction, but their union, or relationship, becomes itself a Third Self. Teilhard calls the Third Self "a psychic unity" or "higher soul" or "higher center." For him, this Third Self has "its own personality." It is a new being with its own "soul." This is how he sees the process working: "Elementary personalities can, and can *only* affirm themselves by acceding to a psychic unity or higher soul."[4]

For example, in a marriage, the husband and wife individually are "elementary personalities." But when they join together in love — with a loving purpose — they create a new unity, one that possesses a "higher soul." The marriage relationship is a new being in the world, a Third Self. Husband and wife affirm themselves as belonging to this "higher soul."

Teilhard goes on to clarify: "But this always on one condition: that the higher center to which they come to join *without mingling together* has its own autonomous reality."[5] Even though a new being, "the marriage," emerges possessing a "higher soul," the husband's and wife's "elementary personalities" do not dissolve, melt together, or lose their own uniqueness. In fact, in the marriage, they experience themselves enriched and enhanced individually.

Teilhard goes on: "*Since there is no fusion or dissolution* of the elementary personalities, the center in which they join *must necessarily be distinct from them, that is to say have its own personality*" (the italics are Teilhard's).[6] Since husband and wife have lost nothing of their personalities, the new "center" (the Third Self of the marriage), being distinct from the husband and wife, will emerge with its own distinct personality. The Third-Self relationship is capable of accomplishing more than either the husband alone or the wife alone. Think, for example, of the achievements of Third Selves such as Marie and Pierre Curie, Franklin and Eleanor Roosevelt, Samuel and Olivia Clemens, or James and Nora Joyce. In our own time in philanthropy, we could begin with Bill and Melinda Gates (of Microsoft), Michael and Susan Dell (of Dell Computers), Priscilla Chan and Mark Zuckerberg (of Facebook), and Meryl Streep and Donald Gummer. You may check the powerful work these couples are doing by researching their names on the Internet.

Mathematically, we might express this view of relationship as two people forming a union that not only enhances each of the members, but creates a third reality, the relationship itself. The relationship is indeed a new reality that is capable of accomplishing more than either of the people in the relationship:

$$1 + 1 \rightarrow \text{“1”} + \text{“1”} + \text{Third Self (the relationship)}$$

Just as you and I are real beings and have a life and personality of our own as "elementary personalities," so our relationships are real. We might describe each of our relationships as an intangible being that enjoys a life, a "higher soul," and personality of its own.

The creation of a new relationship-self is obviously not restricted to a marriage relationship. A Third Self can happen in a close friendship, a research team, a ballet troupe, a symphony orchestra, and in many other contexts. For example, we can see this Third-Self effect most familiarly and most clearly in sports teams, such as a basketball team. First of all, the team is a real entity, because only the "team" can play a game or win a game; none of the individual players can win a game. Second, the fans of the team recognize the team as having its own identity and personality. It is the "team" they cheer for. It is the "team" they want to win the game. Even if, after a season, some of the players leave the team and others join it, the team still maintains its identity. Of course, it is in playing on the team that each of the team members' abilities and qualities are enhanced and developed in ways that would never have happened except for being a member of the team.

A similar Third Self is created in a deep friendship or a marriage, although that Third Self is seldom consciously recognized and identified. Here is where Teilhard's realization of the evolutionary effects of Attraction and Connection come in. If a group of people were asked how to describe what happens to the partners in a marriage, most would choose either the romantic perspective or the individualized perspective. They might say that either the two partners produce one whole person or the two partners enhance each other. But the reality is that, in these caring partnerships, a relationship-self is also created, although the Third Self is usually not acknowledged, recognized, or identified.

SPIRITUAL EXERCISE: PEOPLE AND PERSPECTIVES

Do you know people who see relationships in the first way, the romantic perspective? In the second way, the individualist perspective? In the third way, the third-self perspective? How does this third-self perspective challenge you? How can you "see" a relationship, when all you can really see are individual people?

Some Reactions to the Third-Self Perspective

During the opening of a class we taught on relationship, we introduced the three versions of relationship mathematics. This is one graduate student's reaction. She expressed the thoughts of many on first hearing about the Third Self:

> Tonight you introduced the concept of the third person. I have never really thought of this concept before. In past relationships I was more of the $1/2 + 1/2 = 1$. I always thought I was doing great in my current relationship with John, as we have supported each other's individuality and were $1 + 1 = $ us. (This is my own equation.) I don't believe that either of us have actually conceptualized a "third being" living with us, though. I always thought that it was either us as *individuals* or *us* as 1. This is not to say that we haven't nurtured that third person, whom I have always referred to as "us" — there's you, there's me, and then there's us. I just have not thought of it as its own entity that needs tending to, and I'm quite sure that John has not either. Although we are aware of this relationship, I think seeing it as a whole separate entity while simultaneously being ourselves as individuals will enhance our relationship further.

One of the clearest expressions of this third self is in a marriage relationship. There are three selves: a husband, a wife, and the marriage;

three distinct realities. The children of a marriage clearly relate to all three selves of that relationship—the mother, the father, and the relationship. The children can easily tell when their mother is speaking to them as mother ("Please help me carry the groceries into the house"), and when she is speaking to them on behalf of the parental "we" ("Your father and I don't want you to stay out that late tonight").

When a divorce occurs, the children grieve the loss of that Third Self, the relationship that raised them. After the divorce, the mother may say to the children, "I love you just as much as I have always loved you." The father may say to the children, "I love you just as much as I have always loved you." Yet the children still grieve. They grieve because the parental relationship, the Third Self that they have related to and loved all their lives, has died and is henceforth lost to them. *The parental "we" (the marriage itself) no longer can express its love and care for them.*

A therapist who works with children discovered how the mathematics of relationships could be quite useful as a therapeutic tool even with children.

> I will be using this model to help a teenage boy deal with his parents' very nasty divorce, even though their divorce was finalized years ago. His loss of the "we" of his parents truly does represent the loss of his foundation and base of security. He is now conflicted about his alliance with them, but the relationship equations can help him in other ways. He can see that he may develop a separate relationship with each, and each relationship can enhance and enrich him in new and different ways.

Once you begin to see a marriage as a Third Self, you realize how it so often goes unrecognized and unacknowledged, as one of our students preparing for marriage observed while attending a relative's wedding. She was listening closely to the words of the ceremony.

> When I attended my cousin's wedding, I found myself analyzing the words and actions used for the ceremony. As I listened to the prayers and blessings being spoken, I realized that the words were referencing what each individual would bring to the other in their life together, but I never really felt

as though their relationship was being observed, addressed, and celebrated as its own entity. Seeing this made me want to get creative with the words and actions to be used in my own ceremony. In many ways, I now see a wedding as being a birth or baptism of a third entity. I believe they implicitly saw this in my cousin's wedding, but there just seemed to be something missing.

What was missing for her in the wedding liturgy was a clear acknowledgment that a new being or a new self (the marriage) was the focus of the ceremony. For her, the baptismal ceremony clearly acknowledges that a new individual-being (an "elementary personality") is being formally welcomed into the faith community. Shouldn't the marriage ceremony clearly acknowledge that a new relationship-being (a "higher soul" or "higher center") is being formally welcomed—or "baptized"—into the faith community?

Another, more familiar situation is where the couple is first introduced to the concept of the Third Self. One of our married students expressed the contrast this way:

> Being supportive of each other's development and unfolding has been key in my marriage, but I've never considered the relationship as its own entity. Now that I think of us in this new way, I find that I can sometimes more easily make good choices for our relationship, held in sacredness, than I can for my spouse who might be annoying me at that particular moment. I look forward to talking with him about our relationship, its identity, needs, purpose, and calling. I've felt for some time that he and I as a unit share some sort of spiritual purpose—it's helpful to have some concepts to apply to those vague, yet strong feelings.

SPIRITUAL EXERCISE: STORIES THAT RESONATE

Do any of the stories above resonate with you? Have you ever acknowledged a strong relationship in your life as a Third Self? Have you experienced or known children of divorced parents missing the Third Self that raised them? Have you ever studied the words of a wedding ceremony to see if or how it recognizes the Third Self of the marriage?

Spirituality for the Third Self, a Relationship-Self

Most of this book is about the evolutionary potential of the Third Self, your relationship-self. Although we focused this chapter, applying the mathematics of relationship to two-person relationships, a Third Self may represent more than two people. This may occur in a close-knit family, a sports team, a business team, or even a classroom of students.

Because a true relationship possesses a life and story of its own—a time when it was born and a time when it may die, a time when it was weak and a time when it was strong—a relationship is no less real than a visible person. The relationship-self has needs that will keep it healthy, vibrant, and creative. For example, a relationship needs to spend quality time together on a regular basis. It also needs a shared purpose or a project that requires the commitment of the partners.

The relationship-self has its own set of values. Those values—at least in the order in which they are ranked—may be different from the values of each individual in the relationship.

The truth of this may be seen in a workshop for couples that we often ran. We would give each partner a deck of eighteen cards. On each card was the name of what we called an "ultimate value." These were values such as True Friendship, World Peace, Salvation, Financial Security, and a Good Reputation. Each person was to arrange the eighteen values in order of personal preference. Seldom would the three top values be the same for both partners. We would encourage couples to talk to their partner about their different choices.

Next, we would ask the couples to put aside one of the decks of value cards, and do the same exercise for their relationship. They were to think on behalf of their relationship and identify its top three values. Surprisingly, couples found it an easy task. No pair ever came to us and said, "We can't do this." Universally, the relationship would have three top values that differed, at least in order of preference, from the top three of either partner.

In a few words, a relationship-self possesses its own *values*, *spirit*, and *personality*. During the 1970s and '80s, Bob and Ray had their own radio program called *The Bob and Ray Show*. The gift of their partnership was the ability to make people laugh. A close friend of theirs, the news commentator Andy Rooney, had this to say about their Third Self:

> Bob and Ray have three distinct personalities. There's Bob's, there's Ray's and there's Bob and Ray's. Both Bob and Ray are interesting to meet separately because two duller people you never talked to. Every Sunday morning I meet funnier people down at the news store when I go out to get the paper.
>
> If you run into Bob and Ray together, it's a different matter. Over a year's time they must give away a million dollars' worth of comedy material free to people they meet on the street.[7]

The spirituality and spiritual practices we propose throughout the rest of this book are designed for that Third Self, the relationship-self. Almost any strong relationship qualifies for a relational spirituality. It could be a comedy team, close friends, or a volunteer group. All of these groups, depending on the quality of their relating, can form Third Selves.

Since few people, as far as we can discover, have treated their relationships as new beings or new selves, uniquely different from each of the partners, most people will enter a spirituality of relationship as a newcomer.

A Baby Metaphor

For this reason, we have found it useful to ask relationship partners to view their Third Self as if it were a baby. Usually, one of the first things people do when they have a new baby is to give it a name. That might be a hint that one of the first steps in a spirituality of relationship is to give your relationship a unique name. Sports groups have learned the power of giving a name to their team. Families have unique names that give their relationship its unique identity—the Smiths, the Browns.

We also encourage two-person friendships to honor their relationships by giving them a name. For example, we have named our relationship *Palo*, built from the first letters of our names, Patricia and Louis. Once your relationship has a name, the partners begin to treat it as something real and distinct in their lives.

Giving names to groups is very common. Corporations give themselves names, like Apple, Microsoft, Alcoa, Subway, Google, Yahoo, and Facebook. Native American tribes gave themselves names and erected totems to celebrate their unique identities. Sports teams carry group names like Jets, Dolphins, Colts, and Lightning. Players even wear identical logos or symbols on their uniforms and fans wear T-shirts with their favorite team's name. Why not acknowledge your relationships and their identity by giving them names?

SPIRITUAL EXERCISE: NAMING YOUR RELATIONSHIP

From the two or three important relationships you listed earlier, choose one significant relationship to explore. The first task is to give this relationship its own special name. Please get together with your partner(s) and decide on a name for your special relationship. Then refer to it by that name from now on. If you do so, you will notice a difference in how you relate to each other and deal with relationship issues that arise.

Nurturing Needed

Although a baby has a life and an emerging personality of its own, it still needs much help growing up. The same goes for a relationship. It needs to be watched carefully, lest it come to harm, as happens to many relationships. It needs to be fed and nurtured according to its own special requirements, or it may weaken for lack of nourishment. A relationship, like a baby, needs certain kinds of "food" during infancy, but eventually is able to eat more adult fare. It needs to have a name, a place to be, a setting that is safe and secure. A relationship needs to feel valued and useful, it needs to know that it is contributing something to the wider family and the community, and most importantly, it needs to feel needed and wanted by others.

All these same needs and desires felt by a baby are felt by a relationship, as we will see in the following chapters. But for now, it is important that you realize that the relationship, for which you are choosing to build a spirituality, already has a life of its own.

SPIRITUAL EXERCISE: RELATIONSHIP PROFILE

It is important to recognize some milestones in the life of your relationship, distinct from the individual milestones for you and the other(s) in the relationship. On a piece of paper or in a notebook, write down some important information about your Third Self. Here are some questions for your reflection. Use as much space in your notes as you need to answer them.

1. When and where did the relationship begin? If you can, specify the date and place.
2. How did you meet? What was the source of Attraction? What got it started? How was the Connection made?
3. What gave the relationship the impetus to grow?
4. What are some milestones or turning points that mark your relationship's journey? Give dates, places, and influential people, if possible.
5. In what direction does the relationship seem to be leading? Is there some clear aim or purpose that seems to characterize it and give it special meaning?
6. Has the relationship grown or matured? Give an example.
7. When, where, and in what situation did the relationship end (if applicable)?

CHAPTER 5

"Union Differentiates"

A FEW YEARS AGO, we drove to the University of South Florida at its St. Petersburg campus to attend a lecture by Christopher Bache, a college professor. The theme of his presentation was his discovery of a wonderful phenomenon that he called "collective consciousness."

When he gave assignments to his students as individuals, each performed according to their typical skill level. However, when he gave similar assignments to small teams of students, many of the more ordinary students displayed abilities *as team members* they had never shown before. This was especially true when the team members formed a bond of friendship and mutual trust and acted as a team producing true teamwork. Students presented surprisingly fresh ideas, some with perspectives on how to approach the assignment, others on where to find helpful information, still others on how to organize and divide tasks.[1]

Bache recognized that each of the teams in his classroom had a life of its own; it was a "living" classroom. He recognized that something new and vital had emerged among his small teams, a kind of energy that was refreshingly different from the atmosphere in an ordinary classroom. He also recognized that each small team enjoyed a kind of "collective consciousness." They were thinking as one unit and each person seemed to have access to the consciousness of the others. When someone made a good suggestion, everyone on the team seemed to recognize its value, so it became easy to implement with minimal discussion, without people taking sides, pro and con.

He explained that he was trying to name this phenomenon: *How could a team release new abilities in the individual team members, and why does it happen?* It took him paragraphs to describe the phenomenon during his lecture, but he was looking for a simple name for it.

I (Louis) raised my hand and said that, almost a hundred years ago, a French Jesuit priest named Pierre Teilhard de Chardin had named the phenomenon that Bache was describing. Teilhard had summarized it in two words. Those two words were "Union Differentiates."

In the simplest language, Teilhard's insight revealed that each student team had become a true unity, or "union." It had also become *a new being*. Members of this new "team-being" were somehow sharing or participating in that group consciousness. The team as a unit was more complex than any of the individuals in the team, and their shared consciousness was richer—that is, the team-being enjoyed a degree or intensity of consciousness—than any of the members.

Furthermore, that new being (the Third Self, or the team, itself) allowed each member to find a fuller identity and capacity within that team. Each student was, in Teilhard's words, "differentiating" himself. In other words, each was more fully recognizing and utilizing his or her personal capabilities. Those capabilities emerged as a contributing member of the team and as one who participated in the team's more expanded consciousness. In order to contribute to the success of the team, each member was challenged by that team spirit to manifest latent abilities in themselves that might never have appeared as long as the student was performing solely as an individual.

Some individual qualities that typically appear in members of a team with an assigned task include: leadership abilities, mediating skills, organizing and ordering a series of necessary steps, creative thinking, problem solving, an ability to envision the whole process, a sense of humor, respect for the contributions of others, expressing gratitude, cooperating, mutual trust, joy in being part of a team, and other qualities that might never emerge if each student alone was assigned the same task.[2]

We tell this story here because it is a fuller explanation of Teilhard's "union differentiates" insight that lies at the heart of this book on love. Love is the most powerful force or energy in the universe. That power is multiplied in relationships. Love's potency is released most powerfully among people who have formed a relationship (a *union*). People who truly unite for a purpose beyond themselves become "differentiated" as they unite and work together in a shared consciousness to achieve their larger purpose.

This is the phenomenon that happened in Bache's classroom teams. As "differentiated," each team member could pursue the team's shared purpose (solving a problem, compiling research, producing a report, etc.), both individually and collectively, but they could do it with much more talent, ability, and consciousness than they ever could by working alone. In a true relationship, no one's individuality is lost. It is increased. That is the beauty of Connections.

These unions that enjoy a collective consciousness become the launching pads for the next stage of evolution, as we learn consciously how to create them and use them.

SPIRITUAL EXERCISE: EVOLUTIONARY POTENTIAL

Can you offer some ideas on how these classroom teams and other teams might have the power to nudge the evolutionary process forward? What if teachers and professors, from the start, were to divide their classroom students into working teams? It might prove difficult to grade each student separately, but it might enhance each student's abilities, especially their ability to work collaboratively, an ability seldom developed in classrooms currently.

Two Distinct Processes

It is very important to recognize and identify the two processes that are continually happening in a powerful, loving relationship or team. *The first process is to observe what happens to the team (or union). The second process is to observe what happens to the individual members of the team as they participate in the team.*

First, we consider the team as a new being. Once a cohesive union is formed and the team members are working together at its shared purpose, one can begin to notice what are called "emergent properties" of the team. Emergent properties are abilities, skills, or talents that belong uniquely to the team, not necessarily to any of the individual team members. These emergent properties are produced and expressed only when the team members are together and acting as a team.

Recall some of the great Broadway musicals throughout the last century—*Oklahoma, The Sound of Music, Fiddler on the Roof, Chicago*, and many more. You realize that each musical is the work of a huge team of people, from authors and composers to choreographers and wardrobe people, from financial backers and set designers to promoters and orchestrators, actor interviewers and musicians, and so on. Only the entire team could produce the stirring and inspiring live musical production happening on stage that audiences enjoy night after night.

The term "emergent property" is a term we have chosen to use here; it is not a Teilhardian term. We adopted it from systems-thinking theory, an approach to knowing and decision-making that became popular only after Teilhard's death. Teilhard would have delighted in having access to systems-thinking terms like "emergent property" and using them, for those two words summarize a very powerful concept.

Any unique team ability "emerges" and functions only when the team is operating together. A team is best described not by the actions of each individual player, but by their *interactions*, by what happens between and among them as they play. The ability of a basketball team to play and win a game only "emerges" when the players are engaged interactively together in playing a game.

This emergent ability is called a "property" in that it is "owned" or belongs to the team itself, not to any of its individual members. No individual basketball player can play or win a game; only the team can claim ownership of that ability (or "property").[3]

The team of Bob and Ray were able to produce comedy and laughter. That ability was an emergent property of their team. Neither Bob nor Ray as individuals possessed that property. There was little or no comedy when a person encountered Bob or Ray. The comedy emerged only when the two men came together and interacted as a team.

For example, a married couple through their sexual union may produce a child. The ability to produce a child is a typical emergent property of a marriage. Neither of the partners is able to produce or raise a child alone.

We often mistakenly think that a single parent or a couple can raise a child, but a moment's reflection will clarify that it takes a community to raise a child—the interactive influence on the child of extended family members, teachers, neighbors, clergy, shopkeepers, classmates, playmates, pop stars, TV personalities, books, and so on. Each of these can exert an influence that helps shape a child's personality, attitudes, and values. Raising a child is most properly an "emergent property" of the community.

Many teams are behind the success of familiar companies. Bill

Hewlett and Dave Packard created the computer company Hewlett-Packard. Richard and Maurice McDonald started the fast-food chain called McDonald's. Sam, Jack, Harry, and Albert Warner founded Warner Brothers, the Hollywood movie-making company. Bill Gates and Paul Allen began the computer software giant Microsoft. Steve Jobs and Steve Wozniak gave birth to Apple, who gave us the personal computer, the iPod, iPad, and iPhone. Larry Page and Sergy Brinn invented the mammoth search engine Google. Evan Williams, Biz Stone, and Jock Dorsey developed the social media connector Twitter.

SPIRITUAL EXERCISE: RECOGNIZING AN EMERGENT PROPERTY

Can you give examples of couples, groups, or teams that possess an ability (or emergent property) that none of the individuals in that group possesses? Think of musical groups, scientific groups, teams at work, church, communities, and schools.

The Second Process in "Union Differentiates"

The first process in "union differentiates" was to recognize what happens to the team or *union* itself. The second process is to observe what happens to the *individual members* of a third-self relationship (union) or team. Teilhard says that the individuals acting in their teams become "differentiated." They discover their own personal "emergent properties." For example, while only an entire team could produce a Broadway musical, the talents of every individual involved emerge ever more clearly and distinctly as they participate in its production.

In this second process, we look at the term "emergent property" from a different perspective. While a team in action may reveal its own emergent properties, in this section, we apply the term "emergent properties" to the individual team members. We emphasize the surfacing—or emergence—of personal abilities of each team member that might have been previously undiscovered, undeveloped, or underdeveloped, but now begin to appear and emerge as each individual continues to act within the team.

Anyone who has played on a sports team knows this experience. Players may begin the season operating at a certain skill level; during the season, that skill improves. Or a team member has always played a certain position on the team. Yet when asked to play a different position requiring different skills or abilities, the person discovers a capacity to perform those new skills. These skills are newly "emerging" and the person may claim them as "property." It is what Teilhard called "differentiation." In other words, as I interact with others on a team, I am challenged to discover more fully who I am and what I am capable of being and doing. I am "differentiating" myself from each of the others on the team. I am not separating myself from them, far from it. For it is primarily as I interact with the others that I discover my unique abilities emerging more and more fully.

This second process happens in many areas of union or Connection, where people are brought together to work and perform in teams. We interviewed children attending a music and dance camp[4] where they had to perform together in groups. When the camp sessions were over, each one could identify personal capacities that had emerged from the team experience.

One discovered her capacity for *self-discipline*. She discovered she could freely choose to practice her violin at camp. "I didn't need my mother to make me practice." Another discovered that she could *overcome her shyness*, "jump out of her comfort zone," and have fun.

A young trumpet player proudly announced that he had learned to read the subtle syncopations of jazz while playing in a combo. He also discovered he could *improvise*, a skill he could never have learned on his own. "As I watched other players perform a difficult skill, I said to myself if others could do it so could I. And I could."

A guitar player said, "I got a chance to play in the jazz quartet, which has made me twenty times *better as a musician*." A 14-year-old cellist discovered that playing in an orchestra developed his *team-building skills*. "I'm learning how to work better with people. It's a great experience that prepares you for the rest of your life." An actor summed up his camp experience, saying, "You don't leave the same as when you first came. You come out *stronger, more confident*, and with friendships for life."

Each of these newly discovered abilities had been dormant in these children until they learned to commit themselves to a team. It was the "union" experience that allowed their personal skills to be "differentiated" and revealed. In a team's striving for success or aiming to achieve its purpose, individual members are allowed to make mistakes and to fail; but they are encouraged to try again and persist. Failure is often involved in "developing" a skill or talent. Improvement seldom happens without sometimes making mistakes.

While each of the unions (orchestra, jazz quartet, drama team, etc.) developed its own emergent properties, each of the team members developed their personal emergent properties (self-discipline, overcoming shyness, the ability to improvise, team-building, self-confidence, etc.).

It is important to recognize what happens to both the team and the individuals, but especially how the team brings out the best in the team members. Most likely, without the influence of the team (union), each individual's latent capacities would not have been revealed (differentiated).

Transformations don't happen only to young people. In the early days of our nation, Benjamin Franklin and a number of his most ingenious acquaintances formed "a club of mutual improvement" that they named the Junto Club. Every Friday night, the group of friends met to discuss points of morals, politics, or philosophy. The Junto Club met for almost four decades and, in Franklin's words, "was the best school of philosophy, morality and politics that then existed in the province."

The Junto Club was an experience of union. Its members formed a living being. One of its effects was that it revealed the unique capacities of each member. Members were inspired to read, write, and speak in public, said Franklin. They became excellent scholars and speakers, while remaining close friends without interruption for forty years.

SPIRITUAL EXERCISE:
BEING "DIFFERENTIATED"

Have you ever been part of a relationship or team where you discovered talents and abilities you never realized you had or could develop? Can you name any of those abilities, as these young conservatory people did?

When Geniuses Gather

Teilhard's writings are filled with other insights that are as powerful as "union differentiates."[5] In the relationship between science and spirituality, Teilhard was a seminal thinker of the first order. People who have studied him would call him a genius.

In a TV drama series called Scorpion, we see the power of collective consciousness and how it operates in the team and in its members. The team members of Scorpion are geniuses in their own fields—a computer whiz, a Harvard behaviorist, a mathematical phenomenon, a mechanical prodigy, an awesome programming analyst, and a government contact. The team also includes a normal person who keeps the geniuses organized. She also has a genius young son who often plays a crucial role in solving problems. Together they are Scorpion. That is their team name. They each work best as part of that team. The team consciousness brings out the best in each of them. Together they are able to solve crimes or other problems that no one else can—not even any individual of the Scorpion team—but it is the very closeness of their bonding that brings out the best in their differences.

The insight "union differentiates" belongs to Teilhard. According to Teilhard, it was the force of Attraction that brought people together to form Connections or unions. In various episodes of Scorpion, we learn how Attraction brings each of the members into Connection with the team. We see how these Connections release special abilities of their own, as anyone can observe, not only in the team itself but also in each of its members.

First, their closeness and shared purpose often brings out unrecognized capacities and talents of team members, which otherwise would have laid dormant. Second, Scorpion, the union itself, discovers that it had its own purpose and personality, which is quite different from the purpose and personality of any of the members of the union.

Thus, the best way for you to discover and develop your talents and potential would be to enter into relationships (unions, connections, friendships, teams, etc.) with others in pursuing a shared aim or purpose. In that way, the union itself becomes the pathway and driver of your self's fullest definition and identity.

SPIRITUAL PRACTICE: TEAM SPIRIT

Can you name some relationships in which you experienced a sense of team spirit—everyone working together effectively—and where you experienced "emergent properties" in yourself as well as in the team?

Connections Drive Evolution

What Teilhard also discovered is that unions, or relationships, are the basic driving force of evolution. Some evolutionary pioneers appear to be "loners" like Albert Einstein, Thomas Edison, or Nicola Tesla. And many mistakenly think Teilhard was one of them. The reality is that even these seemingly solitary pioneers are really members of teams or relationships. It's just that their helpers or supporters are not as visible and noticeable as the "rugged individuals" who seem to be functioning out there on the edges of the future all by themselves.

We often think that salvation is an individual thing; that God's focus is on saving each individual soul. However, if we look at the Ten Commandments, we see that God is focused on relationships rather than individuals. The commandments are all about preserving relationships. Among the commandments are prohibitions against stealing, lying, murder, adultery, and coveting what another possesses. Each has to do with the violation of a relationship. In other commandments, God asks people to honor the family relationship, neighbor relationships, and most of all, the sacred relationship with God.[6] God values relationships as the best way to "fullness of life." We are to get to God and the fullness of life through relationships. As philosopher John Macmurray emphasizes again and again, there is no such thing as an individual person; there can only be "persons in relation."[7]

SPIRITUAL PRACTICE: TEAMWORK AND THE TEN COMMANDMENTS

Consider a relationship or team already successfully operating, at work, school, church, or community, and considering each of the "Thou shalt nots..." of the Ten Commandments, show how a team member could harm the Third Self of that relationship or team, for example, by lying, misrepresenting, cheating, stealing, or dishonoring the team.

Static versus Evolutionary Perspective

To correctly and adequately grasp the importance of Teilhard's understanding of love, relationships, and evolution, it is essential to grasp the distinction between a static worldview and an evolutionary worldview. For the thousands of years before the nineteenth and twentieth centuries, most ordinary people were born, grew up, and died holding a static worldview.

In a static world, things don't really change. The Earth may go through its seasons, but it does so predictably and without much variation. People live and die, but the world doesn't really change. People are pretty much the same, generation after generation. All things are much the same as God made them in the beginning. Nothing really changes in any radical way. That is the mindset of a person with a static view of the world.

For centuries, most people saw themselves living in a static world. They lived their lives without noticing much transformation either in the world in general or, certainly, in their local circumstances. For generation after generation, everything seemed repetitive and cyclic, with some minor variation but fundamentally unchanging. The rich were always rich; the poor were always poor. Some people enjoyed good luck; others endured misfortune. Life was filled with much pain and sorrow. Everybody struggled.

In such an unchanging world, the only hope for reaching "salvation" (the fullness of life) had to be *in a different world*, which was called "heaven," a world of unchanging bliss and happiness.

For people who believed they lived in a static universe, there were only two possible worlds, heaven and Earth, both of which were perceived as "unchanging." Life on Earth would always be full of pain, sorrow, and death, while life in heaven would have no pain, no sorrow, and no death. In a static world, the best spirituality was one that taught you how to "escape" or "avoid" the world and get to heaven.

However, science's discovery of evolution changed everything.

The fact that evolution was happening on every level of being forced religious thinkers to reconsider the traditional static-world theology and spirituality, because both theology and spirituality had been based on an inadequate if not an incorrect perspective of creation. Many tradition-minded theologians and religious leaders, however, found it hard to give up a static worldview, since an unchanging perspective is easy to teach and appealing to people in its simplicity. It makes few demands of human beings beyond avoidance of sinful behavior and the patient endurance of painful and sorrowful periods of life on Earth.

In contrast, for those who base their theology and spirituality on the fact that the world is evolving, God's will for them is far from passive and simple. It takes work and commitment to help Earth evolve through ever-richer levels of capacity, complexity, consciousness, and convergence in love.

For people who acknowledge an evolving creation, God's will for them has not really changed; it still is "the fullness of life" (salvation). What has changed is the realization that God wants to begin bringing about that fullness of life, as much as possible, for everyone *now*, while people are living on Earth, not waiting until they die and "go to heaven."

The Lord's Prayer is an evolutionary prayer. We pray, "Thy will be done, on earth…." God's will for us on Earth is much more than avoiding sin. It is to keep developing Earth into a place of peace and love, so that, in time, all of us will be able to enjoy more and more the fullness of life and love on Earth. That the kingdom of God is operating here and now was a basic teaching of Jesus. He encouraged kindness, generosity, forgiveness, sharing of goods, and concern for all. His parables described how this kingdom of God was silently growing and developing. He was doing his Father's will on Earth.

For an evolving world, our task is not primarily or merely to avoid sin and get to heaven, but to spend one's life — in relationships — helping transform the world into a better and better place. Undoubtedly, this is why the universe was created so that "union differentiates."

SPIRITUAL PRACTICE:
AN EVOLUTIONARY PERSPECTIVE

In your spirituality, did you shift from a static-world perspective to an evolutionary one? Can you name some spiritual practices presented in your church that were designed to get you to heaven or assure you that you had a place in heaven waiting for you? Were liturgy and sacraments presented from within a static-world perspective? How would you re-present some spiritual or liturgical practices so that they fit into an evolutionary-world perspective, in which human beings were expected to help move that world forward in compassion and love?

A Reminder to the Reader

It is important to remember that Teilhard sees human love playing a very different role and having a different purpose from that of most other writers on the topic. Teilhard views love—all forms of healthy love—primarily as *energy*. Love is an energy source that God put into all things in order to keep the evolutionary process moving forward toward a final union of all beings. Energy is defined by scientists as "the ability to do work." For Teilhard, love is indeed an energy doing important work for our planet. The work of love energy is to keep the human family evolving. This is God's project in which we are to be fully involved as active participants.

Of course, love still produces very desirable results that other writers describe—experiences of joy, happiness, closeness, affection, fulfillment, security, belongingness, esteem, and self-actualization.[8] Teilhard would not deny the value of any of these wonderful effects. In fact, he rejoices in the immediate blessings love provides. But he is always looking at the human race in its evolutionary progress, since God's project—the most important evolutionary process in creation—remains uppermost in his mind. The primary work God wants our love energy to accomplish is its evolutionary work. To fulfill our promise to God—"Thy will be done, on earth…"—our manner of loving needs to evolve continuously.

In the spirit of our traditional Judeo-Christian tradition, God certainly wants each individual to experience personally the fullness of life in God's presence. But, more than that, for the success of God's project, God wants us all, collectively, to mature in our ability to love.

When we truly mature in our ability to love unconditionally, we will come to experience everything that God loves and we will have learned to love everything the way God loves it. For Jesus told us that God loves all of creation, and loves it as much as God loves the divine Son (see John 3:13). God wants us, as a reflectively conscious human family, to grow (evolve) into a way of unconditional, all-embracing love that God manifests toward us.

Collective growth in all-embracing loving is the goal of God's project for us. We can only achieve it by evolving in the ways we love one another and our planet. We need to maximize our ability to love, to find new ways to love, and to discover the creative potential of love. That is the challenge Teilhard places before us. He wants to wake up the world to its as yet undiscovered ability to love as God loves.

For Teilhard, the evolutionary law of Attraction-Connection-Complexity-Consciousness is the law we are to use to maximize our ability to love. This evolutionary law is a law, not in the sense of a civil law enacted to govern society, but a law inherent in creation—a law of nature—like the law of gravity or the law of electromagnetism. Teilhard's evolutionary law is a law of nature about how energy works and how to use energy. Therefore, Attraction-Connection-Complexity-Consciousness is a law of nature about love energy—how love operates and how to use it.

For Teilhard, this evolutionary law is a *natural law* that affects all creation. Creation "has a natural tendency to associate in groups and to concentrate upon itself (wherever it can, and as much as it can) in systems."[9] Teilhard approaches the study of "love" not only as a man of faith but also the way a physicist or other scientist might. He studies it as a *source of energy*. He would list "love" alongside those other physical sources of energy like electricity and nuclear power.

For example, he might observe the care and respect team members had for each other, and find a way to "measure" how much that "love energy" flowing among the team contributed to their efficiency and effectiveness in their scientific work. Teilhard suspects that if there were little love and respect among team members, their work would not be as efficient or effective as a team operating with love energy.

Teilhard would also place the law of Attraction-Connection-Complexity-Consciousness as a natural law alongside those laws of gravity and laws governing nuclear forces.[10] The more lovingly connected team members are, the more accepting they would be of their complex interpersonal interactions.

Teilhard acknowledges that there are other human experiences that produce energy that can be used to promote the evolutionary process, such as suffering,[11] research, faith in the future,[12] and peacekeeping. Thus, love for God's work in the world is what can activate and redirect the energy spent in suffering, energy that would otherwise be seen as a waste. It is a love for knowledge, healing, and human advancement that drives much research happening in thousands of places across the globe. It is love for family, neighbors, nation, and people in general that motivates most peacekeepers like soldiers and law enforcement. All these people are putting their faith in the future.

When Teilhard uses the word "faith" in the context of energy, he is not talking about articles of faith as in the Nicene Creed, but rather *a faith akin to the motivation and determination* that drives researchers to keep searching for a cure for cancer or Alzheimer's, a new kind of rocket fuel or a more efficient way of harnessing solar energy. Teilhard also described this faith in the "forward momentum of the universe" as "loving the not-yet." In this sense, Teilhard envisions Christianity as "the religion of tomorrow."[13]

Other expressions of love-energy appear as emergent properties of certain groups—governmental, nongovernmental, and philanthropic. Many groups, each in different ways, are caring for some of the three-billion poor who share Earth, our common home. Some find ways to feed the poor, provide clean water, healthy air, adequate healthcare, housing, education, and employment.

Teilhard would also list as energy-conserving groups those dedicated to preserving, protecting, and promoting the health and safety of our planet. This work involves maintaining a thriving physical environment for all human beings and all forms of life.[14] Many Teilhardians feel that Teilhard qualifies as patron of the ecological movement. However, for Teilhard, straightforward loving is the best producer of the energy needed to promote evolution. In fact, he would say that interpersonal love and caring is the underlying energy that basically drives most other energy-producing human activities.

So, as you continue to read, remember Teilhard's perspective on love. For him, *God gave us the ability to love as a source of energy to promote evolution.* Our job as part of those contributing to help accomplish God's project for Earth is to learn to maximize the energy of love we are capable of, and to use the law of Attraction-Connection-Complexity-Consciousness to do so.

SPIRITUAL PRACTICE: PROMOTING EVOLUTION

Where in your life or relationships do you have the clearest opportunity to promote evolution? How could you begin to make it happen?

PART TWO
PRACTICE

CHAPTER 6

A Higher Way for Committed Partners

Exploring Evolutionary Potentials

TEILHARD NOT ONLY recognized the many signs of evolution happening in the scientific world, he also wanted to encourage evolution in human relationships wherever he could. One area laden with evolutionary potential was the institution of marriage. He knew that love in its many forms and expressions offered the most powerful energy for making evolutionary advances. The most common and universal form of shared love on Earth was marriage and the love between committed partners. What would it take to re-envision and repurpose such love so that it would become an evolutionary force?

During his early years, he realized that, for most religions, this most familiar union of husband and wife seemed to have only one purpose, that of propagating the planet with children. He realized that this purpose was necessary but not sufficient to move the human race forward in its potential development. Procreation was only a Level One purpose of marriage.

The potential for Level Two, he realized, was quietly waiting in the "union" of the spouses. The power of the evolutionary principle "union differentiates" had not been tapped for married couples. So, he proposed a new and equally potent purpose for marriage. Although the Church had, in effect, silenced Teilhard from speaking in public, his new insights about a second purpose of marriage resonated with a number of influential theologians who learned of his ideas.[1]

In this quiet way, Teilhard had a powerful, although often unnoticed, enriching effect on the Church's traditional approach to marriage and the purpose of sexual activity in marriage. Before the Second Vatican Council, the *procreation of children* was the single primary purpose for marriage according to the Church. Thus, the Church taught, a married couple's genital sexual acts must always be "open" to conception.

For years, based on the evolutionary principle "union differentiates," Teilhard had proposed that an equally important purpose for a married couple's sexual activity was *to foster the mutual love of the spouses*.[2] Because of Teilhard's (and others') voices, after Vatican II, the Church acknowledged the purpose of sex in marriage to be twofold, both for procreation and the mutual love of the spouses.[3]

Teilhard recognized that sexual activity could provide love energy to deepen the strength of the couple's union, so that the principle "union differentiates" would be operating to bring out the best, both in their committed union and in each of the partners. This gave him the insight how to reach for Level Three.

In this chapter, we see Teilhard proposing a new, third stage—or third purpose—for committed couples. It is a way to release even more evolutionary energy in the relationship. He explores a further evolutionary potential of that spousal union, nurtured in part by sexual love energy. He began to formulate a "higher way," a more advanced stage of married love. He envisioned a spiritually richer purpose for committed couples that included the purposes of procreation and the mutual love of the spouses, yet went expansively beyond them. It would create many new ways to release love energy in small and larger ways to help renew the face of the Earth. Some famous couples may show us how it works.

Paradoxically, Teilhard called this third stage the way of "chastity," but he defines the word in a surprisingly new way.

Chastity in Christian Life

In 1934, while in Beijing doing geological research, Teilhard wrote an essay on what he described as a higher stage of married love, giving it the puzzling title "The Evolution of Chastity."[4] It is puzzling since chastity is usually associated with priests and nuns. It is basically a vow that priests and nuns make not to engage in those sexual expressions of human love that are specifically associated with marriage.

For centuries in Christian times, chastity was considered a requirement for men and women living consecrated lives in religious communities. Priests and nuns solemnized their membership to their religious community by taking a formal vow of chastity. As a member of the Society of Jesus, Teilhard had made the same vow. It is surprising that he would choose to use the concept of chastity, a keynote of life in convents and monasteries, to explore the evolutionary potential of married love.

However, he chose *chastity* very consciously. Following Christian tradition, he considered the ability to observe chastity as the "supreme mark of the triumph of spirit."[5] He finds himself wanting to explore this "supreme mark" idea more deeply in relation to marriage.

Although sexual expression in marriage was seen as good and holy, married couples in the past were consistently taught that spiritual perfection was synonymous with "victory over sexual attraction."[6] Therefore, *traditionally*, couples were advised that sexual activity, even in marriage, must be used minimally and only for the purpose of reproduction, the propagation of the species. It logically followed that, even in marriage, couples should, ideally, live in a state of abstinence—no genital sexual activity at all—because the belief was that, in itself, abstinence expresses a more advanced state of spiritual perfection. As Teilhard understood it, that would be the traditional rationale for married couples to abstain from sexual activity. But this is *not* Teilhard's viewpoint. He tells us why.

Teilhard observed that hidden beneath this traditional reasoning is the unspoken assumption that "sexual relations are tainted by some degradation or defilement."[7] The implication is that the emotional passion that accompanies sexual activity somehow produces animality, shame, fear, and loss of reason in those who engage in it. This assumption, he said, is rooted in the unexpressed belief that "sexuality is sinful."[8]

SPIRITUAL EXERCISE: WHAT WERE YOU TAUGHT ABOUT SEX?

In what you were taught by the Church about sex and sexual activity, was there an unexpressed belief that it was dangerous or sinful? Was any part of sexual expression considered healthy or normal or beautiful?

It is important to bring to consciousness any of the assumptions about sexuality that you still carry, and to identify them.

The Evolving Meaning of Chastity

What Teilhard proposed to develop in his essay "The Evolution of Chastity" was a moral defense of *chastity as a universally significant spiritual practice*. To avoid confusion with the traditional notion of this word, he assigned himself the task "to define precisely what constitutes the excellence of chastity" as it applies in *all* roles of life today including our present understanding of evolution and God's plan.[9] For Teilhard, chastity is not primarily about abstaining from sexual activity, but about the purity or clarity of focus of a person's or a couple's life purpose.

Most importantly, Teilhard was proposing a new understanding of chastity. He was writing not for those who believe that the body is evil, that sexual activity is sinful, and that one's primary life purpose is to save one's soul. Instead, he was writing for those who lovingly embrace the physical world and are hoping to help the human family evolve *through matter* toward spirit.

Evolution is happening primarily through matter — *through matter* toward spirit. The physical body — matter — can release and express spirit in passion, excitement, the longing to be intimately connected. At times, only the physical body can provide the means and resources the spirit needs to express love and welcome love. Only hands can touch, stroke, and caress. Only arms can hold, hug, cling, and embrace. Only lips can murmur loving words and kiss. Only eyes can show longing and joy. Only bodies can cling, join, and tremble in pleasure. Only in the body can one experience the spiritual moment of orgasm. Only through the symbiotic joining of sperm and ovum — two portions of matter — can new human life begin its genesis and gestation as a being capable of human love.

Love is most commonly shown through matter. The evolutionary drive of love is happening through matter. For Teilhard, love is the energy driving evolution. It derives its resources from physical matter and human bodies. Where better to focus this drive than with committed couples — where love is most likely open to the spirit?[10]

Remember, for Teilhard, the very meaning of chastity is evolving just as the meaning of love itself is evolving and as every other facet of life is evolving. In this evolutionary framework, Teilhard expands the horizon of chastity beyond the vow of chastity taken by consecrated religious people. He particularly wants to show how, outside monasteries and convents, chastity—in its much wider meaning—can become a path for married people as well. Teilhard does not exclude men and women who are single or unmarried from this new notion of chastity; in his essay, married people are simply his primary focus.[11]

Teilhard takes his cue from a special expression of the vow of chastity sometimes taken by monks and nuns. In the Christian tradition, members of religious orders or congregations, especially women, were often encouraged to make a further expression of their chastity vow, namely, a "supreme marriage." This was a human-and-God intimate nonsexual relationship experienced in prayer, in which the consecrated person becomes, as it were, "Christ's bride."[12]

Teilhard takes this idea of a "supreme marriage" and develops it—even for people living a consecrated religious life. Rather than just seeing a supreme marriage as living in a kind of prayerful intimate Christ-and-me cocoon, typical of the traditional Christ's bride tradition, Teilhard envisions such a spiritual union with a more outward, action-oriented approach, where chaste people in religious life—priests and nuns—choose to share life with the divine partner, not because they want to hide from the world and be alone with God, but precisely because they want to actively participate in God's work of transforming the world. The desire to be of service is a natural instinct. Based on this instinct, Teilhard might ask an individual or a couple to choose a "supreme marriage" in order to be an instrument of God's work in the world.

Teilhard realized he could transfer this new understanding of a "supreme marriage" to committed couples. When he applies this idea to such couples, it would not exclude sexual activity within marriage, since that activity can help intensify and deepen their union. Rather, as with priests and nuns, the couple's "supreme marriage" with Christ would focus on the couple's *action* in helping transform the world as their union's third primary purpose.[13] From this new and actively involved "supreme marriage" perspective, Teilhard takes a fresh look at marriage as a context of chastity and supreme marriage.

Teilhard proposes that, in the evolutionary scheme of things, a "supreme marriage" is available to earthly lovers. So that, perhaps even while a married couple are giving birth to their own physical children, they are invited to enter—in a kind of new stage of marriage—a "supreme marriage" of their relationship (Third Self) to God. In making this commitment, they discover the *"miracle of a common soul."*[14] That is, the partners commit themselves as a dyadic unit (a union of two) to the evolutionary work of building the kingdom of God on Earth. Thus, as a dyad, *their "relationship" becomes Christ's bride,* doing Christ's work in the world.

Notice that, in his re-envisioning of the evolutionary purpose of chastity, Teilhard has turned around completely the traditional understanding of *chastity.* He has taken chastity from its traditional focus on "giving up" certain activities to a focus on a "commitment to action." Take the time to digest some implications of this radical shift in understanding of chastity, from "avoidance" to "action."

In this dynamic Teilhardian ethic, "chastity is the opposite of waste."[15] It is the creative unification and conservation of energy.[16]

SPIRITUAL EXERCISE: CHASTITY AS ACTION

No one before Teilhard has ever proposed this shift in the understanding of chastity. Ask yourself these questions: Why did Teilhard do this? Where did this understanding originate? Recall that for Teilhard love is a source of energy. In an evolutionary world, love-energy is to be used for building bigger and broader loving relationships. If you are going to create a supreme marriage with God, imagine the love-energy created by that act! What are you going to do with all that energy? Teilhard says that you use it to accomplish God's project.

Some Examples

In an earlier chapter, we mentioned that we authors, Patricia and Louis, named our relationship "Palo." So, in this divine marriage that Teilhard is describing, it would be Palo who "marries" Christ, not Pat or Lou as individuals. This does not exclude either of us as individuals from having a personal spiritual life with Christ—or sexual activity with each other. But the emphasis here is that our relationship becomes one with Christ and his work. Our challenge is to keep the relationship between Palo and Christ chaste.

Here, being chaste means that Palo in its actions remains faithful to the values and way of Jesus. Such chastity does not demand that our way of interacting with each other needs to change. For example, we need not change our sexual behavior. *Chastity's requirement is that we as a couple remain faithful to Christ and his work*. We would be "unchaste," for example, if after promising fidelity to God and God's project, we turned around and dedicated our lives to amassing money or power or living our lives purely for our own fun and pleasure.

To take a classic example from the Middle Ages, Elizabeth of Hungary and Louis of Thuringia came together in a politically arranged marriage but subsequently fell deeply in love. Their loving dyad, wedded to Christ, produced creative work for God and humanity. At the same time, their love for each other also produced a number of children.

In the workings of their dyad, the creative ideas came from Elizabeth but they could only be realized with the "fertilizing spirit of Louis."[17] Together they founded a hospital where Elizabeth herself cared for the sick each day. Her husband supported her charitable work among the poor. Their shared commitment to Christ expressed itself in work for the kingdom of God.

There is a famous story told of King Louis and Elizabeth. Early in their marriage, she was out in the countryside taking bread and gifts to the poor in secret. Some nobles had accused her of stealing money from the castle treasury. On this particular day, King Louis was riding in a hunting party with these nobles. They came across his wife in an area where the poor lived. Louis, surrounded by the nobles, asked her to reveal what was hidden under her cloak. The nobles expected to find her holding money from the treasury. When her cloak opened, out fell a bouquet of white and red roses. This proved to her husband that God's protecting hand was guiding their work. After that, he fully supported their ministry.[18]

Elizabeth's young husband succumbed suddenly to fever in Italy on his way to support the Sixth Crusade. After King Louis died, Elizabeth, as queen, kept their dyadic spirit alive. She assumed control of affairs at home and, on behalf of them both, continued to distribute alms in all parts of their territory, even giving away state robes and ornaments to the poor.

SPIRITUAL EXERCISE: HOW TO CREATE A "SUPREME MARRIAGE"

In a church wedding ceremony, two people promise their love and fidelity to each other as husband and wife. A desire for the sacred marriage of their relationship to Christ will usually emerge later on. Since the Church has not yet created a formal service or ritual for the marriage of a loving partnership to Christ, a couple desiring a sacred marriage will have to create their own ritual and words.

To begin this process, it would be helpful to give your relationship its own name, as we have named our relationship "Palo." You may then draw up some words for a private ceremony to read to each other, formulate some prayers promising fidelity to Christ and his work in the world, followed by some ritual that feels appropriate.

To keep the sense of our Third Self alive, during our shared prayer each day, we commit Palo to be an instrument of God's work in the world. Additionally, we have personally found it helpful when sending letters or giving birthday cards to each other to sign them from within the relationship as "Pat Palo" or "Lou Palo."

Two Key Insights Concerning Chastity

The First Insight: The Heart Dictates Chastity

As Teilhard reflected on this idea of a "supreme marriage" for a married couple, he had two key insights. The first is that "it is the heart that dictates chastity."[19] This first insight has two aspects.

First, *the choice for a "supreme marriage" form of commitment must flow from the heart*; it must be utterly free, chosen without any coercion or obligation. This holds true both for religious sisters and priests as well as committed couples.

Second, *it is the heart that defines one's meaning of chastity and its expression.* This is so because chastity is an evolving love process. Its meaning and expression are able to change and develop as human love develops.

For example, for a married couple at an early stage, chastity need not involve abstinence from physical sexual expressions of love, because the essence of chastity for a married couple is not primarily that they abstain from genital expressions. It is primarily that they commit their "relationship" in a supreme marriage to God. In this regard, chastity is their hearts' commitment of their relationship to God and to God's work in the world. Their fidelity is to God and God's plan. King Louis and Elizabeth did not abstain from sexual expression of their love. They had three children, even though as a dyad they had committed themselves to God's work in the world. In this new sense, a violation of their chastity, or their relationship's marriage to God, would have meant that, as a relationship, they had chosen to live and act in ways that are contrary to God's work.

As long as sexual activity and other loving gestures will help deepen that commitment (their supreme marriage) to God and God's work, such expressions of love are still within Teilhard's definition of chastity, since *it is the heart that dictates chastity's meaning and its expression*. As a couple evolves spiritually, their hearts may choose to redefine their chastity's manner of expression.

SPIRITUAL EXERCISE: CHASTITY'S MEANING

Although this chapter has focused on the marriage relationship, could this insight—*it is the heart that dictates chastity's meaning and its expression*—also be applied to religious sisters and priests who take a traditional vow of chastity as a "requirement"? Are there ways within their hearts that they could reinterpret the meaning and expression of that vow? Return to this question again and again as you read the rest of this chapter and future chapters. It may provide insights into the evolution of religious and priestly life.

The Second Insight:
A Transposition into Religion

The second insight about chastity is that Christian chastity, as Teilhard understands it, is ultimately *"a transposition into religion of the lover's fidelity."*[20] Here, we understand the work of religion is to tie or bind together all the ways of loving and of bringing people together in love. The fidelity of the couple's relationship with God is measured by how dedicated their partnership is to God's loving work among people.

For example, if Palo were to become unfaithful (or adulterous) in its relationship to God, such infidelity would take the form of activity

79

that would violate the "supreme marriage" or break up Palo's sacred relationship to God, such as a commitment by Palo to pursue greed, power, or prestige.

We often read the term in the Hebrew Scriptures of an "adulterous nation." What does adultery mean for a nation? Adultery means to break or violate a sacred covenant. Israel has a (marriage) covenant with Yahweh; God alone deserves Israel's worship and fidelity. Israel the nation becomes adulterous when it worships other gods and is thus unfaithful to its covenant with Yahweh. For Teilhard, the same understanding of adultery applies to couples. Thus, if a couple has entered a sacred marriage to God and God's work, then chooses to serve another "god," (money, prestige, power, and so forth), their sacred marriage has become "adulterous."

By contrasting his approach to chastity with the traditional approach, Teilhard shows how each of these two ideas regarding chastity is genuinely new.

For all the priests, brothers, and nuns living in religious communities until now, Teilhard might say, the vow of chastity was for the most part neither "dictated by the heart" nor "a transposition into religion of the lover's fidelity." Rather, the vow of chastity in religious life was taken as an expression of one's conformity with a traditional restrictive and penitential asceticism. In this context, one's fidelity to the vow of chastity was seen primarily as privation and deprivation, as a giving up of a normal human life of physical intimacy. In this context of "giving up," the idea and ideal of a "lover's fidelity" is hard to discern. It was not the heart primarily dictating chastity in religious life, but a canonical obligation. There was no "lover's choice" in the matter. In religious life and in priesthood, chastity was never an option. It was a requirement.

SPIRITUAL EXERCISE:
TRANSFORMING A REQUIREMENT

Teilhard took a "required" vow of chastity when he joined the Society of Jesus. If he really believed he could not transform the meaning of his vow through his "lover's fidelity," he probably would have left the Jesuit order. But he didn't. He stayed a Jesuit to the end of his life. What do you think he did in his interpretation of his vow of chastity to make it *a transposition into religion of the lover's fidelity*"? Teilhard never told us what he did. It is a reflective challenge for us to try to envision what he did and how he did it.

Sanctification Rooted in Love

Teilhard firmly agrees with the traditional theology of Christian sanctification, both for those inside and outside of monasteries and convents: *the process of sanctification must be rooted in love, specifically in the gradual purification of love.* Teilhard calls this process of the gradual purification of love "sublimation." It is important to clearly understand what Teilhard means by this term. For him, the sublimation process involves converting—or better, re-envisioning—the energy of love's natural sexual impulse from being used simply for its immediate goal *of personal and shared pleasure* to a broader purpose with a loving social, moral, or aesthetic value. In other words, sublimation, as Teilhard understands it, does not suppress love's natural sexual impulse. He affirms that sexual activity may help deepen the love of the partners for each other as an immediate interpersonal effect. But he sees a larger picture. For Teilhard, sublimation invites committed couples, in addition, to use the very energy of their shared love to seek a new and wider effect in the larger world. For him, chastity is not a refusal to show love, but "an increasing refinement of the power to love...a growing interior unity...a concentration and spiritualization of that power."[21]

Sanctification, like sublimation, is a gradual process that moves in stages. In some cases, sanctification—that is, the love-of-God purification process—may begin at a very basic stage. For example, from fear of the "pains of hell," it may develop into true sorrow for sin as offending God. From there, it may grow into a further stage called "obedient love," where love is shown by obeying God's will. From there, it may mature into a pure and direct love of God, even an all-consuming love, as happened with many saints. Such purification and sublimation of love is meant to develop naturally, in a kind of spiritual evolution.

In a similar way, love's evolution among couples might begin with predominantly physical and genital expressions of love. Later on, it might—or might not—choose to minimize genital sexuality to favor an emphasis on related shared displays of affection and intimacy—kissing, hugging, and loving touches. In time, displays of love might move toward

81

ever more spiritual expressions. For example, when Samuel Clemens (Mark Twain) was off lecturing and physically away from his beloved wife, Olivia, they kept in close contact with each other by writing love letters to each other, "every day and, many times, twice a day."[22]

In one sense, Teilhard is looking at this gradual purification of love as a scientist looks at converting physical energy in useful ways. He knows that with the energy of electricity, for example, we can "convert" electrical energy in a number of ways, from wasting it and using it in frivolous ways, to using it productively, for example, in conducting an important research project in medicine or making an important communication of life and death. In such ways, we are "purifying" our use of electrical energy.

SPIRITUAL EXERCISE: CONVERTING ENERGY

How might Teilhard have used this principle of converting physical energy as a process for "purifying" love energy? Do you see ways you and your partner might do so?

Sanctity and Sexuality

While some would argue that there is no direct relationship between sanctity and sexuality, Teilhard asserts very emphatically that there is an important connection. He says that we know psychologically that "the energy which fuels our interior life and determines its fabric is in its roots of a passionate nature."[23] Those passions are most often felt and expressed physically and affectionately in loving relationships.

For example, Samuel and Olivia Clemens were very affectionate lovers. While Samuel came from a very undemonstrative family—he claims he never saw his mother and father kiss each other—it was Olivia, he says, who introduced him to the energy of passion. She poured out "her prodigal affections in kisses and caresses, and in a vocabulary of endearments, whose profusion was always an astonishment to me."[24] Their physical passion provided the fuel for their sanctification and energy for their work.

Teilhard's focus is on the married couple as the most typical of loving relationships that can promote sanctity and the service of God. Remember, for Teilhard, "it is the heart that dictates chastity." The more mature and fully human the partners' love is, the more they can consciously and wisely dictate their expressions of their shared commitment to serving God's work in the world.

The more mature and complete we human beings become, the better we can see what needs to be done to make the world a better place and how we, personally and with others, can contribute to that improvement in our lifetime.

SPIRITUAL EXERCISE: THE MATURE HEART

Teilhard is now introducing a new dimension to the "heart that dictates the meaning and purpose of chastity." This new dimension is the layer of personal emotional maturity or immaturity of the people in a relationship. Is an emotionally immature person really ready to comprehend a vow? Or how emotionally mature must a person—or a committed couple—be to be able to understand and carry out the purpose and meaning of a vow?

CHAPTER 7

More Fully Human

Loving Involves Becoming More Fully Human

AN IMPORTANT THEME in Teilhard's essay "The Evolution of Chastity" is the need for individuals and partners to develop their humanity to its maturity or fullness.[1] For him, the process of becoming more fully human is essential. It is crucial in the practice of chastity in Teilhard's sense. Some of the more positive theorists in modern psychology have attempted to define some of the factors involved in becoming a mature human being. These factors may include compassion for others, accepting responsibility for the welfare of others, willingness to contribute to the betterment of the community, and the ability to grasp another's viewpoint and acknowledge its merits and value.

For Teilhard, there is a wide range of healthy relationships that may provide a powerful influence in nurturing growth in some of the deepest human capacities, especially love. Based on the law "union differentiates," Teilhard would assert that such relationships, like those of Jacques and Raissa Maritain and Samuel and Olivia Clemens, provide the experiences that most effectively foster mutual completion and human maturity.

Human beings naturally tend toward unions that bring about and foster mutual completion. This is usually why people build friendships and enter into marriage. They want to feel more fully human. They sense that caring and respectful relationships will release dormant potentials that will help them become so. The impulse toward such unions has its roots in our physical bodies. Teilhard says that it is "from the storehouse of passion that the warmth and light of one's soul arises, transfigured."[2]

Two famous philosophers of the early twentieth century were Jacques and Raissa Maritain. They were a married couple, he a Christian, she a Jew. One might say that when they met as young university students in Paris, "they saw each other's face," instantly knew each other, and recognized their mutual destiny.[3] Jacques had noticed Raissa's slender grace, her "marvelous smile," and the "extraordinary light of her wonderful eyes." Such physical qualities are typically the first ones to create the necessary Attraction[4] to bring two people together. It is the physical presence and shared physical Connection that allowed their more intellectual and spiritual union to blossom.

> They became inseparable, walking and talking, discussing with the passion of young people the ultimate questions of life, politics, religion, and the meaning of it all, if any. They sometimes walked for miles, forgetting to go home, not turning up for meals, and causing both sets of parents to worry. Raissa wrote, "Did anything else exist in comparison with all we had to tell each other? Together we had to think out the entire universe anew, the meaning of life, the fate of man, the justice and injustice of societies."[5]

To maintain the continuous drive toward spiritualizing any deep union, each partner needs to fill up with fuel. That fuel comes, not from the body alone nor from the spirit alone, but precisely from the constant interaction of body and spirit as an integral union, which is their Third Self.

Universally, in the evolutionary process, spirit emerges from within matter. Teilhard insists that, if we want to understand love, we must first explore the "spiritual power of matter."[6] Paradoxically, it is in the tangible physical elements of life that we must first look for the power and evolutionary possibilities for spiritual growth.

SPIRITUAL EXERCISE: THE SPIRITUAL POWER OF MATTER

The phrase "the spiritual power of matter" is a paradoxical expression, because in our culture, we have made "matter" and "spirit" opposites and almost contradictory in meaning. Teilhard asks you to transcend this apparent contradiction and find the power and evolutionary possibilities of chastity in "tangible physical elements of life." How would you begin this quest? Think of Jesus' parable of the merchant searching for fine pearls (Matt 13:45). If you were a merchant searching for these evolutionary possibilities, where would you look? What tangible physical elements suggest a place to start exploring to find the source of spiritual power that Teilhard talks about?

The Feminine

In Teilhard's essay on chastity, Teilhard tells us where he would look to find the spiritual power of matter. He begins by making some very bold and puzzling claims. For example, he writes, both beneath and above "the spiritual power of matter lies the spiritual power of the flesh and of the feminine."[7] He adds, "Woman is, for man, the symbol and personification of all the fulfillment we look for from the universe."[8]

In his essay, these statements about the feminine seem to come out of the blue and surprise us. We are not yet ready to grasp their meaning or recognize their import. Perhaps, we think, they are just Teilhard challenging a cultural tradition of patriarchy. Certainly, Teilhard's comments here clearly affirm women's equality with men. They surely sound like feminist thinking emerging a quarter-century before the rise of feminism.

Remember that this essay on the evolution of chastity is not focused on consecrated religious life but primarily on the marriage relationship and its evolution.

In so many stories of famous couples, the work they produce for God is primarily attributed to the husband. Yet the husbands consistently attribute their success to the contributions and inspirations of their wives. In our terminology, we would say the work is produced by the couple's Third Self.

Mark Twain wrote his most powerful novels after his marriage to Olivia and he credits her inspiration: "Ever since we've been married I have depended on my wife to go over and revise my manuscripts. I have written scarcely anything in twenty-five years that she hasn't edited."[9]

The famous poet William Blake was healed of an illness the

moment he told his beloved Catherine he loved her. Together for years, they produced books of poetry and art. He created the poetry while she copied it in beautiful script and drew the stunning illuminated artwork that illustrated and gave tangible life to his verse.[10]

The Tales of the Hasidim was published under the name of Martin Buber, and it brought him worldwide recognition. But much of it was written and all of it was inspired by his wife, Paula, during the months they were in hiding to complete the manuscript. Martin dedicated the book to her in acknowledgment of the "enormous impact" she had on him and on the writing of the book.[11]

To acknowledge his wife Raissa's contribution to their union, Jacques Maritain wrote, "She sacrificed everything in spite of all her suffering, and, at certain moments of an almost total exhaustion… and because the collaboration I had always asked of her was, for her, a sacred duty… revising in manuscript everything I have written."[12]

These are all examples of the spiritual power of the feminine.

Remember also another biased assumption about women. In the traditional scriptural understanding of marriage, reflective of ancient cultural practices, the woman belongs to her husband, first of all, as his property and, second, as essentially an instrument for the propagation of the human race, that is, she produces *his* children, children that become the husband's property (see Exod 20:1–17).

Teilhard finds this traditional exclusive focus of the woman's role in marriage as a child-bearer severely limiting. No matter how funda-mental and necessary a woman's physical fertility may be, he says, "it is almost nothing in comparison with her spiritual fertility"[13]—her intel-ligence and wisdom.

People, he says, have always known that a woman brings "fullness of being, sensibility and self-revelation to the man who has loved her."[14] But human beings—especially church leaders—couldn't acknowledge the true value of a powerful male-female union before now—even in marriage. The human community needed many centuries to evolve to a certain level of consciousness before it could acknowledge the true potential of an equal man-woman union.[15]

Although married couples knew, of course, that sexual expres-sions of love between spouses helped deepen and solidify their union, it wasn't until the Second Vatican Council that the Church[16] acknowl-edged this obvious fact. As already noted in the previous chapter, the Church teaches that there are two primary purposes of sexual activity in marriage: (1) to procreate children and (2) to foster the love between the spouses. Teilhard had been writing about fostering love between the spouses as a primary purpose of marriage many decades before Vatican II. His insights on this matter undoubtedly influenced those theologians composing documents for the ecumenical council. Unfortunately, he never lived to delight in how his ideas came to find acceptance in these solemn church documents.

SPIRITUAL EXERCISE:
THE POWER OF THE FEMININE

Can you recall stories from your own life, like stories of the famous couples you have read about, where the feminine influence was very powerful in the development of some work or effort that had a positive spiritual effect?

Evolutionary Forms of Union

In his essay "The Evolution of Chastity," Teilhard is writing about much more than fostering love between spouses. Through his evolutionary theories about marriage, he is looking further into the future. He thinks that people today are searching for "a form of union which will be richer and more spiritualized than that which is limited to the cradle."[17] However, for love to evolve enough to take us into "another universe," he acknowledges, we must first master the energies of the feminine.

Teilhard is exploring the spiritual potential of the combined union of the masculine and feminine energies. He envisions the energies of that union rising upward toward God, not separately as man and as woman, but "as two portions of nature in composition." In his words, "Spirituality does not come down upon a 'monad' but upon the human 'dyad.'"[18]

For Teilhard, a man cannot fully know himself or become himself by himself. He can do it only through interaction with women. If that development of fullness remains undeveloped or underdeveloped, and the person attempts to go directly to God, that person's vow of chastity remains inadequate and cannot evolve. Teilhard's reasoning is that such a person does not know himself in any complete sense of the word.

The same goes for a woman as for a man. If her human fullness remains undeveloped or underdeveloped through lack of loving interaction with men and the consequent development of her masculine capacities, her vow of chastity remains incomplete and cannot evolve. Teilhard is *not* saying that men should become more like women, or women more like men. Rather, he is talking about the energies or qualities traditionally associated with the feminine that men are not likely to develop normally, perhaps for cultural reasons, but need to develop to become a whole person.

Because of mistaken assumptions and biased cultural expectations, the spiritual power of the feminine in our world today has yet to be fully tapped. Nevertheless, the need for development is mutual between the genders. Men have not been completely revealed to themselves by women, nor have women been completely revealed to themselves by men. In this specific evolutionary process, the two genders should not be separated from each other or treated unequally while their development and mutual self-revelation is still going on.

In a passing comment, Teilhard observes that this spiritual growth and maturity typically happens in paired units, whether the pairs are married or unmarried. His point is that one's fullest self-revelation happens best in a loving union with a complementary person, whether the partners are spouses or close friends. For example, Pope John Paul II attributed his close friendships with women as powerful influences in his development as a human person.

Polish Cardinal Karol Wojtyla (who would become Pope John Paul II) met a Polish married philosopher, Anna Teresa Tymieniecka, in Krakow in 1973, and for more than thirty years carried on an intimate friendship with her, until his death. It began after she had written to him congratulating him on his philosophical treatise *Osoba i Czyn* ("Person and Act").

Twenty years before they met, in 1954, Anna Teresa had moved to the United States to accept teaching positions at Yale and Penn State. She was married to an economics professor from Harvard and had three children.

The cardinal first encountered her in Krakow in 1973 and began an intense relationship "carried on in letters sent by circuitous routes to avoid the prying eyes of Poland's secret police." They also had arranged meetings, "such as in 1976, when Wojtyla stayed at her home in Vermont on a visit to the United States, during which time she arranged meetings with the cardinals who would help elect him two years later." During this visit, they camped and skied together.[19]

Cardinal Wojtyla saw this friendship as providential. "He believed her presence in his life was a God-given gift, and that the relationship was a kind of vocation." He believed God's grace was guiding their relationship. After he was elected pope, he told Anna Teresa he wished to continue their relationship. This collaborative relationship—their Third Self—produced an English language edition of his philosophical treatise titled *The Acting Person*.

In a letter he wrote to her, speaking of the divine gift of their relationship, he said,

> Once—I remember exactly when and where—I heard these words, "I belong to you." For me, first of all, the gift of a person resonated in them. I was afraid of this gift; but knew from the beginning, and I know still better and better now, that I have to accept this gift as a gift from heaven.

Anna Teresa was one of the few people allowed at his bedside in the clinic during his recovery after he had been shot in May 1981, and again her presence, from time to time in Rome, offered emotional support during his final years as he was suffering from Parkinson's disease.

Pope Francis, who knew of the pope's friendship with Anna Teresa, was quoted as saying, "Any man failing to have a good friendship with a woman" was "missing something." He also said that being friends with a woman is not a sin, and that Pope John Paul had been capable of "a healthy, holy friendship with a woman."

Because the official lives of the saints have been censored by the Church for centuries, we will perhaps never know how many men saints' lives have been shaped by their friendships with women, and vice versa. Some of the most public cases were between Francis of Assisi and Clare of Assisi and John of the Cross and Teresa of Avila.

Any one individual, of course, can be a partner in many such self-revelatory paired units or teams. Partners can be found among colleagues, parents and children, teachers and students. Teilhard himself, although a celibate priest, attributes much of his personal development as a male to a number of caring relationships with women throughout his life—his mother, his cousin Marguerite, and a number of women friends with whom, for decades, he maintained significantly close relationships (although always observing his traditional vow of celibacy).

Pope John Paul II also had other close friendships with women. A 2009 book revealed Pope John Paul II's deep friendship, beginning in the 1950s, with another woman, Wanda Poltawska, a Krakow psychiatrist.[20] He often spent time in her home with her family. In one of his letters to Wanda, discussing his spiritual development, he credits her "with nurturing his thoughts on family values and the theology of the body." At the age of 94, Dr. Poltawska claims to have a "whole suitcase" of unpublished letters to and from Pope John Paul, but has been under pressure to destroy them. If she does, it will deprive us of rich insights into the human sensitivities of Saint John Paul.[21]

Similarly, most men and women have or had close relationships with a number of people of the opposite gender that helped them grow and develop as a human person. All caring male-female relationships, especially those with a purpose beyond the relationship, can nurture this mutual self-revelation and personal development.

As far as Teilhard was concerned, the kind of energy of which shared love is capable is still largely in its potential stages in our day. Although we can find a number of examples of the power of loving dyads throughout history, especially in more recent times, that power still remains quite dormant. The kinds of intense partnership we meet in some of the couples mentioned earlier—William and Catherine Blake, Samuel and Olivia Clemens, Martin and Paula Buber, Jacques and Raissa Maritain—are the exceptions, but they prove that a higher kind of loving union is possible. It is an evolutionary process just emerging and will require a long period of development on the "natural plane" before such loving unions become predominant.

Before that happens, a man's full spiritual potential waits to be revealed and emerged through loving interaction with the women in his life, and vice versa for the revelation of a woman's full spiritual potential emerging through loving interaction with the men in her life.[22]

Notice that this Teilhardian claim is quite different from the traditional religious assumption about union with God for husbands and wives. Traditionally, in spirituality and spiritual practice, even in marriage, it was encouraged that the natural drive toward maintaining a loving union of man and woman could and should be redirected, so that each partner might individually aim directly toward union with

God. Tradition claimed that such unions of individuals with God were the ideal of spirituality and required no need of support from another human creature. Thus, almost all traditional spirituality is structured essentially as a me-and-God relationship. For Teilhard, this traditional approach describes "spirituality coming down upon a 'monad.'" For him, if spirituality is to continue to evolve, it must be based on "relationships." However long this evolution of chastity may take, the exploration and experimentation will happen not primarily in individuals by themselves, but rather in loving, caring unions.[23]

SPIRITUAL EXERCISE: FULL HUMAN POTENTIAL

Can you recall some relationships with people of the opposite gender who helped you develop parts of your own personality that needed to grow to reveal your potential as a human being? Especially the parts or qualities of you that are typically associated with the opposite gender?

Beyond the Natural Manifestations of Love

Instead of a traditional focus on reducing and denying the natural and normal physical expressions of loving, the real challenge, says Teilhard, is to harness that dyadic energy and transform it. Don't cut back on those natural manifestations of love, but go beyond them. Let the energy of love suggest ways your relationship could make a difference in the world. This is the new ideal of chastity—the *spirit* of chastity.[24]

Once we understand the spiritual power of matter, we can drop the distinction between "holiness of body" and "holiness of spirit." Moreover, we can no longer maintain traditional distinctions between what is sacred and what is profane, what is pure or impure. In an evolving world, says Teilhard, there is only a good direction and a bad direction. There is either an ascent into chastity or a descent into pure egoism or materialistic enjoyment.[25]

In the old asceticism, the word *detachment* implied a rejection of matter through self-deprivation. Teilhard graphically described it as "purifying oneself from the refuse of earth."[26] Much of traditional asceticism involved a formally chosen form of self-deprivation, an unnatural attempt to separate spirit from body.

In the new asceticism, the word *detachment* emphasizes the "divinization" of creation. Instead of "purifying oneself," the challenge is to "purify creation." We do this, says Teilhard, by plunging into the flood of created energies, not to wallow in them but in order to (1) uplift them and (2) to be uplifted by them. For Teilhard, the first and foremost of those created energies to be purified and refined is love.

In this new context, detachment does not need to be chosen or artificially imposed; it happens naturally. It happens inevitably as one enters and moves through these created energies and carries them along in order to share them. Teilhard says that this was the kind of natural detachment or self-emptying Christ entered in his Incarnation. When the Divine Person plunged into the flood of created energies, Christ entered matter, moved through it, and *carried with him in his body the whole material world.* His body, like ours, was made up of tangible matter—water, minerals (calcium, magnesium, sodium, etc.), metals (iron, zinc, copper, manganese, etc.), gases (nitrogen, oxygen, carbon dioxide, etc.), bacteria, viruses, emotions, and a host of inherited animal characteristics (carried over into his DNA). From animal evolution, like all of us, Christ inherited a tripartite brain: first, a *brain stem* developed by the reptiles; second, a *limbic system* evolved for us by the primitive mammals and birds; third, a *bilateral cortex* from the higher mammals, including a *prefrontal cortex* developed by earlier hominin species. He didn't discard or deny any of these material realities. He uplifted them and let himself be uplifted by them.[27]

SPIRITUAL EXERCISE: PURIFYING CREATION

What does Teilhard mean by helping to "purify creation"? He says you do it by "uplifting creation." How do you "uplift" physical creation, and how are you uplifted by it? He says that Christ in the incarnation did it. From your own life, can you give any examples of people where this "uplifting" process has worked? Here are some obvious examples to get you started: Your voice is a physical thing; you uplift it by using it to comfort or console others, to give them important information or directions to help them find what they are looking for. Your mobile phone is a physical thing; you uplift it by using it to seek driving directions to a certain location or to purchase something needed for your health. Your body is a physical thing; you uplift it by learning and training, perhaps to become a musician, a teacher, a nurse, a scriptwriter, or a computer programmer.

The Threshold of Another Universe

Teilhard likens this divinization of matter in the marriage relationship to an artist in the emotional excitement of discovery. For Teilhard, human love in its emotional excitement of discovery can provide the energy to move us into the next stage of evolution on Earth. At present, he says, "Love is at the threshold of another universe."[28] For him, the spirit of chastity (in Teilhard's understanding), as found in marriage and deep friendships, is destined to release the power of love hidden within matter. It hasn't achieved a great deal yet, but the capabilities and its limitless potential await release.

For example, Teilhard hopes that the stories of intense partnerships described on earlier pages will show that there is available a third and evolutionary purpose for marriage (and deep friendships). Currently, the two purposes are as follows: (1) the procreation of children and (2) the mutual love of the spouses.[29] The third (3) would be for the couple to *commit to advancing the further development and growth of the human community*.[30]

This evolutionary purpose could happen through *scientific research*, as with Marie and Pierre Curie's work with radiation; through *technological invention*, as with partners like Steve Jobs and Steve Wozniak, the founders of Apple; through *art and music*, as with collaborators like Rogers & Hammerstein; through *human rights programs*, as with husband and wife Bill and Melinda Gates; through *caring for the environment*, as with movie star Johnny Depp and his partner, Vanessa Paradis, investing in solar energy. In each case, these partners have used their time, talents, and financial resources to promote human development.

Teilhard says there are two opposing ethical ideas or theories of chastity and purity. The first theory says, in effect, "Above all, break no rules and, not even at the cost of some richness." The second says, "Above all, increase your richness even at the cost of some contamination." Teilhard prefers the second way.

In using the word "contamination," Teilhard acknowledges that if a relationship is going to commit to the third, evolutionary purpose of marriage (or friendship), the partners are going to meet resistance from others, even their closest relatives and friends. Moreover, simply by getting involved in exploring new avenues of service, they are bound to make mistakes, take wrong turns, get bad advice, step on some toes, or alienate some people on the way. These are the kinds of "contamination" pioneers and explorers will inevitably experience. However, they are no reason to stop exploring.

Nevertheless, Teilhard believes that it is the second approach that holds much truth and, in time, will be shown to be a true source of movement toward God. It will foster God's project.

For Teilhard, chastity's ultimate purpose is *to facilitate the Holy Spirit's work of renewing the face of Earth*. As he says, "Chastity, then, is a virtue of participation and conquest, and not a schooling in restriction and avoidance."[31]

There are, what Teilhard called "lower radiations of love" that have been operating in human society beyond the use of sexual actions for reproduction. Some of these "lower radiations" arise from the passionate love of money, power, prestige, comfort, sex, or pleasure. Because of their power, these lower radiations can become intoxicating, addictive, and even corruptive. Despite the possible pitfalls of sexual passion and "lower radiations," we need not abandon them. Rather, we need to find ways to use such passions for human growth and development. After all, he notes, "Fire can destroy and electricity can kill. Should we therefore stop using them?" Danger, Teilhard observes, is usually a sign of power or energy.

In the past, it was morally more important to avoid the risks of breaking any rule than to try something difficult to promote God's project. According to the principle of evolution, Teilhard says, "The more dangerous a thing is, the more its conquest is ordained by life."[32] For this reason, Teilhard says, "Our religion must be reborn."[33] Our focus must shift from "keeping safe from sin" to "trying anything for God." Our focus is no longer primarily on "saving our soul" but on "saving Earth."

For example, in the late nineteenth century, the passionate love between Marie Curie, physicist and chemist, and her husband Pierre, a professor at the university, challenged the pair to do painstaking research to isolate the first identifiable radioactive substance, radium. Their discovery of radioactivity ushered in a host of new areas in science and medicine. But their research also endangered their physical health.

In the early twentieth century, the passionate love between Frank Sheed and Masie Ward challenged them to start the first Catholic theological publishing house in England, Sheed & Ward, which catered to intellectual readers. Other Catholic publishers offered only Bibles, missals, and prayer books.

Through their writings, Raissa and Jacques Maritain were instrumental in changing the worldwide anti-Semitic attitudes of Christians during World War II.

In Paris, Leon Bloy and his wife were reduced to abject poverty because of their unrelenting commitment to writing and speaking out for social justice.

In other words, instead of focusing on our personal safety and security, Teilhard feels we should be concerned about how God is trying to transform the face of our planet and how we can contribute toward that mission. We show our love for God by committing ourselves, both individually and in partnerships, to God's project for creation. This is the true reason for a commitment to chastity. If it is the heart that dictates the choices chastity makes, it is the physical passion of love that gives chastity its energy.

SPIRITUAL EXERCISE: RELIGION REBORN?

In order for our religion to be reborn, Teilhard says, our focus must shift from "keeping safe from sin" to "trying anything for God." Our focus is no longer primarily on "saving our soul" but on "saving Earth." Can you spell out what these statements might mean to you personally, if you truly believed them and wanted to live them out?

A Passionate Response

To describe the evolutionary process, Teilhard uses the image of people climbing toward a mountain peak. The peak symbolizes the completion of God's project. Many abandon the quest because our traditional spirituality has promoted the primacy of safety and security, private lives of devotion, and avoidance of contamination by the world. Teilhard cannot understand why some people claim that a commitment to keep ascending toward the peak would *not* bring us closer to God. Instead, he challenges us to explain why we, as Christians in today's world, remain committed to safety and security, avoiding the greater challenge.

In light of the evolutionary evidence of the divine project and God's plans that we get from science, Teilhard feels there is no excuse for us not to use all our effort to work "to renew the face of Earth." The effort calls for a passionate response.

Teilhard notes that there are two kinds of passion at work in this divine project. There are evolutionary passions of an *impersonal nature*. These may be observed in things such as scientific research (as in the Curies' work in radioactivity) and the exploration of ideas and insights in philosophy, theology, science, and the arts (as in the Sheed & Ward publishing house). However, there are also evolutionary passions of an *interpersonal nature*—compassion, forgiveness, and encouragement—that can only come from interpersonal bonding between men and women (as in the charitable works of Elizabeth and Louis of Hungary).

Some may argue that we must reserve our loving hearts only for God.[34] This is true, admits Teilhard, but note that God is not an ordinary person like us. He says God is a super-person or a hyper-center of people. For a person in love to center his or her heart on some man or woman, Teilhard says, does not neutralize or diminish that person's potential for union with God, since God is the center of all centers.

Here is where Teilhard's understanding of chastity becomes most functional. The spirit of chastity releases the power of love hidden in matter. "Love is the threshold of another universe," says Teilhard.[35] As one learns to master the energies of love, a progressive shift emerges from the physical "attraction and possession" toward the spiritualizing of love. If two beings are to attain deepest unity with each other, they are obliged to explore the potential of their love at progressively deeper and more intense levels of union, each one more spiritual and more broadly encompassing of others than the level before.

For example, at the first level of married love, couples give one another the gift of their bodies for their mutual enjoyment and delight, for that is the way the "natural power of matter offers itself."[36] But at the same time, this natural expression presents itself for sublimation, for possible transformation into a higher form of love. Teilhard likens the physical expression of love in marriage to a kind of spark, waiting for the human spirit to be set on fire.

Here, Teilhard is suggesting that instead of warning and worrying young married couples about mutually exploring "the gift of their bodies," perhaps such stimulation and exploration (granted that it might even be misused for a while) would, in time, give rise to—and "spark"—

deeper expressions of love and a gradual mastery of love's potential in its ability to make positive changes in their world. Teilhard's vision is that such partners would begin to transform their expressions of love to become more all-embracing of the larger human family, and that they would become so closely bonded to each other and open to the needs of the world that they could begin to envision God's project and their possible contribution to it.

Consider the great surge of energy (Teilhard always sees love as a source of energy) released by physical love. Speaking of physical expressions of love, he asks, "Is it not precisely this which should be our first concern to stimulate, to master and to transform?"[37] In this gradual transformation of love energy, we continue to find other ways of loving, where our spiritual richness accompanies our material rich-ness ever more closely—and ultimately the spiritual purpose becomes the primary justification of physical union.

Thanks to science, Teilhard says, we human beings have learned to master all the physical forces available to us. The challenge before us now is to master the energies of love. As that happens, we will see God's project move forward confidently toward its accomplishment.

SPIRITUAL EXERCISE: TWO KINDS OF PASSION

Teilhard talks about passions that are *impersonal* in nature, like scientific research or book-writing, and other passions that are *interpersonal* in nature, like caring for the sick and elderly, as a physician or nurse would, or teaching students as a teacher or professor would. Do your passions tend to be more impersonal or interpersonal, or do you have some of both?

CHAPTER 8

Invisible Partners

Inner Union of Masculine and Feminine

A MONG THE RELATIONSHIPS that offer promise to further the evolutionary process, one is seldom noticed: *the inner union between the masculine energies and feminine energies in each of us.* The quality and maturity of the interaction between those inner partners affects all of our other outer relationships. For example, in a marriage or a deep friendship, the degree that each has developed the potentials of their inner masculine and inner feminine energies suggests the degree that their outer relationships can impact the world for goodness and growth.

As mentioned in the previous chapter, Teilhard makes some very bold claims about the power of this inner union.[1] Here are three of those that still startle us today. First, below *and* above the spiritual power of matter lies "the spiritual power of the flesh and of the feminine."[2] Second, "Woman is, for man, the symbol and personification of all the fulfillment we look for from the universe."[3] Third, people have always known that a woman brings "fullness of being, sensibility and self-revelation to the man who has loved her."[4]

Are you surprised at the powerful role Teilhard gives to woman and the feminine? Think about the Judeo-Christian tradition and its negative view of women and sexuality. For example, Eve is presented as the first to commit sin by disobeying God and the first to tempt the man. For tradition as well as for Teilhard, the feminine energies are those most closely associated with the Earth, the physical, and the flesh, all inescapably connected to "matter." Tradition sees the connection of the feminine to "matter" as leading *away* from God. Teilhard sees this connection as leading *toward* God. If God loved material creation one might say "passionately," as John the Evangelist has assured us (John 3:16), then feminine qualities are precious to God. This is clearly Teilhard's position.

In 1917, while he was serving in the French military as a stretcher-bearer during World War I, Teilhard wrote a most fascinating poem or hymn called "The Eternal Feminine." In it the Eternal Feminine is speaking. She describes herself as "being from the beginning," the "female essence of life" and as the source of attraction for all things — "through me everything moves and relates." She also describes how men are confused by her presence in their lives.

The poem's themes suggest that Teilhard knew of Carl Jung's work on archetypes in the collective unconscious, especially of the feminine archetype. The Swiss psychoanalyst Carl G. Jung (1875–1971) was a contemporary of Teilhard, who most deeply explored and described the working dynamics and pitfalls of the inner marriage between masculine and feminine energies. It is known that Jung had read and was impressed by Teilhard's *The Phenomenon of Man*. It is also known that Teilhard was familiar with Jung's ideas, certainly through Teilhard's connection with the magazine *Psyche*, the international review of psychoanalysis and the human sciences. Jung was a frequent contributor to the magazine as well as Teilhard, who was also on *Psyche*'s editorial board.[5]

"Though they never met, Teilhard and Jung shared a common vision of the inner dimension of life, a dimension that underlies the process of evolution on planet Earth."[6] While Teilhard stressed that outer relationships between men and women will help them integrate missing masculine and feminine elements in their lives, Jung, in exploring the human unconscious, showed that each person already holds both masculine and feminine potentials within the self.[7] Thus, any missing or undeveloped qualities are already present in each person's psyche and need only to be consciously nurtured.

Teilhard and Jung had much in common. Teilhard was seeking to build the bridge between science and religion; and Jung was seeking to build the bridge between psychology and religion. In his essay "The Evolution of Chastity," it is clear that Teilhard recognized that, as Jung suggested, men needed to integrate some feminine qualities in themselves to become fully human. But rather than develop these latent qualities directly through conscious effort in psychoanalysis, as Jung suggested, Teilhard recognized that the way men, as they matured, typically acknowledged and accepted these feminine qualities was through interaction with living women.

SPIRITUAL EXERCISE: TREATMENT OF WOMEN

Think of the many negative cultural and religious attitudes toward women that have held sway over the past six thousand years. Identify some ways women have been seen and treated unfairly—politically, socially, economically, religiously. Why? What are the reasons men have offered to subjugate—and even fear—women over the centuries? Do we still see this bias against women in our own era? Is it still based on the same cultural and religious beliefs? In what ways might these attitudes be changing?

Anima and Animus

According to Jung, every male person has an invisible feminine inner partner whom he must learn to recognize, identify, respect, and welcome fully into his life. The name he gave to a man's invisible partner is his *anima* (a feminine Latin word for "soul," from the verb *animare*, meaning "to animate" or "to give life"). The *anima* lives in a man's unconscious mind, says Jung, therefore he is usually unaware of it.

For example, in the shaman tradition, the primitive healer or medicine man typically took a *spirit wife* (he may have a physical wife as well). His spirit wife—for Jung, his *anima*—would teach him and assist him in his work of healing. Together he and his spirit wife, an invisible inner partner, would function like a single entity. As one shaman put it, "She has been coming to me ever since I took her as my spirit wife, and I sleep with her as with my own wife."[8]

Similarly, every female person has an invisible masculine inner partner whom she must learn to recognize, identify, respect, and welcome fully into her life. The name Jung gave to a woman's invisible partner is her *animus* (a masculine Latin word for "spirit," from the same verb *animare*). The *animus* lives in a woman's unconscious mind, therefore, she is usually unaware of it.

Referring to the inner partner as a "principle," Russian philosopher Nicolas Berdyaev wrote,

Man is not only a sexual but a bisexual being, combining the masculine and feminine principle in himself in different proportions and often in fierce conflict. A man in whom the feminine principle was completely absent would be an abstract being, completely severed from the cosmic element. A woman in whom the masculine principle was completely absent would not be a personality....It is only the union of these two that constitutes a complete human being.[9]

These invisible partners, according to Jung, want to be acknowledged and integrated into each one's personality. To deny the existence of these inner partners can damage one's personality and even prevent healthy and productive outer relationships between men and women.

Teilhard wisely recognized that, because of mistaken assumptions and traditional cultural expectations, the spiritual power of the feminine has yet to be fully tapped.[10] Moreover, he notes, the need for personal development and fulfillment is mutual between the genders. Men have not been completely revealed to themselves by women, nor have women been completely revealed to themselves by men. In this specific integrative process, which is evolutionary, the two genders should not be separated from each other or treated unequally while their development and mutual self-revelation is still going on.[11]

The human maturation process is mutual, says Teilhard. A man's full spiritual potential waits to be revealed and it emerges through loving interaction with the women in his life. And vice versa for the revelation of a woman's full spiritual potential emerging through loving interaction with the men in her life. Billionaire Bill Gates's mind was opened to the world of philanthropy through the compassion for others of his wife, Melinda. President Franklin Delano Roosevelt became an advocate for the poor and women's rights through the influence of his wife, Eleanor.

Note that Teilhard is not saying that men should become more like women, or women more like men. Rather, he is talking about the energies and abilities traditionally associated with the feminine that men do not normally develop, perhaps for cultural reasons. Yet these need to be developed for him to become a whole person, and similarly for women.[12]

SPIRITUAL EXERCISE:
IS GOD MASCULINE AND FEMININE?

In the first chapter of the Book of Genesis, it says, "Then God said, 'Let us make humankind in our image, according to our likeness'.... So God created humankind in his image, / in the image of God he created them; / male and female he created them" (Gen 1:26–27). These words seem to imply that God possesses all the best qualities of the masculine and feminine. What if each human person, man or woman, in order to grow into the fullness of life, is called on to develop all the best qualities of the masculine and feminine?

The Invisible Made Conscious

Invisible partners (the *anima* in men and the *animus* in women) typically operate primarily at an unconscious level. In human development, the challenge is to bring them into consciousness. These invisible partners also pack a lot of energy, so it is wise to learn consciously how to tap into their energy.

According to Jung, only when a man has consciously loved and integrated his *anima* can he hope to become a fully energized and whole human being. Likewise, only when a woman has loved and integrated her *animus* can she hope to become a fully energized and whole human being.

In his deep exploration of the unconscious mind, Jung was perhaps the first psychiatrist who differentiated the traditionally accepted differing psychological makeup of men and women, especially noting those differences to be found operating in the unconscious mind. These differences provide tremendous, often untapped energy for people.[13]

Today many want to stress the equality of men and women, saying, for example, that women can do any job men can do and excel in any field where men were thought to be superior. We do not deny the equality of the genders in terms of talent, skills, and abilities, but simply point out that men and women may be structured differently at certain unconscious levels. As long as that deeper level of differences goes unrecognized or denied, it will be difficult for a person to fully mature, whether male or female. To the degree that a full development is lacking in a partner, so too, will the evolutionary potential of a marriage, friendship, or team be hindered.

Let us explore some of those unconscious feminine energies[14] of the *anima* and corresponding unconscious masculine energies of the *animus*. For simplicity, we will consider four basic expressions of what might traditionally be called "feminine" energies. These four are *Mother Energy*, *Companion Energy*, *Solitary Energy*, and *Medium Energy*.[15] In the following section, we will consider four corresponding "masculine" energies. These four are *Youth Energy*, *Hero Energy*, *Teacher Energy*, and *Sage Energy*. All eight of these energies represent characteristically different ways of relating and participating in relationships and teams. Potentials for all eight capacities are found in each human personality, yet in any particular person, each of these eight energies may be developed to a certain degree or not at all.

Not every woman has developed all four of the feminine energies. Most women specialize in or favor one or two of them. For example, Elizabeth of Hungary might be known for her *mother energy* and *solitary energy*; in contrast, Maisie Ward, wife of Frank Sheed and cofounder of Sheed and Ward Publishers, would be known for her *companion energy*, for supporting and nurturing her husband's development as a public speaker. She would also be known for her *medium energy*, for her vision in seeing the need for a Catholic publisher of theological books for educated readers. So, for these two women's full human development, each would want to develop, at least to some degree, all four of the feminine energies as well as all four of the masculine energies.

Similarly, not all men have developed all four of the masculine energies. Most men specialize in or favor one or two of them. King Louis of Hungary would have been known for his *hero energy* and *teacher energy*, while Frank Sheed, Maisie's husband, would have been known for his *youth energy*, managing all the details of their publishing house and speaking engagements, and *teacher energy*, as a commandingly powerful public speaker. For each man's fullest human development, he would want to develop, to some degree, all four masculine energies plus all four of the feminine energies.

Four Basic Feminine Energies[16]

Because all eight of these energies need to be developed in both men and women, we will try not to associate the feminine energies exclusively with women, nor the masculine energies exclusively with men, but to describe them as energies that anyone is capable of developing.

Mother Energy

Mother Energy channels the *energy of caring for the needs of those who are underdeveloped or helpless, whoever they may be.* Mother energy is basically indiscriminate; it goes out to whoever needs caring—family, friends, enemies, animals, flowers, and so on.

This caring energy (or archetype) represents a bundle of associated energies. Among the bundle of mother energies, we could list the following: *nurturing, feeding, comforting, supporting, affirming, encouraging, listening, cleaning, loving, caring for the weak, healing, guiding evoking growth, defending the helpless, nursing the wounded, protecting the powerless,* and *being compassionate toward the handicapped.*

People who most frequently exemplify aspects of this energy include mothers, nurses, day care workers, veterinarians, physicians, teachers of handicapped children, and those who work with the poor and homeless. One example is Mother Teresa of Calcutta; another is Elizabeth of Hungary. In their care for the poor and sick, they expressed strong mother energy.

Mother energy is perhaps the most common and easily identifiable energy among all the feminine energies. It is manifest in many, many mothers in all ages. Many men enjoy a great amount of this energy as well. Pope Francis has shown the ability to express mother energy in his concern for the poor. Many saints such as Francis of Assisi and St. Vincent de Paul possessed mother energy to a great degree. Jesus certainly manifested mother energy with healing, comforting, feeding, and so on.

There is a saying among psychologists that every man at every age is looking for a mother. Women, who possess strong mother energy, whether consciously or unconsciously, seem to attract men who want to be with them and enjoy feeling those nurturing, affirming, and protective energies.

SPIRITUAL EXERCISE: MOTHER ENERGY

Is mother energy one of the energies you possess and express? How and where in your relationships do you express it?

Companion Energy

Companion energy operates in the *domain of special interpersonal relationships, reflecting the ability to relate intimately as one individual to another.* This energy differs from mother energy in that mother energy's caring for those needing help is rather indiscriminate and goes out to all those in need. In contrast, companion energy is focused completely and intimately on one single person. Companion energy is one-to-one energy. It is symbolized in the person who chooses just one partner and is truly faithful to that partner.

Companion energy wants the partner to succeed and achieve the best—to do significant and even heroic deeds. In its expression, the person using this energy is content to remain in the background and play a consistently supportive role for the partner. A person who wants to accomplish great things is fortunate to find a partner with strong companion energy, one who will never give up the vision of the partner's success.

The bundle of energies associated with companion energy include *friendship, trust, loyalty, fidelity, presence, constancy, inspiration, stimulation, interdependence,* and *complementarity.* The companion is capable of strong and powerful emotions, such as erotic love. However, when this energy is distorted or threatened, jealousy may take over. Healthy companion energy is focused mostly on the other, bringing out the best in the other, and arousing the other to heroic deeds.

James Joyce's wife, Nora, possessed strong companion energy—working, caring, moving, and supporting—while her Jim searched in cities across Europe for work to support the couple as he wrote his great novels *Ulysses* and *Finnegan's Wake.* These are powerful works that changed the face of nineteenth-century literature. Nora stayed in the background, yet was ever present, as she helped her partner achieve his dream and his fame.

Olivia Clemens also possessed great companion energy. She believed her husband Samuel (Mark Twain) was meant to be a great American man of letters. She refused to let him think of himself as he used to be, a cynical satirist and buffoon. She knew of his great compassion for the poor and downtrodden, his sense of social justice. Like a true companion, she would not let him lose sight of the powerful author he was destined to become.[17]

It is certainly possible for professionals like coaches, counselors, or supervisors to provide companion energy to a number of the people working with them. Counselors can evoke the best in their clients. Sports coaches can help bring out the potentials of their team players, just as bosses or supervisors with companion energy can dedicate themselves to helping their staff accomplish difficult goals.

SPIRITUAL EXERCISE: COMPANION ENERGY

Is companion energy one of the energies you possess and express? How and where in your relationships do you express it?

Solitary Energy

Solitary energy moves through the *channel of independence and self-containment*. Unlike companion energy that operates primarily when connected to another, the person with strong solitary energy *can operate alone*. Solitaries can choose the single life and live it fruitfully, productively, and happily. Unlike the mother who is focused on individual needy creatures, the solitary is more broadly focused—on the good of the *community*. In literature, the solitary is also at times called the Virgin, the Amazon, or the Nun.

The solitary is a person in her or his own right, typically dedicated to *social concerns, spiritual values, or scientific research*. The solitary is dedicated to the betterment of the community. As examples of those who channel solitary energy, one immediately thinks of religious sisters working for social justice, or of scientific lab technicians quietly dedicated to research in medicine, and pathfinders in information technology. Pioneers in space, court judges who rule on those who violate community values, and even CEOs who make decisions that affect the entire corporation—all these people may get help and advice from others, but ultimately major decisions fall on their individual shoulders.

The bundle of energies associated with solitary energy include *commitment to social concerns, making a difference in the community, dedication to values and projects important to society*, and *wanting to make the world a better place*. Solitaries are typically *self-contained, independent, valiant, warm*, and *socially aware*.

Solitary energy reflects the person who is independent, yet welcomes instructions from a teacher or guide on how to grow, learn, and develop as a human being. People who excel in this energy often do well in jobs like scientific research, nursing, engineering, writing, and politics.

Both Raissa Maritain and Olivia Clemens expressed this solitary energy, not in writing great books that would positively affect the larger society, but in doing the lonely, thankless task of editing and critiquing them.

Madame Curie also displayed this energy to a great degree in her dedication to research in radioactivity that would one day benefit the entire human community.

In terms of women's rights, we might suggest people like Golda Meier, Betty Friedan, Margaret Thatcher, and Gail Sheehy as possessing solitary energy. Among famous men who possessed great solitary energy, one might include Thomas Edison, Alexander Graham Bell, Nicolas Tesla, and Albert Einstein.

SPIRITUAL EXERCISE: SOLITARY ENERGY

Is solitary energy one of the energies you possess and express? How and where in your relationships do you express it?

Medium Energy

Medium energy operates in the domain that gives shape to what lies beneath the surface of society. This energy is in touch with the world that is yet to be born. While mother energy responds to the many creatures in pain, companion energy focuses on the success of the hero, and solitary energy pays attention to the larger needs of society, medium energy *envisions what is yet to happen on Earth*.

We typically associate medium energy with wise women, crones, psychics, poets, prophets, fortune-tellers, mystics, myth makers, and science-fiction writers, and we can also include here philosophers and theologians, like Teilhard himself in his predictions for the future of spirituality and human evolution.

The bundle of energies associated with medium energy include *intuition, wisdom, clairvoyance, extrasensory perception, self-awareness, prophecy,* and *healing visions.* Mediums seem to be socially predictive and in touch with unconscious sources of motivation. They have the ability to penetrate into the future and predict what is likely to occur in society.

In literature and fairy tales, this energy is personified in the psychic, the good witch, the fortune-teller, and the helpful crone. The Jewish yenta, or matchmaker, is attributed with the ability to predict which boy should wed which girl for a successful marriage. Medium energy is usually associated with older men and women, but sometimes it appears in the very young. In men, medium energy is usually associated with religious and secular prophets and healers.

Coauthor, Patricia, had a six-year-old daughter who seemed to be wise well beyond her years. One day, walking alone together on the beach, Patricia asked her daughter where she learned all these observations she made that people told her were so wise. Her startling reply was something like, "You have no idea of the things I know."

SPIRITUAL EXERCISE: MEDIUM ENERGY

Is medium energy one of the energies to which you have access? How and where in your relationships do you express it?

SPIRITUAL EXERCISE: SELF REVIEW

As you reflect on the four feminine energies—Mother, Companion, Solitary, and Medium—which two stand out as most characteristic of you? Which do you prefer?

Which of these four feminine energies do you need to get in touch with and consciously develop in yourself?

If you began working on this least developed feminine energy, how do you envision it might change your life and the way you relate to others?

Four Basic Masculine Energies[18]

Youth Energy

Youth energy (called Eternal Youth in Jungian psychology) channels the *energy for doing small deeds and tasks*. This energy learns by doing, but needs lots of support and approval. Youth energy is most evident in people who enjoy having a list of things to do and delight in accomplishing each item on the list. This energy does not like to deal with large, difficult, dangerous, or heroic deeds. (Great deeds are for someone with strong *hero* energy.) When given a rather large assignment, youth energy will typically break down the large work into a series of smaller tasks, each of which may be checked off on a list as it is accomplished.

The bundle of energies or qualities usually associated with youth energy include *creativity, eagerness, spontaneity, optimism, activity,* and *busyness.* A youth is easily fascinated—and also easily distracted. He or she shows love by doing little things—a note, a card, a joke, a gift, a small task done for a loved one without being asked.

In adult life, the person with strong youth energy will find it easy to excel in certain professions like accounting, inventory work, receptionist, secretary, typist, filer, telephone operator, travel agent, handyman, actor, newscaster, athlete, and the like.

Youth energy naturally relates to mother energy, for it is often that the "mother" (coach, boss, director) creates the daily list of small tasks that the youth is assigned. These two energies—mother energy and youth energy—are closely related and reciprocal. A person with youth energy can easily understand and develop mother energy.

SPIRITUAL EXERCISE: YOUTH ENERGY

Is youth energy one of your favorite energies? How and where in your relationships do you express it?

Hero Energy

Hero energy operates in the *channel of great deeds* and is usually motivated to use that power in the service of good and in the liberation of others. This is the energy that makes one capable both of greatness and of facing danger. It gives the person who has it the ability of getting up when knocked down and returning to the fight, in whatever area of life the battle may be raging. This is the energy of the brave warrior, of the person who looks for dragons to slay and for damsels in distress to save.

The opposing forces it confronts are symbolized by wicked enemies, witches, evil forces, satanic powers, those who enslave people, and the symbolic "dragon." In its pursuit of great and often dangerous deeds, hero energy is most unlike youth energy, which prefers safe, small tasks.

The bundle of other energies or qualities that hero energy gives access to include *fortitude, daring, bravery, will, strength, idealism, discipline, determination,* and *loyalty.* With this energy one is willing *to attempt the impossible* and is *motivated by the highest of aspirations.*

Author James Joyce was not content to churn out dime novels. He was determined to write the novel of the century, which he did in both *Ulysses* and *Finnegan's Wake.* Mark Twain was not content to remain treated at parties as a cynical humorist who wrote clever columns for newspapers. He was destined to write *The Adventures of Huckleberry Finn,* the novel that would expose the sin of racism in the United States, and do it in a most humorous way.

Be careful not to discount women who possess hero energy. Witness, for example, Amelia Earhart, the daring pilot; Harriet Tubman, the black woman slave emancipator and founder of the Underground Railroad; and Theresa Kane, the Mercy Sister. She was the woman who dared stand up in the congregation at the National Shrine in Washington, DC, in the presence of Pope John Paul II and protest directly to the pope on behalf of women's rights in the Church.

The feminine energy counterpart to hero energy is companion energy. A hero needs someone who is worth doing a great deed for, and a companion needs a hero to be proud of, to wait faithfully for, to pray for his (or her) success, and to enjoy participating behind the scenes in his (or her) victory. Such companions were Olivia for Mark Twain and Nora for James Joyce.

SPIRITUAL EXERCISE: HERO ENERGY

Is hero energy one of the energies you possess or aspire to? How and where in your relationships do you express it?

Teacher Energy

Teacher energy operates in the *domain of words of wisdom gained through study,* in order to help people discover themselves and call them forth to make their proper contributions to society.

We see teacher energy symbolized all around us in fathers and mothers, professors, lecturers, journalists, guides, mentors, managers, bishops, theologians, philosophers, counselors, spiritual directors, and authors of how-to books. A person with strong teacher energy can organize thoughts and ideas in ways that can be conveyed to others, so that others grasp them and learn from them.

The bundle of qualities that flow from teacher energy include *learning, the ability to inspire, knowledge, insight, discipline, study, reflection, clarity, reason,* and *decisiveness.* Teacher energy is able *to arbitrate and resolve disputes, is protective of its students or charges,* and *is familiar with those books, laws, and regulations related to each field.*

The natural complement to the Teacher is the Solitary, the willing student who wishes to learn, who accepts instruction and can follow through by using it.

Both Frank Sheed and Maisie Ward were excellent and persuasive public speakers and writers, who had fully developed this teacher energy.

SPIRITUAL EXERCISE: TEACHER ENERGY

Is teacher energy one of the energies you clearly possess and express? How and where in your relationships do you express it?

Sage Energy

Sage energy operates in the *channel of transcendent experience.* This energy is familiar and at home in the unconscious depths of the human spirit. It evokes the deepest aspirations in others and guides them through the sage's witness, experience, and presence.

The bundle of qualities that flow from sage energy include *truth, beauty, wisdom, unity, inspiration, wholeness,* and *integration.* Sage energy is at home in the deepest states of consciousness. By witness and example, the sage inspires people to great spiritual heights and holiness.

Sage energy is the energy of lived experience talking. This is the energy of the Wise Old Man who has lived life and has been through it all. While teacher energy may come from book learning and job training, sage energy is derived from lived experience in exploring the depths of the human mind and heart. Sage energy speaks from personal knowledge: knowledge gained through deep exploration of reality. The wisdom of the sage comes not from books, but from deep inspiration and his or her own personal experience.

Sage energy is often found in the priest, healer, shaman, wise old man, magician, and saint. The complement to sage energy is the medium energy. If medium energy is in touch with what lies beneath the surface of society and makes prophetic predictions from intuition, the sage makes predictions based on past personal experience and familiarity with pathways in our unconscious depths. It is the sage who can always say, "Been there, done that" or "Let me show you the way to what is deepest in you."

SPIRITUAL EXERCISE: SAGE ENERGY

Is sage energy one of the energies you aspire to release in yourself? How and where in your relationships do you express it?

SPIRITUAL EXERCISE: SELF REVIEW

As you reflect on the four masculine energies—Youth, Hero, Teacher, and Sage—which two stand out as most characteristic of you? Which do you prefer?

Which of these four masculine energies do you need to get in touch with and consciously develop in yourself?

If you began working on this least developed masculine energy, how do you envision it might change your life and the way you relate to others?

When Feminine Energies Are Misused or Used to Excess

According to Jung, these eight masculine and feminine sources of energy wait to be revealed and expressed in every human person. Deep in the unconscious mind, they wait for us to access them in order to help bring us to our fullest human maturity. However, these powerful energies can be repressed, misused, or used to excess. When they are misused, usually unconsciously, they can at times overpower the person's thoughts and behavior so that they distort one's personality. Each of the four feminine sources of energy can be misused or used to excess in different ways.

When *mother energy* takes over or consumes the personality, such people can lose that healthy sense of loving, trusting, and caring, and become overprotective in the extreme, suffocating others in sweetness, and keeping others totally dependent on them. Such people may eventually become overly possessive of those in their care, smothering, controlling, and "devouring" them. Some, taken over by distorted mother energy, may nag others persistently instead of supporting and affirming them; others, instead of being the protector, play the martyr, or in some cases, the obsessive controller.

When *companion energy* takes over or consumes the personality, it turns people into seducers or tempters, leading their partners away from—instead of toward—their highest aspirations. Such people, overtaken by companion energy, may sacrifice their own identity, living only for the partner, thereby becoming codependent and unable to find emotional security in themselves. Some with distorted companion energy become manipulative, exploitative, and go on power trips, crippling rather than supporting those they claim to love.

While *solitary energy* is typically warm and concerned, when misused it can make people cold, isolated, closed-minded, locked in their own world, distant, and uninvolved. It can keep them in a state of emotional immaturity. Instead of serving the community, they become self-centered and ego-driven. They may become success-oriented or power-oriented, wanting the glory and accolades only for themselves. People with distorted solitary energy may show a lack of tolerance of weaknesses in others, and they can even become aggressive and brutal toward others on their team.

While *medium energy* gives a person access to what lies beneath the surface of society, when distorted it can turn someone possessed by this energy to believe that they are a witch, a psychic, or a fortune-teller. They get so lost in the occult world they become swamped by inner unconscious forces. Such people lose the boundaries between the conscious and unconscious mind and are unable to distinguish themselves from the "collective" unconscious forces that have taken over their personality. They may also become wildly destructive, using their power to subtly control others. To people who see them both under normal circumstances and when inflated with medium energy, they may seem to have a split personality.

When Masculine Energies Are Misused or Used to Excess

Likewise, each of the four masculine sources of energy can be misused or used to excess in different ways. While *youth energy* can be playful, optimistic, and busy, it can easily become distracted, remain immature, and even demanding when it takes over a personality. Self-absorbed youth energy can focus relationships, not around people, but around tasks and projects. When the task becomes the total focus, youth energy tends to make the person lack compassion and concern, become sullen, withdrawn, withholding, or even angry and rebellious. In love relationships, distorted youth energy can make one promiscuous.

When *hero energy* becomes inflated, this energy can make a person see enemies where there are none, in order to create a need to exercise violence. In youth, distorted hero energy may initiate gang wars or start fights for no apparent reason. Such a person can become cruel, blunt, a bully, and even destructive of what one loves. When hero energy dominates a personality, that person is most easily seduced by a jealous person with strong companion energy. For example, a gang leader's girlfriend (companion) may falsely tell him (hero) that a rival gang leader has called her names, thus inciting a gang war.

Distorted *teacher energy* can make a person become cold and distant toward others. When out of control, this energy wipes out rational control and can turn a person into a know-it-all tyrant, violent despot, punishing ogre, or inquisitor. At other times, it simply moves a person into an ivory tower, where he or she remains out of touch with reality.

When overtaken by *sage energy*, a person may embark on a narcissistic power trip, inflating his or her own psychic powers, either by becoming a messiah who can save the world or a wicked magician who wants to get even with those who do not appreciate his (or her) powers.

Although it may not be pleasant to acknowledge such extreme uses of these unconscious masculine and feminine energies, it is important to acknowledge their potential power. People need to consciously develop them as well as restrain and contain them.

SPIRITUAL EXERCISE: EXCLUSIVITY

As you review these eight energies, is there one of them that you favor exclusively and call on most frequently? If so, be conscious that this energy is capable of taking over your entire personality. It calls to mind a psychiatrist who could never stop being a psychiatrist. Even when he had left his office and was having dinner at home or standing around at a cocktail party, he was unable to stop analyzing and diagnosing everyone he encountered.

CHAPTER 9

Parent-Child Relationships

Evolution in the Noosphere

TEILHARD LIKED TO PICTURE Earth's four-plus billion year evolutionary history as a series of concentric spheres. As each new sphere emerges, it is larger and more complex than the sphere before it. In its very early history, Earth was most likely a molten hot ball of metals, mostly iron. That was the first sphere. As the surface of this sphere cooled, it formed a hard crust of metals and minerals that we call the earth or the ground. That was the second sphere, or *lithosphere* (from the Greek word *lithos*, meaning "stone" or "rock"). The next sphere was made up of water that covered most of the earth. Scientists call this the *hydrosphere*, after the Greek word *hydros*, meaning "water." The next layer was that of oxygen and other gases that we call the *atmosphere*. About two billion years ago, life began to happen, and for the next two billion years, a new sphere made up of millions of emerging living species appeared, beginning in the water and then covering Earth, which scientists call the *biosphere*. We human beings are part of the biosphere.

Humanity began creating the most recent sphere to cover the earth. It is a sphere of thought, knowledge, emotions, spirit, and love, which Teilhard named the *noosphere* (from the Greek word *nous*, meaning "mind"). For him, it is in the noosphere where the most important stages of evolution are currently happening.

During Earth's deep history of the biosphere, over many millions of years, most evolutionary advances happened primarily among fish, plants, insects, birds, animals, and eventually human beings. Teilhard believed that the next evolutionary stages occurring on Earth in the biosphere are less important than those happening in the noosphere. He believed that in the noosphere is where human beings will be creating a dynamic movement toward a future unity of mind and heart in the human family. In the noosphere, he envisions a kind of unity of spirit in humankind happening that we have not yet achieved—or probably not even imagined.[1]

Teilhard is envisioning a "collective transformation" of humanity. "Even in spite of ourselves, every day [we become] more one in our common thoughts and enthusiasms….[It becomes] less possible…to dismiss the evidence that we are *here and now* the subjects of a profound organic transformation that is *collective in type*" (his emphasis).[2]

For Teilhard, while nonhuman species—bacteria, viruses, insects, plants, and animals—will continue to evolve in their various biological forms, human evolution will happen primarily in the noosphere, in that layer of human minds and hearts that covers Earth and grows more complex and conscious each day. The noosphere will allow evolution to happen in relationships in the areas of knowledge, innovation, compassion, and love. In Teilhard's culminating vision for the noosphere, he says, humanity will eventually develop a "single heart."[3]

For Teilhard, relationships in the noosphere will provide the key drivers of the evolutionary process. There are other domains operating in the noosphere besides science, technology, and communication. These include fields such as morality, religion, economics, politics, ecology, commerce, global security, and other areas of social concern.

We need to remember that, for Teilhard, the evolutionary process going on around us is central to God's plan and is therefore the most important process happening on Earth. When human beings act to evolve in any of these many areas of the noosphere using the law of Attraction-Connection-Complexity-Consciousness, we are participating in God's own action. They are helping further the God project.

One may therefore ask what all this evolution in the noosphere has to do with infants. This book is focused on the evolution of humanity through adult relationships. Shouldn't we be thinking about university students finding the most forward-thinking professors and studying with them? Shouldn't we be fostering scientific research? Shouldn't we be thinking about ways to enlarge and enrich our adult relationships? Of course!

Then why is there a chapter in this book on parent-child relationships, especially with infants? Babies are years away from school and any possibility for evolutionary development. The answer is because human babies are *born into the noosphere*. It is within the relationships formed in infancy and early childhood where interpersonal development has the best chance to emerge and flourish. Forming a loving bond or attachment between parent and infant marks a crucial first step in the evolutionary process. For in these very first months and years, a child learns to become a person and to develop as a person capable of evolving, forming loving relationships, and making a positive difference in family, community, and world. *Infancy is where the evolutionary spirituality of relationship must begin.*[4]

This is because each child is born into an evolving noosphere. The child is important because he or she needs to have the best chance of influencing that continuing evolution. "Man is not yet complete in Nature, that is, he is not fully created—but that, in and around us, he is still in the full swing of evolution."[5]

SPIRITUAL EXERCISE: BONDING AND EVOLUTION

How might one introduce into family spirituality an awareness that parents could look at their infant and realize that, by the way they form a loving bond with their children, they have the best chance to prepare them to participate in future evolutionary projects for God?

What Is a Human Being?

Aristotle defined the human being as a "rational animal." According to this Greek philosopher who lived almost four centuries before the Christian era, a human being was unquestionably an animal, and the primary way of distinguishing human beings from other animal species was the ability to think, reflect, and reason. Therefore, Aristotle concluded, a human being must be a reasoning animal. For centuries, no one challenged his "rational animal" definition.

In the seventeenth century, René Descartes, a Jesuit-trained philosopher, supported Aristotle's definition, when in his proof of existence, he declared, *Cogito, ergo sum*. I am able to think and reason; therefore, I exist.

John Macmurray, a more contemporary philosopher, was probably among the first who dared to disagree with Aristotle's definition.[6] He disagreed with each term. He said that the human should not be classified as an animal, nor is the ability to think rationally the most significant distinguishing characteristic of human life.

So, if human beings are not really *animals*, what are we? If *rationality* is not really our distinguishing feature, then what is? Let's take thinking—or the ability to reason—first.

Human Beings as Agents

For Macmurray, the human being is most characteristically an *agent*, not merely a thinker. *An agent is one who takes action, conscious and thought-out action.* Unlike animals that act instinctively, human beings can also act consciously out of motivation and intention to accomplish some envisioned and desired result.[7]

Of course, human reasoning is used in this agent process, but *thinking is merely a servant of action*; rational thinking is at the service of one's motivations and intentions to act. The human being is primarily one who is able to plan and accomplish something that will make a difference. That choice to act arises from one's motivation and intention. Human beings don't merely live on the planet, they participate in Earth's life and purpose. They affect it and change it.[8]

In general, Macmurray's own motivations and intentions as a philosopher-agent are to shift the center of philosophy's concern from thought to action. He would like to have had Descartes say, "I am an agent; therefore, I am." Macmurray writes,

> We know existence by participating in existence. This participation is action. When we expend energy to realize an intention we meet resistance which both supports and limits us, and we know that we exist and that the Other exists, and that our existence depends upon the existence of the

Other....What is given is the existence of a world in which we participate.[9]

From the standpoint of evolution, Teilhard might recast Macmurray's ideas to say something like, "Evolution will not move forward and upward merely by individuals cogitating, but only when people in relationships have the motivation and intention to act and interact positively on the evolutionary processes happening within the noosphere."[10]

People also need to be told and reminded of their personal role in helping Earth evolve. In her counseling practice, Patricia encourages people to think of themselves as "God's instruments in the world" and to work with others in making our world a better place.

Teilhard calls this kind of action "conspiration." We usually give a negative connotation to the term *conspiracy*. We associate it with a group of people joining together and conspiring to bring about an evil outcome. In contrast, Teilhard uses the term in a positive way, as a group of people conspiring to produce a good and evolutionary outcome. Teilhard sees "conspiration" happening most often in scientific research. He writes, "Research is the form in which the creative power of God is hidden and operates most intensely."[11]

Basically, conspiration describes the *collective energy of a group of agents that share the same spirit*. They breathe the same motivation and intention, for good or for ill. The needed evolutionary advances here on Earth will happen only when people conspire for good, that is, when they form relationships that build new levels of complexity in motivation and intention, so that human consciousness is forced to rise to a new level capable of integrating that new complexity.[12]

For example, it takes some complexity for parents to prepare a surprise birthday party for one of their children, but far greater complexity when a group of people conspire to get a candidate elected to political office. There is an even greater level of complexity in moving the human race to combat an epidemic in a far off nation.

Another example of the human race reaching a "higher level of consciousness" might be when the majority of human beings realize the need for a planetary government, or the need to establish and ensure basic human rights to all people, or the need to cease the use of fossil fuels worldwide because of their polluting effects.

Teilhard recognized that conspiration is a uniquely human form of union. From conspiration, he says, is born an "entirely new form of connection that distinguishes the human layer from all other departments of earthly life."[13] While some people conspire to do evil, Teilhard shows us the power of conspiracy to do good. In conspiration, each agent of the "conspiracy" is aware of his or her fundamental connection of mind and heart to all the others involved.

We experienced the power of conspiration in the United States when women suffragettes at the turn of the twentieth century conspired to obtain the right to vote; when people conspired to end Jim Crow laws during the 1960s; when the people of the United States in the 1960s conspired to put a man on the moon within a decade; when people conspired to give basic civil rights nationwide to homosexual partners in 2015.

Thus, conspiration serves as a powerful tool in human evolution. You may recall that at the beginning of chapter 4, we spoke of Christopher Bache and his "living classroom," where his student teams enjoyed "collective consciousness."

SPIRITUAL EXERCISE: AGENT AND THINKER

Why is being an agent, rather than a thinker, a much more comprehensive way of describing how human beings operate differently from other animal species?

To take it a step further, do you think Teilhard would have preferred to define a human person as a conspirator rather than as an agent? Recall that *an agent is one who takes action, conscious and thought-out action,* and *a conspirator is a person who belongs to a group conspiracy committed to produce a certain outcome.*

Human as Person

Macmurray also disagrees with Aristotle, who defined human beings as animals. The human being, Macmurray insists, is not an animal but a *person*. For him, this is not quibbling about semantics. The distinction is crucial, he says, if you want to understand the meaning and purpose of human life. Personhood is the distinguishing characteristic of humanness.[14]

Teilhard agrees. He expresses it slightly differently. The human being, he says, "belongs to another level, another form, another species of life in the universe." He adds, "Man is not simply a new species of animal...he represents, he initiates, *a new species of life*."[15]

Of course, Macmurray acknowledges that human beings possess many of the same kinds of biological organs and functions of dogs, cats, pigs, cows, horses, mice, chimps, and orangutans. We have lungs, hearts, kidneys, livers, genitals, and brains just like the animals. However, as long as we keep thinking of our infants as little animals or mere organisms, Macmurray says, we will never be able to help them realize their evolutionary potential.

What makes human beings different, Macmurray asserts, is that all animals have built-in instincts that guide their behavior and relationships from birth.[16] As a rule, when animals come out of the mother's womb (or crack open their egg), they are almost fully formed. They're just not as big as their parents.

Newborn animals don't need to be taught how to walk, run, or swim, and how to chew or recognize their mothers. They know how to do these things instinctively. They do not have to be taught how to distinguish a member of their species from one of a different species. They do not have to be taught to recognize strangers or an enemy. They just know how instinctively. They do not have to be taught not to put certain things into their mouth that might be harmful, as human adults have to do to protect their infants. For an animal, there is very little need to go to school to learn rules of social behavior as human children do; animals are born mostly preprogrammed. Basically, animals function instinctively. If a single animal has food and a protected environment, even without others of its same species to care for it, many very young animals could probably survive.

In utter contrast, the human infant at birth, and for many weeks and months afterward, is helpless. It cannot survive as an individual. It takes days for human infants to learn to focus their eyes and to coordinate hand movements. It takes months for them to learn to crawl, to walk, and to run. Aside from the instinct to suck, the human baby has almost no other in-built rules of behavior. Their neck muscles are so weak that they cannot lift their heads by themselves. They must be cradled in an adult's arms. The infant is made to be cared for.

Although thousands of human capabilities are present potentially in the infant at birth, *each new kind of movement and response must be taught or evoked by other human beings.* Sitting, standing, walking, speaking, eating, grasping, and distinguishing people—all these basic skills must be learned painstakingly, usually step-by-step, under the purposeful guidance of other caring people. Dependence on other human beings is essential to survival. This dependence on others remains essential throughout life. Each infant is born into a loving relationship and will grow and spend the rest of its life enmeshed in a network of interpersonal relationships.

Only other human beings can raise a human child and develop its capabilities because that child is a person. To raise a person requires the work of agents, people who know how to take action with clear intention and motivation. Although there are stories of human babies raised by caring animals in the wild, the stories are all fictitious. Only other people can raise a person to take purposeful action.

Imagining a child's potential is as complex and as simple as this: When you ride a bicycle, throw a baseball, use a knife and fork, speak a sentence, type a text message, or drive a car, you are engaging in physical and mental movements so complex you can't describe or even comprehend them. Neither can anyone else. These familiar activities are only a very few of the capacities that are enfolded in every child, waiting to become realized. Think of playing a musical instrument, learning a foreign language, mastering the rules of chess, inventing a new app for a smartphone, graduating from college, and learning to calculate the trajectory of a rocket. Children have thousands of other capacities within them that are phenomenal. We are only beginning to learn how to release them.

SPIRITUAL EXERCISE:
RATIONAL ANIMAL AND PERSON

How do you feel about relinquishing the definition of yourself as a rational animal? Do you agree with Macmurray that the "rational animal" definition is very limiting? Are you content with his redefinition? If not, how would you change it?

Mutuality of Interpersonal Relationships

The human child is a person at birth, and can only become fully so through interaction with other people. A child needs to mature and develop into a competent, compassionate, self-reflective social being, who can act consciously, with motivation and intention, create relationships, and make a difference in the world. He or she can do so only with the continual help of and interaction with other people.

From birth, your personal life is determined by the mutuality of personal relationships. Thus, Macmurray echoes Teilhard in asserting that the basic unit of human life is not the "I" alone, but the "You and I."

The human being is not primarily a *rational animal* but is much more adequately described philosophically as an *interpersonal agent*. Teilhard might add that the human family is made up of *interconnected interpersonal agents whose intention and motivation is to create a better future*, in other words, to keep evolution moving forward.[17]

For this reason, states Macmurray, in the human community, there is no such thing as an individual person. There are only people in relation to one another. There are no individuals, only relating people, people interconnected to each other, ever depending on each other, either directly or indirectly.

There is almost nothing that touches or influences one's life, even in adulthood, that hasn't already been touched or influenced by another person, usually by many other people. The foods you eat were prepared by other people. Even if you are the cook, the ingredients you use to make a meal came to you via other people. The clothes you are wearing were made by other people. Even if you are your own seamstress, then the fabric you use to make your own clothes came from others, as did the sewing machine you use. The appliances in your kitchen, the electronics you use, the car you drive, the phone in your pocket—all these were made by other people, provided for you by other people, or sold to you by other people. Even the money in our billfold was printed or minted by other people.

Most of the information and knowledge in your mind was put there by others. Either you read that information in a book written by another person, or you were taught it in school by a teacher. Perhaps your parent explained it to you, or you learned it from a friend, or you saw it on television, or you looked it up on the Internet, and so on. You learned to speak your native language only with the help of others. In short, you and I—the people we have become—are primarily a product of our relationships and interactions with other people.[18]

With regard to the theme of this book, the lesson is that we all learn to love and relate socially and compassionately in relationships with others and through the influence of others. And we do it from infancy onward.

The human potential of every child is enormous, and we come into life with a variety of inborn, biosocial systems that favor the actualization of that evolutionary potential. The process begins with essential nurturing connections established in early childhood.

SPIRITUAL EXERCISE:
REDEFINING AS EVOLUTIONARY

Even though Teilhard probably never heard of John Macmurray, why do you think Teilhard would be grateful for his redefinition of the human being? How does this redefinition help us understand Teihard's theories of love and energy? His ideas about evolution and God's project?

"Attachment" and the Law of Attraction-Connection

A person's ability to love and form healthy relationships begins in early infancy. Every infant feels a drive to be connected to another significant adult person, most often the mother. Psychologists call this connection "infant bonding" or "attachment." Attachment may be defined as a deep and enduring emotional bond that connects one person to another across time and space.[19] This is the infant's first and most powerful experience of being part of a loving connection. The infant's crucial first experience of unconditional love usually occurs in the interactions between the infant and the mother. The need for this bonding process between the infant and a significant adult caregiver appears universal across human cultures.

The psychological theory of attachment offers an explanation of why the parent-child relationship is crucially important and how it affects the child's later development.[20] The mother or caregiver expresses the connection by holding, hugging, kissing, and rocking the young person as well as singing to the child, using loving words and tone of voice. The infant responds with signs of pleasure and contentment. The child quickly learns to recognize the mother's bodily scent, her voice, her face, her kiss. In this bonding process, the infant's sensory capabilities become associated with love and care. In the physical presence of this consistent caring adult, the child learns to trust and to reciprocate the loving expressions in whatever ways the child can.

The effects of "attachment" are lifelong. The child that experienced a strong loving attachment as an infant will be better able, as an adult, to build loving and trusting relationships with others. Research shows that, after bonding, when parents continue to show understanding, offer love and affection consistently, and provide for their child's needs for food, play, rest, and entertaining stimulation, it positively affects the young person's brain development. Cared-for children typically do better in school academically and socially. They usually enjoy healthy self-esteem and are better able to cope with stressful situations. In this way they are most able to make positive contributions in society.

If a human child misses that early attachment experience, psychologists tell us, it can cripple his or her ability as an adult to relate to others with loyalty, deep trust, and commitment. Naturally, this lack of loving connection reduces that child's ability in adulthood to develop fully and healthfully.

SPIRITUAL EXERCISE: CHILDHOOD EXPERIENCE

Consider your childhood experience and the childhood of others you know, how true does it seem to you that a loving attachment in infancy makes a difference in how loving and trusting the person becomes as an adult?

Lacking Attachment

During the 1960s in communist Romania, government policies led many parents to abandon their newborn children who were then placed in state-run institutions. "As babies, they were left in cribs untended for hours. Typically, their only human contact was when a caregiver—each responsible for 15 to 20 children—came to feed and bathe them. As toddlers, they hardly received any attention."[21]

Researchers from the United States began a study in 2001 of 136 of the most recent group of these Romanian orphans. They decided to investigate the impact of early neglect on the children's subsequent psychological and neuropsychological development. Many of the deprived children studied were less than two years old. In observing

these toddlers, researchers found aberrant behavior, showing no attachment to their caregivers. Even when these children were upset, they
didn't go to their caregivers. "Instead, they showed these almost feral
behaviors that we had never seen before—aimlessly wandering around,
hitting their heads against the floor, twirling and freezing in one place."[22]

If the need for that primary unconditional loving connection is
not met during infancy, the drive toward attachment and bonding is so
strong in a human infant that the infant will continue to seek it throughout early childhood. The infant will continue to long for a primal loving
connection. If it is not offered by the mother, the infant still needs and
craves it for healthy development. In some cases, other family members
or a loving nanny may provide the needed emotional bonding.

If Teilhard had known the theory of "attachment," he would have
agreed that it is precisely in "attachment" where the infant first learns
about love, the most powerful energy on Earth and in heaven. As a
child of a loving God, the child's essential need is to have love ignited
in her or him by the mother's spark of loving and the sparks of other
family members, so that the child, once set on fire by love, can learn
how to love itself and others. Infant attachment is not only the child's
first tangible experience of human love, Teilhard would say, it is also
the child's first experience of God's love as well.

When some of the Romanian children under two years were
placed with caring foster families, they were eventually able to attach
to their new caregivers and develop normal social abilities. By the age
of four, these fostered children were able to relate to their new families
much as typical children would. Research showed that "there's enough
plasticity in the brain early in life that allows children to overcome
negative experiences," as long as there is enough good nurturing given
within that critical developmental period.[23]

If the infant's drive to attachment is neglected or rebuffed during
that critical period, it creates a psychic wound in the child. Research
shows that neglectful and abusive care can negatively affect brain
development in a child. Not having loving care and interaction with a
parent or guardian can even change a child's body chemistry, stimulating chemical responses of fear, aloneness, and abandonment throughout life as well as the ability to feel compassion and respect for others
and for life. These deprived emotional responses, in turn, can limit
the chemical responses of contentment and pleasure that are needed
to trigger the hormones for development of brain, heart, and other

organs. Children who were mistreated or uncared for during early childhood and missed having early emotional attachments may have lifelong problems relating to their peers because they tend to grow up fearful, suspicious, and expect to be mistreated and rejected by others. Unfortunately, these children remain stunted in their emotional, psychological, and social growth as human persons. Many lack the ability to feel remorse or empathy.

In conditions and communities where the infant's drive to attachment is typically neglected and nurturing environments are lacking, there is a need for parental training and intervention programs.

SPIRITUAL EXERCISE: CURRENT TRAINING

With the information and ideas discussed thus far, how would you make or modify current training for pregnant mothers? What points would you emphasize?

Creating a Nurturing Environment

Here are four essential elements of a nurturing environment necessary for a child from birth to school age.[24]

First is *to minimize toxic events or experiences* that would harm physical or psychological development. One obvious parental practice would be to shift from scolding a child every time they do something to displease you, to noticing and affirming the child every time they do something pleasing. This is a shift from giving put-downs to giving affirmations that build healthy self-esteem.

Second is *to teach and reinforce appropriate social behavior, self-control, and human skills*, especially the child's specific talents and abilities. Here, a child may learn the ordinary courtesies people show to one another, be trained in paying attention and self-observation, learn to identify and name the emotions they are feeling, and recognize and affirm their own artistic, mechanical, or academic talents. The goal is to help them through cooperative play to become productive adult members of society.

Third is for caregivers *to monitor and limit opportunities for problem behavior*. Since children tend to get into trouble—putting harmful things into their mouths, fighting over the same toy, behaving in ways that are interfering with others or dangerous to the child—the challenge for the adult caregiver is not simply to stop the undesirable behavior or to reprimand the child. Rather, the intent is to intervene in a distracting but positive way by offering the child alternative behaviors that would not create problems, saying, for example, "That's not something you should be doing right now. How about playing with this toy or this bottle? That could be fun. Or maybe you would like to sit quietly here and draw a picture for me."

Fourth is for caregivers *to foster emotional flexibility in the child and to show how to choose actions that serve important values.* One might say, "In our family, we value kindness toward one another and sharing things we enjoy doing. Sometimes, when you and your brother want to play with the same toy at the same time, instead of fighting over the toy, you might say to him, 'It's okay. You can play with the toy now. I'll play with it later.'"

If we want to prevent multiple problems and increase the likelihood of young people developing successfully, we must increase the prevalence of nurturing environments.[25]

SPIRITUAL EXERCISE: LEARNING TO MAKE CHOICES

Consider the fourth point above. We seldom give young children—or adults, for that matter—the opportunity to make choices. Most of the time, we tell children and other people what to do. We make choices for them. How can we train children to make choices and provide plenty of opportunities to practice making choices?

Person-to-Person Interaction

Person-to-person interaction proves consistently to be the best way for young children to develop socially, psychologically, and intellectually. The richer and more varied the very young childhood experiences are in relating directly with other people, the richer and fuller will be the repertoire the child has to build and maintain deep, lasting relationships.

In its featured article on child development during the first years,

National Geographic tells two stories.[26] The first recollects a famous story from a few decades ago, where two child psychologists, Todd Risley and Betty Hart, recorded hundreds of hours of interactions between children and adults in scores of families across the socioeconomic spectrum. Their study covered children from the age of nine months to three years. In one aspect of the study, Risley and Hart measured the number of words a very young child hears in a day and over a week. They did this by attaching small voice recorders to the child and counting the number of words that child has heard spoken that day. If the recorder captured a word, then the child heard it, even though the child may not have paid attention to it.

The researchers simply counted the average words per hour that children heard spoken to them by other adults. In the more well-off families, children heard an average of 2,153 words per hour, while children from more disadvantaged families or those on welfare heard 616 words spoken to them per hour on average. By the time these children were four years old, the word gap between the two groups of children would have been close to 30 million words. Needless to say, the children in the well-off group got significantly higher scores on IQ tests and performed better in school.

A wide vocabulary and a broader intelligence stems from the conversations a child hears and participates in early in life, when learning language is easiest.

SPIRITUAL EXERCISE: EVOLUTION AND THE POOR

The Church has always had a special preference for caring for the poor. While the traditional emphasis has been on providing food, clothing, housing, and other necessities for survival, providing what else would be most helpful in preparing poor young people for making their contributions to society and the evolutionary process?

Only Person-to-Person

The second story was about testing an assumption about very young children learning language skills delivered by means other than person-to-person interaction. The hypothesis was that teaching language skills to very young children using television, Internet, or audio could be just as successful as person-to-person interaction. The comparisons would be made using babies during an age range when they possess the keenest ability to discriminate between sounds in any language, native or foreign.

In their study, a team of researchers led by neuroscientist Patricia Kuhl tested English-speaking nine-month-olds for language discrimination in Mandarin Chinese for twelve sessions using three approaches. One group had tutors who played with the toddlers, spoke to them in Mandarin Chinese, and read to them in that language. The second group of children watched and heard the same tutors speaking in Mandarin Chinese only in video presentations. The third group heard only the audio track of the tutors' voices.

The researchers expected the children in the video group to have the same language discrimination response as the kids tutored face-to-face. They were surprised. Children in the tutored face-to-face group learned to distinguish sounds as accurately as native Mandarin speakers. The infants in the other two groups showed *no learning whatsoever.*

Kuhl said of the results, "We were blown away. It changed our fundamental thinking about the brain." From subsequent experiments with infants and toddlers, her conclusion was that, for young children, social experience—physical person to physical person—is a significant portal to linguistic, cognitive, and emotional development. Nothing else, including television, really works, at least for the very young.

The children in her experiment interacting with Mandarin tutors had become bonded to them. "The babies were entranced by these tutors," Kuhl said. "In the waiting room they would watch the door for their tutors to come in."

Perhaps in later childhood years, interaction with people via television might prove an avenue to learning as well as to psychological and social development, but for very young children, the *face-to-face interaction in the context of emotional bonding is the surest way to help an infant become a person.*

These stories reinforce Teilhard's evolutionary law that Attraction leads to Connection, and the bonding relationships thus formed allow for new complexity to emerge—in this case, in the child's ability to grasp and use sounds in a foreign language. This learning would never have happened without the face-to-face bonding, or person-to-person union, with the caring tutors. At this early age of development, bonding or connecting with a person's image alone on screen or voice alone on a tape recording proved ineffective. For an infant or toddler, nothing can replace the caring physical-psychological-social presence of another human person in fostering human development.[27]

Infants who successfully form a loving attachment to the mother or primary caregiver are more likely to form healthy and productive bonds with others during childhood and throughout life. Without that early physical loving attachment, a child is less likely to be someone who moves the evolutionary loving process forward.

SPIRITUAL EXERCISE:
LEARNING PERSON-TO-PERSON

Were you as surprised as the researchers were in realizing that very young children learn something new only in direct, person-to-person experience?

Summary

If Teilhard were to give advice to parents and teachers on raising children to help evolve the noosphere, he might say, *teach them how to cooperate, collaborate, and conspire.*

Cooperation is a skill that is seldom emphasized today. Instead, competition reigns supreme. While competition promotes *winning*, cooperation promotes *success*. In winning, there are always losers; in success, everyone wins. Evolution moves forward only when everyone, in the long run, wins. Many board games such as Monopoly and World Power are cutthroat, competitive games that promote winning as their sole purpose by eliminating others from the game.

Rather, teach children to play cooperative games where a successful outcome may be enjoyed by all. For example, putting together a jigsaw puzzle, building things with construction toys, playing house, decorating a Christmas tree, preparing for a party, cooking together, and so on. Encourage the child to improve sensory skills using the eyes, ears, nose, and touch. Encourage children to develop talents that require continual improvement, such as music, dance, computer programming, cooking, woodworking, and so on. Encourage children to develop abilities that will enable them to work with a wider range of others on cooperative projects. Such abilities might include building facility in a foreign language and studying the literature as well as social and cultural customs of other religions and cultures.

Collaboration goes one step beyond cooperation. Here, the focus is on teaching children teamwork and team spirit. Its opposite might be an emphasis on "rugged individualism." In individualism, one learns to say, "I'll do what I want." In teamwork, one learns to say, "I want to do what's best for the team." In teamwork, one says, "I'm willing to play any role to make our work a success. If you want me to help set up before the event or clean up afterward, that's fine because I want to work for the success of the team." In teamwork, one learns to forgive and let go, for the sake of the team's success.

Conspiration goes beyond collaboration and teamwork, which is basically simply a willingness to work together. In conspiration, members choose not only to join hands and work together, but also to join hearts and minds together in "one spirit" in order to achieve success. In conspiration, an element of bonding in love and affection emerges. To learn conspiration, invite children to help plan in secret a surprise birthday party for mom to show her your love and appreciation.

SPIRITUAL EXERCISE: CONSPIRATION

Can you think of some other specific examples or ways to give children you know and love an experience of a "conspiracy of love"?

CHAPTER 10

Love and Friendship

Friendship's Universality

ECHOING TEILHARD'S INSIGHT about the universal energy of love, lyrics of the popular song "Love Makes the World Go 'Round" make a powerful point.[1] The lyrics describe Love acting "high in a silent sky" making Earth turn softly. They are referring to the divine force. But, upon study, the lyrics hold a double meaning. Not only does divine love make the physical Earth go 'round in its daily orbital dance; human love also makes our hearts and minds on Earth move gently but powerfully in their own dance. One of those familiar dances is the dance of friendship.

Friendship is perhaps the most universal form of love because no one is excluded from the love of friendship. Everyone has friends. Children have friends. Grown-ups have friends. Even cloistered nuns have friends in the convent and, by letter, with friends outside the convent. Most couples say that the most treasured blessing of married life is to have a spouse who becomes their best friend. Even in the business world, managers say that teams where the coworkers are friends make the best teams. The same goes for sports; team spirit is highest where teammates are friends.

Seasoned members of the United States' Congress lament the fact that today on weekends many members fly to their home state to be with their families. Consequently, these lawmakers seldom get to meet each other as normal human beings. In earlier times, men and women from all over the United States elected to Congress typically moved their families to Washington. As a result, weekends in the nation's capital were filled with dinners, cookouts, and get-togethers in homes where members of Congress from different political parties enjoyed time together as friends. Often, over food and drink, they got to know one another and their shared interests and were able to sort out differences or come to compromises on legislative matters, long before the issues came to a vote in the Capitol. Today, those seasoned members tell us, they get to know other members of Congress, especially newcomers, only through public statements or what newspaper articles say about them. This makes it hard for them to become friends and work together for the common good of the nation.

In marriage, you are limited to one spouse. There is no limit to the number of friends you can have. Friendships transcend boundaries or restrictions. Friends can be of the same gender or not. Friends can be intergenerational, interracial, interreligious, interpolitical party, and international. Friends can even be interspecies, as a friendship with a pet dog or cat. Some would claim that one can have an *inanimate* friend. Anne Frank described her diary as a friend, and even named it "Kitty."

A surprising number of people have *imaginary* friends. We usually associate them with children talking to a teddy bear or religious figurine, but many adults have imaginary friends, like the shaman with his "spirit wife."

Mountain climber Hermann Buhl was the first man to reach the summit of the Himalayas. He did the last stages of the climb technically alone—but not really alone. During hours of extreme tension and loneliness, he claims to have had a "partner" with him, an imaginary friend who looked after him, took care of him, and strengthened him.[2]

Teilhard had close friends among his family, some who were fellow Jesuits, others who were colleagues in geology and anthropology from many countries. He also had a number of women friends. Although he spent decades doing fieldwork in China, he was an avid letter writer. His letters reveal a man who cherished friendship and who was true to his friends.[3]

Like Anne Frank, Teilhard was a daily journal keeper during his years in China. In that journal, he would write his spiritual thoughts and scientific ideas. He also related to his journal as to a friend pouring out his fears, frustrations, and sadness at being so far from his home base and close friends in Paris.

SPIRITUAL EXERCISE: CHERISHED FRIENDSHIPS

Think of a few cherished friendships you enjoy and note the different ways you stay in contact and ways you nourish each relationship.

I-Thou Friendships

Philosopher Martin Buber pointed out in his book *I and Thou*[4] that there are fundamentally two very different ways that people relate to each other, one he calls "I-Thou" and the other "I-It." In an "I-Thou" relationship, I treat you as a *person* with some degree of reverence, while in an "I-It" relationship, I treat you as an *object*, a thing. One way of relating is heart-and-mind to heart-and-mind; the other way treats the other not as person but as thing, not as a he or she but as an "It." An "It" is something I use, such as a phone, a car, a kitchen stove, a television set, or even certain people.

We treat people as an "It" when we simply use them or view them as objects that provide services for us. We usually do not treat people such as cashiers, janitors, law enforcement officers, or people who pass by on the street as Thou, that is, we do not see them as individuals with hopes and fears and desires just as we have. In our culture, many men have been conditioned to look at women who pass by as sexual objects and evaluate them in terms of their physical appearance. Whenever we speak of "using" someone, we are talking about an "I-It" relationship.

Although Teilhard does not make this I-Thou/I-It distinction in his writings, he would assume that the loving relationships he talks about are, at least potentially, in the category of I-Thou.

SPIRITUAL EXERCISE:
RECOGNIZING I-THOU AND I-IT MOMENTS

It is interesting to note that, even with close friends and family, we sometimes relate to them as I-Thou and sometimes as I-It. While two friends may share some of their deepest feelings and work well together (I-Thou), they may sometimes "use" one another as an object to help them (I-It). "Hey, Charlie, can you do me a favor with your boss." "Joan, here's a list of things I need for my project. You're not doing anything today. Would you get them for me?"

Consider a close relationship you enjoy and see if you can recognize the times when you relate heart-to-heart to each other and when you, more or less, "use" each other.

Feminine and Masculine Energies in Friendship

Some relationships are so shallow and primarily utilitarian — "You help me; I'll help you" — that they do not deserve to be called friendships. We see such buying and selling of "friendship" among businessmen and politicians and elsewhere. Other relationships are deep and true. In such cases, the truly mature friend can display or provide, at different moments, any of the eight masculine and feminine energies.

Among the feminine energies, friends may offer to each other *mother energy* (nurturing and comforting you), *companion energy* (challenging you to be the best you can be), *solitary energy* (listening carefully to your ideas), *medium energy* (predicting how your ideas might be received by others).

Among the masculine energies, friends may offer to each other *youth energy* (carrying out a list of small tasks you may need help with), *hero energy* (defending and protecting you), *teacher energy* (giving you new information), or *sage energy* (bringing wise experience to bear on your plans) — whatever energy may be needed in a given situation.

In a true friendship, these eight energies are usually reciprocal. Each friend spontaneously provides them to the other, as needed.

SPIRITUAL EXERCISE: MASCULINE AND FEMININE ENERGIES

As you reflect on the various kinds of services friends typically offer each other, can you identify situations where you have been called on to offer a friend some of those masculine or feminine energies? In your imagination, recreate scenes where such an exchange of energies happened.

Look at yourself as a recipient of such services from various friends. In your imagination, recreate scenes where such an exchange of energies has happened.

Five Factors in Friendship

1. A New Being

Teilhard would have us recognize at least five factors in a true friendship. The first factor of a true friendship *is a new being*. As described in chapter 4, "Relationships Are Real Beings," a true friendship generates a Third Self, the friendship itself. This union is given birth and maintained in its new and separate life by the love energy that flows between the partners. This new friendship-being exists, not only in me and you but primarily in our interactions. Martin Buber says that relationships live in an intangible place that he named the "realm of between."

We most often identify and recognize the Third Selves of friendship by the things they produce—the songs they write, the books they collaborate on, the children they raise, the technological innovations or scientific discoveries they make, the charitable foundations they create, the colleges they endow, the work they accomplish together, and so on.

What is much more difficult to "see" is the Third Self itself—not this partner or that one, but the intangible and invisible relationship that exists "between" them. Teilhard often said that he wished he could teach people to "see" the way he sees—to see the invisible and to love the invisible. We wonder what human sense organ can see the invisible. There is no doubt we can see or feel the invisible, because we do it every day. According to psychiatrist Dr. Thomas Hora,

> We all have the faculty to discern spiritual qualities in the world. We can see honesty; we can see integrity; we can see beauty; we can see love; we can see goodness; we can see joy; we can see peace; we can see harmony; we can see intelligence; and so forth. None of these things has any form; none of these things can be imagined; none of these things is tangible, and yet they can be seen. What is the organ that sees these invisible things? Some people call it the soul, spirit or consciousness. Man is a spiritual being endowed with spiritual faculties of perception.[5]

Although we may all have the faculty to see the invisible, most of us need to develop it. We do this by learning to look through appearances to the deeper invisible dimensions, especially in the people and friendships we encounter. It is often the memory of those moments of inner seeing that give us the motivation to keep going forward in times of setbacks.

SPIRITUAL EXERCISE: YOUR SIXTH SENSE

Cultivate that sixth sense that God has implanted in each of us. Practice grasping the beauty that hides behind appearances. Soul-seeing is an approach to relationships that is seldom explored or taught in books. "Learning to love the invisible" is a basic element in Teilhard's spirituality.

In the context of friendship, first of all, your physical eyes can see two people whom you admire and who form a friendship. Next, try "seeing" the invisible Third Self, which these friends continuously create and within which they operate. Name the qualities of the Third Self you are observing as they interact.

When you develop some skill discerning a Third Self in others, see if you can begin to discern the invisible Third Self of a relationship in which you are a partner. In an earlier chapter, we suggested it helps if you give your relationship a name. Begin this soul-seeing process by identifying some of the qualities of that Third Self as its energy flows "between" you and your friend.

---

2. Transformation of Individuals

The second factor of a true friendship is that it *transforms the individuals in it*. According to Teilhard, a friendship, like any union, "differentiates" the partners as well as unifies them. Friends discover much more about themselves than they were aware of before the friendship. The friendship itself challenges each partner to become more of himself or herself, to reach for talents and abilities that may have been dormant. Teilhard might say that in a true friendship, our personalities are superanimated.

For Dorothy Day, it was her friendship with Peter Maurin that enabled her to translate fully her concern for social justice and the poor into a practical system. Through her friendship with Maurin, where he served not only as her teacher but also as her partner, she developed a clear focus for her work. Maurin suggested they start a newspaper. Because she was a trained journalist, it was her idea to "bring the best of Catholic thought to the man in the street in the language of the man in the street."[6] This newspaper became *The Catholic Worker*, which began appearing in 1931. During the depths of the Great Depression, Maurin's ideas also served as the inspiration for a number of projects. They started "houses of hospitality" for the poor, a farming commune, and regular "roundtable discussions for the clarification of thought." All of these began shortly after the publication of the first issue of *The Catholic Worker*. It was the friendship with Peter Maurin that evoked and matured many of her capacities.

SPIRITUAL EXERCISE: EMERGENT PROPERTIES

Write down the names of two or three friends you have had (or still have). Next to each name, write down qualities about yourself or elements of self-awareness that began to emerge in that friendship that you had not been aware of before. In other words, how were you newly animated in some way by each friendship? What did interactions with that friend bring out of you?

3. A Friendship's Unique Abilities

A true friendship *has its own unique capacities and abilities*. A friendship itself produces emergent properties that only the friendship could possess. Thus, the friendship can do things that neither of the friends could accomplish alone. In other words, the friendship is greater than the sum of its parts.

While Ira Gershwin wrote beautiful lyrics, his friend and brother wrote beautiful melodies. It was not either Ira or George, but their relationship that created beautiful songs. Only through their friendships with producers, directors, actors, singers, and musicians could their songs be performed on stage and get recorded.

Wilbur and Orville Wright were not only brothers but, more importantly, friends and partners in everything they did. They ran a bicycle shop in Dayton, Ohio, but their shared desire and purpose in life was to design a machine that could take off, stay in the air, and be maneuverable while aloft. They had no college education, no university backing, and no foundation grants. They accomplished their purpose using their friendship's own wits and with their own money. They demonstrated that it could be done. They taught the world to fly.

It was the friendship itself between Dorothy Day and Peter Maurin that produced and marketed a daily newspaper, organized and ran settlement houses, and started a farming commune—not Dorothy or Peter alone.

Any sports team playing and winning a game provides an example of the relationship's ability to produce something that none of the players by themselves could have done. None of the players alone could have won the game. Only through the careful coordination of team members working together as a unit can a game be won.

SPIRITUAL EXERCISE: TEAMWORK

Consider some of your more productive friendships. Name some product or process that your relationship produced that neither you nor your partner could have produced—or produced as well—alone.

---

4. Outward Focus

The fourth factor of a true friendship *is a shared outward focus or purpose.* While lovers face one another and tend to remain focused on one another, in contrast, friends are usually pictured standing side by side, facing forward and acting together with a shared purpose. Typically, their purpose lies beyond themselves, and their shared energy is directed beyond themselves.

For Dorothy Day and Peter Maurin, their outward purpose was very clear: to support workers, especially those out of work; to support the unionization of workers; to publish the Church's social justice teachings; and to provide a home in the city for the homeless and unemployed and a rural commune for those who preferred farming.

Among the deep friendships whose perseverance has helped transform the world, Marie Curie and her husband Pierre Curie labored for years to isolate and identify radium and the theory of the radioactivity of elements. Millions of cancer patients whose illness was cured by radiation therapy can ultimately thank the Curies for their renewed health.

For the Church as a community of brothers and sisters who love one another in friendship, their outward focus is to bring God's message of love—the good news—to all people. Beyond bringing the good news of God's love to all, Teilhard, following St. Paul's example, recognized that God had an evolutionary project that involved everyone. In God's plan, not only does every individual have a unique outward life purpose; so does each relationship. It is also true that most of us can better accomplish our individual life purpose through friendships, and often best through more than one friendship.

Teilhard's life purpose was to show the Church that its teachings could be integrated with the discoveries of modern science and the theory of evolution. Although the official Church and the leadership of the Society of Jesus put up great resistance to Teilhard's ideas and writings, he had enough friends who gave him support during his lifetime and others afterward who saw that his writings were published. Even today, there are Teilhardian societies all over the world. These people consider Teilhard a friend and promote his work as providing a great theological vision as basis for the future of the Church and hope for the world.

SPIRITUAL EXERCISE: OUTWARD PURPOSES

Can you identify some outward purposes for friendships you are in or those you have had? Many married couples might choose one obvious outward purpose of raising their children. Do you know any married couples that have found other outward shared purposes in addition to raising their children?

5. To Love Me Is to Know Me

The traditional belief says, "To know me is to love me." In other words, once I get to know you as a person, I can begin to relate to you as I-Thou, and I thereby begin to love you for who you are as a person, a Thou.

But there is an additional step that happens in the process of friendship. Once you allow yourself to love someone as a Thou, you begin to learn things about them that you never could have seen or recognized before you allowed yourself to love them. It's as though loving gives you a new set of eyes and a new depth of intellect to learn more about your friend who is a special Thou.[7]

This starts an evolutionary cycle. A typical friendship begins with knowing ("To know you is to love you"). As love enters the relationship, I begin to want to know more about you—to love you is to want to know you more deeply. Now that I come to know even more about you through loving you more deeply, I come to love you even more deeply. Then, as I love you even more deeply, I come to learn and know even more about you, and so on. Friendship love, like any kind of love, cannot remain static, it must continue to evolve in its knowing-and-loving cycle or it begins to lose its energy and weaken.

It is not that your friend must keep telling you deeper and deeper secrets about himself or herself. It is more like, because you love your friend, you are more observant and sensitive to your friend's behavior, attitudes, and feelings. You keep making discoveries about each other through your mutual interaction. In time, you can begin to say things like, "I know what will make him laugh. I know what will get him angry. I know when he's had enough. I know how to surprise him. I know what will delight him. I know what will inspire him."

SPIRITUAL EXERCISE: EVOLVING FRIENDSHIPS

For the success of any of your relationships, it is important to remember this fifth point about keeping a friendship evolving in its mutual love and mutual knowing. What are some ways you already use to keep your friendships alive and growing? Do you know of friendships that were once very vital but have begun to stagnate?

Two Halves of Life's Joy

At this point, Teilhard offers a paradoxical observation. Half the joy of life, he says, is "to center, individualize and personalize oneself." He is referring to the process of self-development as we each personally put in the effort to grow into a fully human and mature person. The other and better half of the joy in life, he adds, is "to de-center oneself [and re-center] in a being greater than oneself."[8]

In these two stages of joy, Teilhard is describing a very common experience people all go through many times in life as they form friendships, join teams, get married, and raise children. But there are problems involved.

Our culture, in its extreme focus on the individual and the rights of the individual, tells us that one's goal in life is to become self-actualized. "You are important and you must focus on your personal development and fulfillment." A very mistaken understanding of that notion might suggest to someone very immature or naïve that "I am the most important person" and "Everything is all about me" and "People should always do what I want" and "I should always get my way." Such a person, Teilhard would say, is stuck in that first joy.[9]

Nature and society, however, force us to realize that we are not the center of the world. There are higher relationships that demand to be recognized, such as family, friendships, marriages, neighborhoods, society, and so on. For example, a self-focused individual who gets married but remains stuck in that first stage of development will refuse to recognize that the marriage relationship is a higher unity. Such a person enters marriage primarily to see "what I can get out of it." If that person doesn't get enough out of the marriage that proves satisfying, he or she will simply leave the relationship. We might label such an individual as selfish, but the case is rather of the person's lack of social maturity.

Individual self-development remains a very important challenge to all of us, as Thomas Merton points out. "It is true that we are called to create a better world. But we are first of all called to a more immediate and exalted task: that of creating our own lives."

Although the task of individual development is perhaps never quite done, the mature person recognizes that there are times, as in a marriage or friendship, when each of the partners must de-center. They no longer see themselves or their wants as the most important factor in the situation. They need to re-center themselves in the marriage or friendship, which is a higher and more important union. In other words, once they are re-centered in the Third Self of the partnership, they recognize that the needs of the partnership in many cases take precedence over their individual wishes or needs.

Teilhard sees this second stage of joy—the de-centering from self-centeredness and re-centering in a higher relationship—as much more self-fulfilling and joyful than the first stage. The reason Teilhard prefers this "better half" joy is that, for him, only in the process of de-centering and re-centering oneself in a union of persons can one become fully human and fully oneself. In other words, you don't really succeed in the first kind of joy (self-fulfillment) until you enter into the second kind of joy (self-de-centering).

In a newspaper article from his book *The Road to Character*, New York Times Columnist David Brooks tells a de-centering story about Dorothy Day that exemplifies what Teilhard is talking about:

Dorothy Day led a disorganized life when she was young: drinking, carousing, a suicide attempt or two, following her desires, unable to find direction. But the birth of her daughter changed her. She wrote of that birth, "If I had written the greatest book, composed the greatest symphony, painted the most beautiful painting or carved the most exquisite figure, I could not have felt a more exalted creator than I did when they placed my child in my arms."

That kind of love de-centers the self. It reminds you that your true riches are in [relationship with] another. Most of all, this love electrifies. It puts you in a state of need and makes it delightful to serve what you love. Day's love for her daughter spilled outward and upward. As she wrote, "No human creature could receive or contain so vast a flood of love and joy as I often felt after the birth of my child. With this came the need to worship, to adore."

She made unshakable commitments in all directions. She became a Catholic, started a radical newspaper, opened settlement houses for the poor and lived among the poor, embracing shared poverty as a way to build community, to not only do good, but be good. This gift of love overcame, sometimes, the natural self-centeredness all of us feel.[10]

SPIRITUAL EXERCISE: ZEST FOR LIFE

Can you recall a loving friendship experience that took you out of yourself and placed you in a context where you felt especially loving and a new zest for life?[11]

Continual De-Centering

The ability to consciously de-center and re-center oneself in a higher union as Dorothy Day did is, for Teilhard, an important evolutionary ability. In the evolution of the noosphere, where most of evolution seems to be happening today, unities of ever-higher complexity are continually being formed in society, intended for an ever-more-complex kind of organization. Each higher unity invites another de-centering and re-centering in a level more complex than the existing level and requiring a higher level of consciousness to understand and adapt to it.

For example, during childhood, each of us must learn to de-center our little self and re-center ourselves in a family, first in the nuclear family, then in the extended family. We slowly learn that the world does not revolve around us. Next, we learn to re-center ourselves in a school classroom, since we discover we are not the center of attention there either. We also re-center in the neighborhood and community. In each new re-centering, we must cope with new relationships, new customs, new expectations, new awarenesses, new contrasts, new understandings, and so on.

As we grow into adulthood and spend many hours in the workplace, we learn to re-center ourselves among coworkers and organizational commitments. Again in an even larger context, as we realize we are citizens of a state and nation, we again must re-center and broaden our attitudes and thoughts. As we consider for whom to vote in an election, we as citizens must think not merely of our own personal welfare, but the welfare of our fellow citizens. Many people cannot make this larger de-centering step and will vote only to protect their very personal interests.

SPIRITUAL EXERCISE: A RE-CENTERED CITIZEN

When you go to the polls to vote, do you make your choices more often based on protecting your personal interests rather than on the welfare of the citizens of your community, state, or nation? As a voter, do you find it easy or difficult to re-center yourself as "a member of a nation" sharing responsibility for the well-being of that nation rather than as an individual with strong personal interests? Do you vote strictly along party lines or do you examine each candidate regarding their approach to protecting the welfare of all citizens?

Evolutionary De-Centering

Teilhard notes that in our own day, we have a much larger de-centering and re-centering process to carry out. We have both the opportunity and the obligation to re-center ourselves as responsible *members of the planet*—not merely of our home country.

The new consciousness required of planetary citizens is focused on global matters that reflect the common destiny of all creatures. Only in this much larger re-centering process will we be able to make wise decisions regarding ecology, nuclear disarmament, establishing peace, conserving energy resources, feeding the poor and hungry, and establishing a world government, among other matters. Then, as we begin to explore other planets and moons and dream of exploring other solar systems, we will again have to re-center ourselves as *citizens of the cosmos.*[12]

But it is in this most common process of building and nurturing personal friendships where we first learn to de-center and re-center. Teilhard called this learning challenge "the crisis of puberty."

Learning to re-center becomes a very important lesson that we all must grasp and practice. We will use and reuse this process as we evolve toward what Teilhard calls "a sense of the earth." He describes it as "the passionate sense of common destiny that draws the thinking fraction of life [i.e., humanity] ever further forward."[13] It is the "call of the earth" that already functions within us according to Teilhard's evolutionary law.

Once we have learned to re-center in our friendships, we will be challenged to learn to re-center in teams.

SPIRITUAL EXERCISE:
DE-CENTERING AND RE-CENTERING

Can you describe what it took for you to de-center and re-center in a personally challenging situation, perhaps at a new job at work or with a new pastor at church? What part of the process was easier? What part more difficult? What does this tell you about yourself? What, if any, kind of joy did the re-centering bring?

CHAPTER 11

Love in Teams

FRIENDSHIP LOVE, a most beautiful experience, has thrived among human beings—and animals—for millennia. However, Teilhard realized that to push evolution forward, there must arise all over the world a kind of love that brings together the hearts and minds of much larger groups of people. What he envisioned would be a kind of group cohesion that would generate a Third Self of the group, a Group Self with its own personality and purpose in God's plan.

This would mean that everyone in the group or team would have their hearts and minds converge and integrate into one mind and heart—into a group heart and mind, as it were. In this unified state of conspiration, they would be committed to achieving the group's shared purpose.

Some obvious contemporary positive examples of conspiracy might include Doctors Without Borders, volunteer medical professionals that serve the sick worldwide in areas that lack adequate medical care; Red Cross teams that bring food, water, and medical supplies into active war zones; environmental groups that advocate to protect the ecology and endangered species; volunteer political groups that are committed to supporting a candidate for office; charitable groups that raise financial support for medical research; and educational groups that advocate for better school services for poor and minority kids.

The individuals in such a team would still be able to maintain their own personal lives, their own families, and their own friendships. Participating in such a large Group Self would also mean that a significant portion of their time would be devoted to this group project.

Teilhard certainly recognized that it is possible to create conspiratorial teams whose shared purposes are harmful, violent, vicious, and destructive or motivated by humanly immature drives such as greed, power, lust, anger, revenge, terror, or even religion. In the spirit of Teilhard, we are focusing here only on those conspiratorial teams whose shared purposes are positive ones—humanitarian, peacekeeping, charitable, spiritual, intellectual, scientific, artistic, or athletic.

Teams and Team Spirit

We are all familiar with such group selves; they already exist and function everywhere. The most familiar to us are sports teams. These are groups of young men and women who devote many hours to disciplined practice together in their sport. In this way, they become familiar with one another's strengths and weaknesses, learn to coordinate movements in harmony with each other, study team playbooks together, and so on. Interacting in close contact with each other for many hours each week, team members learn to care for and respect one another, develop caring bonds with one another, and share a strong commitment to achieve the goals of the team.

We recognize the Group Self of a sports team by giving the team its own name and having players wear similar uniforms. The Third Self of a sports team is recognized and cheered by their fans. If their team wins a game, they celebrate the Third Self of the team, not primarily individual players. If some players after graduation leave the team and others join it, the team's identity does not change. The team continues to be supported as a Group Self by the school and community.

In small farming communities in the Midwest in the mid-twentieth century, where a high school graduating class might be as few as fifty students, a basketball team might be the school's only chance to produce a statewide winning sport. At home games, almost the entire school's farming community would be at the game in the gym cheering for their team. Teachers and students would be there. During a home game, if someone in town needed a doctor in an emergency, the doctor would most likely be found in the stands. So would the local dentist, fire chief, police chief, school principal, and mayor. As supporters and cheering fans, they all felt connected, physically and in spirit, to the high school's basketball team's Third Self.

The factor that gives birth and energy to a team's Third Self is called "team spirit." Some teams have it and some don't. The most obvious way to tell the difference is by the attitude of individual players. When individual team players, in order to enhance their self-image or ego, compete with each another on the field or court to see who can score the most points in a game, it is a clear sign of a lack of team spirit. *Team spirit can thrive only when the team is a conspiracy*, that is, when every player's heart and mind is committed to the success of the team, and when every bit of success, achieved by any team member, is rejoiced at by every team member.

Sports teams in their own way make contributions to the evolutionary process, perhaps by showing what teamwork can accomplish or by giving examples of what a physical human body is capable of accomplishing. However, sports teams do not typically produce innovations that stimulate and advance the evolutionary process in the noosphere, the primary setting for evolution in our time.

SPIRITUAL EXERCISE: TEAM SPIRIT

Among the teams or groups in which you have personally taken part—at home, in sports, in the workplace, or at church—have you ever experienced team spirit? Have you ever reflected on that experience and how it has affected you? Team spirit provides a taste of an evolutionary process in operation, which is why Teilhard sees the team experience as important.

Team-Selves during Wartime

Teilhard does not appear to have been a great sports fan or a participant in sporting activities. It was as a stretcher-bearer for the French military during World War I that he first learned of teamwork and team spirit.[1] Amid intense fighting on the front lines of the Verdun, he saw, first hand, teamwork, team spirit, and love combined.[2]

Working side by side with his fellow French servicemen, Teilhard realized he had become an integral part of a greater whole, a military team. In letting go of his individuality, and entering into this larger unity created by fighting men with a shared purpose, he experienced what it felt like to expand freely his own energy and abilities, while living and acting within a group that possessed a larger mind and soul.

Teilhard called the process he experienced as "dis-individuation,"[3] a letting go of his own personal concerns and letting himself become fully an integral part of a larger Third Self. Participating in this "new being" formed by groups of soldiers was what Teilhard called "some human essence higher than himself." Here is how Teilhard himself described what he felt as he made his personal transition into the Third Self:

> I do not hesitate to say that this special dis-individuation which enables the fighting man to attain some human essence higher than himself is the ultimate secret of the incomparable feeling of freedom that he experiences and that he will never forget.[4]

Soldiers on the front lines not only fought side by side, but also shared a love for their families and country. Doubtless, it was this motivation as well as their love for one another that brought them together to achieve this shared purpose. They not only protected each other, some actually gave their lives so that others would not be killed or wounded. If a fellow soldier was killed or wounded, they would risk their lives to bring the man's body back to camp to be cared for. They saw themselves as fighting for a cause that was greater than any individual. They were protecting the world for freedom, liberty, and other human rights that were being threatened.

SPIRITUAL EXERCISE: INNER FREEDOM

Consider your experiences of team spirit in sports, the military, or some other context where you felt the oneness of the group, being part of a team that had a shared goal. Did you ever experience in these contexts what Teilhard called "an incomparable feeling of freedom"? Many servicemen and women remember their time in active duty abroad as among the most powerful times in their lives, where they experienced oneness in mind and spirit with their comrades.

The Cyclotron

Teilhard had another powerful, almost mystical, experience of team spirit in the summer of 1952, when he was invited as a special

152

visitor to the cyclotron, the first atom-smasher (or particle accelerator), at the University of California at Berkeley.[5] This mammoth machine, which weighed over ten thousand tons, had not appeared on the scene like some new automobile just off the assembly line in Detroit. The cyclotron was one of a kind, a unique product of many years of research involving people from many different disciplines covering a whole range of highly specialized knowledge and techniques. Physicists, mathematicians, architects, mechanical engineers, and others from electronics, chemistry, photography, and metallurgy helped conceive, create, and build the cyclotron. There were many welders, carpenters, electricians, masons, and the like who actually constructed it.

When Teilhard looked at the cyclotron, he "saw" much deeper than those who only marveled at its technical advances.[6] For him, here was a machine that never existed before with a purpose that never existed before, a machine that no single human mind could conceive and that no individual discipline could build. Yet there it was, right in front of him, in its overwhelming size, functioning successfully in its intended purpose: *a perfect expression of evolution in the noosphere.*

What Teilhard began to envision behind and beyond the machine itself was the tremendous invisible team spirit—"a whole range of specialized knowledge and skills—a whole spectrum of energies too"—that had to come together in a shared purpose in order for this cyclotron to emerge into the physical reality that stood overwhelmingly before him.[7]

While his guide went on chatting about accelerators and interacting fields, protons, deuterons, and alpha particles, Teilhard was seeing invisible evolutionary forces emerging within the human race. Among this team of cyclotron-creators had arisen a new kind of love-energy that Teilhard had only dreamed of before now. Many would not call it "love," but for Teilhard, the cyclotron team was a group of hearts and minds that came together to uncover and discover things about creation that human beings had never known before. It was a shared desire for knowledge and truth, a shared love to know what was as yet unknown.

The evolutionary step forward that Teilhard had dreamed of was not something still far off in the future. It was functioning here now. This is what impressed him, much more than "electromagnetic fields of millions of volts":

...to see how, when what are reckoned to be our most firmly established categories are taken to a certain degree of intensity and concentration they tend to synthesize into some completely new psychic reality whose nature is as yet unexplored.[8]

Standing before the cyclotron, Teilhard realized that the evolutionary law, in its stages of Complexity-Consciousness, had already been at work in a new way. Here was a new moment in evolution. He was witnessing it—a new use for teamwork and team spirit. No longer is a team trained just for winning a sports game or a military battle. Both of those functions of teamwork have been operating for thousands of years. This cyclotron was a machine that had never been conceived before. It reflected an advance in complexity and consciousness, and it was something that required a new kind of teamwork—evolutionary teamwork—in order to bring it into existence. The job also required a new kind of team spirit—evolutionary team spirit. This cyclotron team had to conceive and build something that existed "never before," something that was "not yet."

This team had to envision and love the not-yet. They had to love the cyclotron and want it to be born as much as any pregnant mother loves her baby and wants it to be born. While a mother has a good idea of what her born baby will look like, with its ten fingers and ten toes, the cyclotron team, in its "pregnancy," had no idea what their cyclotron would look like when it was born and how it would work. All they had was its name, cyclotron, and its purpose: to split the atom, a purpose that had never been conceived before.

As Teilhard stood before the mammoth machine, he wondered if the individuals who worked there—the carpenters, masons, electricians, machinists, and so on—knew that they were participating in a great evolutionary experiment. Did those men and women realize they were engaged in planetary advancement? Did they realize that they were part of an evolutionary movement, a "flood" or "a wave that spreads out," an irresistible force? Did they imagine how others would take ideas and discoveries from the cyclotron and apply them to future innovations in physics, chemistry, medicine, aeronautics, space travel, even war and peace? Did they know they were doing work essential to God's project?

SPIRITUAL EXERCISE: ONE SMALL STEP

The next time you read about some advance in science, technology, aeronautics, psychology, or some other field, try thinking about it with Teilhard's mind and see it with his "eyes," as one more small step for humanity's growth in consciousness and its ability to turn the "not-yet" into reality.

The Ultra-Human

For Teilhard, the people who came together to conceive and then help build the cyclotron—whether they realized it or not—were engaged in the earliest emergence of what he called the "ultra-human."[9] For him, the ultra-human meant the evolutionary appearance on Earth of a grand Third Self that could be born only through the dedicated cohesion of multiple minds and hearts—like the team that conceived and helped build the cyclotron. Such a team would be dedicated to envisioning and bringing about things that waited to be discovered in the realm of the "not-yet."

To achieve what they envisioned, this ultra-human team would be called on in their teamwork to use a diversity of new forms and procedures, new processes of concentration and synthesis. These procedures were so new to Teilhard that he could not describe them in any more specific terms or details other than that they revealed the emergence of something "ultra-human," something like the next step in human evolution.[10]

He could see, at least, that this kind of large-scale teamwork had a strong effect on the broadening of consciousness of the individuals who were team members. Not only did it awaken in them capacities they never imagined they possessed, but it also demanded that, for its success, each member of the team had to "reach unanimity with his fellows and in himself."[11]

In addition, at the end of each of these stages of creative advancement, not only the creators but also the rest of humanity continue to reap its benefits. Humanity has grown greater because of cyclotron research. That research not only penetrated into the immense and the infinitesimal, but has also multiplied and accelerated the human ability to think and relate—and to create things that build on and penetrate more fully into the "not-yet."[12]

SPIRITUAL EXERCISE: EVOLUTIONARY STEPS

Teilhard died in 1955, and since then, a number of evolutionary steps have been taken in the noosphere—space travel, the personal computer, GPS, strides in miniaturization, robotics, artificial intelligence, and so on. Using your inner eyes, revisit some of these advances and see them, as Teilhard would, as evolutionary steps, bringing the human race closer together, helping to move the God project forward.

A Multitude of Evolutionary Teams

During those moments in Berkeley, Teilhard had a powerful awareness that went beyond the cyclotron. He realized that the team that created the cyclotron was not the only luminous example of the emerging ultra-human. He had simply never before noticed that innovations like the cyclotron were already happening all over the world. Once he began to look around, he could see that the entire planet was "dotted with luminous points" of the ultra-human.[13] Such teams were already at work everywhere. Each luminous point corresponded to some university center, pharmaceutical laboratory, or industrial research facility—or someone's basement or garage—where human teams, much like the cyclotron team, were attempting to give birth to the "not-yet" in medicine, communication, transportation, farming, electronics, or some other area of growth and development. He had simply never made the connection before. Once he realized where to look, he noticed these signs of the ultra-human happening everywhere, a multiplication of examples of the ultra-human appearing on all continents.

It was not enough, however, to see these "luminous points" as separate and isolated like stars in the sky. Many of them were joining forces and "concentrating among themselves." Not only was each luminous point a generator of human energies, but also in their joining, they were converging into even more powerful concentrators and generators of human energy.[14] Think, for example, of the many currents of research that converged to produce a single handheld unit like a smartphone, which is also a map, a camera, a video recorder, a music collection, a library, a television set, a search engine, an arcade of games, a texting tool, and more.

Even back in the 1950s, Teilhard talked about a "whirlpool of research." A century ago, he said, people thought that "the greatest modern human event was the appearance of the machine and industry. Today, we are beginning to suspect that this estimate left the heart of the phenomenon untouched."[15] Humanity has advanced from the factory to a more powerful agent of human transformation, the research laboratory.

Teilhard would be amazed at the degree to which research in every field has blossomed in the twenty-first century. Twenty-five years earlier, in classic fields of research such as physics, chemistry, anthropology, geology, biology, education, information, and medicine, there had been one or two professional journals in which researchers could publicize their new findings. Today there may be ten or fifteen such journals covering specialties in each of those classical fields. Moreover, there are many fields of study today that Teilhard probably never dreamed of such as computer programming, robotics, rocketry, search engines, missile science, space medicine, drones, astrobiology, satellite design, space telescopes, organ transplants, and so on.

In addition, as soon as new inventions or drugs are being researched, popular science magazines, newspapers, and television programs quickly bring knowledge of them to the general public. Among us today there is a thirst for knowledge, a thirst for progress, a thirst for the future, and a hope for what it can offer. This is the noosphere bursting with new knowledge and discovery.

For Teilhard, here in the noosphere is where the major forces of evolution are at work today. After his sort of mystical experience standing before the cyclotron, he said,

> Before my bewildered eyes, the Berkeley cyclotron had definitely vanished; and in its place my imagination saw the entire noosphere, twisted back upon itself by the wind of research, forming but one single vast cyclone, whose specific effect was to produce, instead of and in place of nuclear energy, *psychic energy in a continually more reflective state*: and that is precisely the same as saying to produce the ultra-human.[16]

What Teilhard was seeing was not separate silos of research, but researchers from one field looking at the findings of dozens of other researchers from many different fields. There they would discover information and ideas that would enrich their own research and approach to research. For example, astrophysics and biology combined to create the field of astrobiology, the study of plant life in space. Geologists and biologists combined to create the field of paleobiology, the study of plant life millions of years ago. Marine biology combined with photography to record the behavior of sea life. Satellite science combined with photography to develop the Hubble telescope and cameras on exploratory rockets designed to send photos back to Earth from the far reaches of space.

Scientist Brian Swimme comments on the emergence of Teilhard's ultra-human:

> This is the power and cohesiveness of entities that are social constructions of humanity, collectives of humans and consequences of human thought that synthesize into a greater whole that contributes its own interiority and personhood to the noosphere. These might take the simple form of dynamics that occur in small or large groups, the more complex dynamics of an institution or organization, or on a broader plane, that of human systems such as corporations, the internet, or our global economic system and its subsystems.[17]

SPIRITUAL EXERCISE: A NEW LIFE FORM?

How are people worldwide being brought closer and closer together these days using the tools of the noosphere? Are we slowly becoming one large human system? How can Teilhard claim that the noosphere is a new kind of "being"? A new kind of life-form?

A Single Thinking Being

In many ways, the noosphere has become a presence in and around us of a psychic field sufficiently powerful to cause the human family to become evermore interconnected so that it becomes almost a single thinking being. People using the Internet, or World Wide Web, reveal a primitive sample of the human race enfolding itself in thought and emotion. Unfortunately, many are still using the noosphere in very immature and potentially self-destructive ways—promoting hatred and violence, bullying, pornography, and the like. But much of what flows through the various cyber tools is helpful information and has a positive emotional component. The Internet is meant to be a tool for releasing the power of knowledge and love.

As far back as 1982, in his book *The Global Brain*, the futurist Peter Russell foresaw in the burgeoning popularity of the personal computer a living system of human beings sharing not only data and information but also their personal thoughts, feelings, and dreams. Before the Internet had been developed, Russell wrote, predicting the potential interconnectedness of the interior lives of individual human beings through technological connectivity.

Like Teilhard, Russell anticipated the emergence of a single interacting human complex system. It would be created from the many individual contributions of human beings and of their collective enterprises, and it would continue to grow and evolve. Both men envisioned the noosphere becoming a single, globe-encircling entity. According to Brian Swimme, Russell even viewed "the minds of connected humanity as forming an organ, a nervous system that is a subsystem of the larger whole of the planet, of Gaia."[18]

Almost half a century before Russell's book, Teilhard was seeing potentials beyond those of Russell. Teilhard envisioned two things:

First, Teilhard saw that any large complex entity, where people's hearts and minds shared the same purpose, could become far more than an organ or a nervous system; it would become a collective being, an immense Third Self. As Teilhard said, such a large whole "cannot but have its own proper character" and personality.[19]

Second, for Teilhard, this emergence of a globe covered with such collective beings marks a new evolutionary step for humanity. It is a stage of growth that the universe is undergoing as it makes a further evolutionary ascent in the direction of extremely high complexes.[20]

The fullest maturation of that single worldwide "being" might take humanity hundreds of centuries more effort until every field of endeavor would be intermingling with every other. Every individual would have instant access to all human information currently available, and each person's consciousness would become capable of welcoming the presence and insights of hundreds and thousands of others.

This was the vision of the "not-yet" far into the future that Teilhard was seeing in his imagination that day in Berkeley.

SPIRITUAL EXERCISE: A SOURCE OF JOY

When Teilhard realized these many examples of the ultra-human were happening all over the world, instead of letting it make his head reel, he said, "All I experienced was a feeling of peace and joy, a *fundamental peace and joy....It* came to me as a reassurance for the terrified monad."[21] What was it about these examples that could have given him such fundamental joy and peace?

The Moon Landing

Can you imagine how thrilled Teilhard would have been if he had lived another twenty years? For example, on July 21, 1969, he would have been able to turn on his television set and watch *live* the first human beings set foot on the moon. He also could have watched and heard Neil Armstrong, standing on the lunar surface, describing the event as "one small step for man, one giant leap for mankind." What excitement would have stirred Teilhard's heart hearing those words "one giant leap for mankind"!

For certain, he would have recognized in this great event the work of a Third Self of an entire nation. That "national being" had been sparked into life through the words of President John F. Kennedy in a speech before Congress in 1961, when he proclaimed and promised, "Before this decade is out, we will see the landing of a man on the Moon and returning him safely to Earth." From that moment, thousands of men and women would put their hearts and minds together as a single team to achieve that audacious purpose. They would become a conspiracy of love.

Even the housekeeping staff at NASA felt themselves an integral part of this new entity committed to that great vision. As the story is told, some nighttime visitors to NASA headquarters stopped a janitorial worker mopping the corridor and asked her what she was doing. Teilhard would have loved her reply. She said matter-of-factly, "I'm helping put a man on the Moon."

160

SPIRITUAL EXERCISE: EVOLUTIONARY TEAMS

Reflect for a moment on how getting a man on the moon required creating an immense Third Self, and how all the people involved—from the project managers to the cleaning crew—saw themselves as part of this great being that had a shared heart, mind, and purpose. What if we learned how to create hundreds of such dedicated conspiratorial communities to accomplish such stunning advancements?

Summary

So many breakthrough events have happened since Teilhard's day that he never got to see: an International Space Station orbiting Earth, the Hubble telescope taking thousands of stunning photographs of the universe, scores of communication satellites constantly circling our planet enabling millions of people to connect simultaneously all over the world. If he were alive today, Teilhard could be watching the heart and mind of humanity, which he named the "noosphere," growing by leaps and bounds.

But back in the 1950s, even as Teilhard saw the existing vortex of research spinning and bringing everyone closer together in heart and mind, he could also see that these efforts and hopes of humankind were moving in the direction of some divine center, a center that was capable of providing a center of all centers.[22] He would be echoing a vision for humanity of the person whose vision Teilhard was carrying on and promoting two-thousand years later. In his heart, Teilhard could hear his spiritual leader uttering these evolutionary words:

> And now I am no longer in the world, but they are in the world, and I am coming to you. Holy Father, protect them in your name that you have given me, so that they may be one, as we are one....that they may all be one. As you, Father, are in me and I am in you, may they also be in us, so that the world may believe that you have sent me. (John 17:11, 21)

In the 1950s, the scientists and technicians at the cyclotron had become "one." They formed a new collective entity whose center (or group heart and mind) could unify hundreds of men and women to create and build this great machine. In the 1960s, a nation had become "one." It had shown that it could come together and find its national center through a shared purpose and act as one being to achieve a lunar landing.

If he were alive today, Teilhard would be telling us that we, as a human family, will never stop being driven to de-center and re-center ourselves in ever higher unities until we have finally learned to center ourselves and our world in the heart and mind of that Center-of-all-centers who gave birth to the universe.

SPIRITUAL EXERCISE: ONE MIND AND ONE HEART

Can you enter into Teilhard's excitement and confidence that our world will eventually mature and find its way, as one mind and heart, back to God as its center? Or does something temper your peace and joy?

CHAPTER 12

A Theology of Love

A New Perspective

TEILHARD ASSERTS THAT the most fundamental and powerful energy in the universe is love—love in all its forms. Yet nowhere in his writings does Teilhard develop a theology based on love. Nevertheless, the basic elements of such a theology may be found in his writings, especially in his claim about the power of love's energy in accomplishing God's work on Earth. If God's work on Earth is all about human beings learning to love and coming together in love, then as we grow in understanding love's many dynamics and expressions, it must reveal to us something of what and who God is. It must reveal the beginnings of a theology of love.

However, for all our public Christian professing about God's love, we are still fundamentally a religion based on rules and regulations, that is, laws. The Catholic Church has canon law, and almost all Christian denominations have catechisms. Those documents tell us who belongs and who doesn't, who is right and who is wrong, who will be saved and who won't. What if, in our preoccupation with rules and regulations, we are missing the most fundamental and universal quality of God? What if we are basing our theology on a God whom we image as king, ruler, and judge rather than as Unconditional Lover?[1]

What happens to theology and morality when we base our theological reflections on a definition of God as Love? Not "love as one of the many of a long list of attributes of God" but God as defined simply by "Love"? It can't be wrong to make Love—God's unconditional love—the basis of our theological reflection, since St. John explicitly says, "God is Love" (see 1 John 4:8, 16.)

SPIRITUAL EXERCISE: A GOD WHO IS LOVE?

What kinds of things would have to change if our Church were to acknowledge that God is Love? Could we ever do without rules and regulations? How would we know what to believe and what not to believe? Carefully read the Nicene Creed and look for a description of God as Love. Can you find it? Is it really there?

A God of Law and a Religion of Law

Through Moses, Yahweh gave his people a Law,[2] which the Hebrew people were required to obey in fidelity to their sacred covenant with Yahweh. They loved their Law; it was their pride and joy. It was proof that Yahweh loved them. Violation of any of the many hundreds of prescriptions of that Law was called *sin*.

The Hebrew people became obsessed with sin. Much of their religion and worship was focused on sin. There were lists of ways sin could be committed and how it could be atoned for. Besides disobeying any of the Ten Commandments, the Hebrew people were taught that they could sin against the Law in hundreds of other ways. Many of these sins were categorized as "ritual impurity." The Hebrew prophets on Yahweh's behalf often rail against the infidelity of the people and their leaders as they apparently break their covenant with Yahweh again and again.

Interestingly, other religions of the day were not focused on sin. In fact, when Greek-speaking Hebrews wanted to translate their Scriptures into Greek, the closest Greek word they could find for "sin" was *hamartia*, which means "missing the mark," as when an archer's arrow misses the target's bull's eye. Judeo-Christians in Greek versions of Scripture and Tradition used the word *hamartia*, but gave it the Jewish meaning of sin, that is, the violation of a sacred law. Hindu and Buddhist writings seldom mention "sin," certainly not in the Hebrew meaning and connotation of the word.

When religious people put such a primary focus on sin, the qualities of divinity that naturally get emphasized are justice, judgment, and punishment. God as Lord and Ruler exercises justice as a primary quality. This emphasis on sin, judgment, and punishment, in turn, generates human responses like fear, shame, and guilt. Religious rites reflect a need to atone for sin and to offer sacrifice in order to obtain mercy, forgiveness, and avoidance of hell and final destruction.

SPIRITUAL EXERCISE: CONNECTING LAW AND SIN

How are laws and sin connected? Make a distinction between moral laws (that violate God's love) and civil laws (e.g., traffic laws and the like that regulate and protect human life and welfare). Can you name some civil laws that are based on moral laws (murder, perjury, arson)? What are some signs of people who are morally immature? Suggest examples of the ways laws can help people mature morally.

Early Christian Founders

Perhaps unfortunately, all the earliest founders of Christianity were Hebrews, with centuries of awareness of sin imprinted on their minds and flowing through their cultural veins. Even though the early Christians soon realized that they did not need the Deuteronomic laws in order to be followers of Jesus, and even though they had been set free from the Law, culturally they still remained preoccupied with sin. Although Jesus, while on Earth, tried to modify their obsession with sin, it was too ingrained in their minds and hearts. So, Christianity inherited that obsession with sin. That obsession has retained its powerful hold on us as part of our faith tradition to the present day.[3]

Forgotten were Jesus' own claims about salvation: "I came that you may have life and have it in abundance" and "I am the Way, the Truth and the Life."

During his life, Jesus was offering us so much more than mere forgiveness of sins. For him, in the Aramaic, when Jesus said the word that we translate as "salvation," he meant the "fullness of life." And he wasn't limiting that fullness-of-life experience merely to a future existence in heaven. We don't know exactly the contents of a full life, as Jesus imagined it. But we can all begin to list the qualities: peace, joy, companionship, creativity, trust, hope, health, vitality, play, and other elements that we imagine would be part of a full life. It seems that Jesus' willingness to heal sickness was an expression of his wanting people to enjoy a fuller life.

As a side note, during his life on Earth when Jesus would heal, he often began by assuring the person that his or her sins had been forgiven. In our English translations of those passages, it sounds as though Jesus is performing an act of forgiveness at that moment. But in the original Greek texts, when Jesus says, "Your sins are forgiven," his words, in the original Greek text, are spoken in the aorist perfect tense. An aorist perfect verb describes an act that was begun in the past and completed in the past. What Jesus was in fact saying to the person was that his or her sins had already been forgiven by God. The act of God's forgiveness was started *and completed in the past.*

Just as the father had forgiven the prodigal son's sins long before the son felt sorrow and returned home to ask his father's forgiveness, so it seems Jesus is telling us that God is forgiving our sins as soon as we commit them. From Jesus' perspective, God sees our spiritual immaturity and our temptations much as a parent would understandingly forgive a baby for vomiting on one's clothing, a child for spilling a glass of milk, or a self-centered prodigal son for wanting all his inheritance just so he could spend it on himself.

SPIRITUAL EXERCISE: JESUS' ATTITUDE TOWARD SIN

Did the early Christians "miss the mark" about Jesus' teaching on sin? If so, how is it revealed in the writings of Scripture or in Christian worship and liturgical practices? In what ways does a preoccupation with sin show itself, if at all, in religious rituals? For example, how often in a liturgical service is *sin* mentioned?

God as Lover

In so many ways, Jesus is trying to describe God's loving nature to us, and we never seem to get it. God is not vindictive, Jesus is telling us. God is not seeking evidence of guilt in every corner of our lives as an excuse to punish us. When something bad happens, it is not a direct punishment from God.

In Luke's Gospel, Jesus recalls the story of the Tower of Siloam falling on eighteen people. He assures his disciples that these people were no more guilty or innocent than any other eighteen people.

The tower just happened to fall on this group of people. Jesus is explicitly contradicting the deep-seated belief of the Jewish people that *every act that happened on Earth was directly willed by God* (see Luke 13:1–5).

If Jesus was speaking in Teilhard's language, he would have been telling his disciples, "In an evolutionary world, it is normal that some bad things happen, because an evolutionary world is an incomplete and imperfect world."[4]

If Jesus was concerned about sin, it was not at all about people's personal sins of commission. He readily looked beyond those personal faults. What he found so destructive to the human family were the social sins. Even a cursory reading of the four Gospels shows Jesus in his public confrontations focusing, not on individuals and their personal sins, but rather on social sins, those destructive practices built into the cultural system, typically practiced and supported by the Pharisees, Sadducees, and temple priests. For example, the collective hypocrisy of the Jewish leaders at the time, their obsession with maintaining power over the people, their failure to practice what they preached, and their lack of care for the poor, the sick, the social outcasts. Basically, they lacked compassionate love. More importantly, they consciously supported and maintained social policies that avoided concern for the poor and forgotten.

For Teilhard, it was what people, especially people in power, were *not* doing that was the greater sin. Instead of making the world a better place by changing the unjust social structures that prevailed, the leaders were more interested in preserving those customs and laws that allowed them to maintain their power base and wealth. They were content to leave the rest of the community—which was most people—to fend for themselves.

Jesus himself found it easy to declare "forgiven" the personal sins of individuals. What he kept facing head-on and what gave him the most resistance were those ingrained destructive patterns of society. He bore them throughout his life and they brought him to the cross. For Teilhard, Jesus was forced to live within these destructive social sins to his death in the direct experience of their power. On the cross, he came into collision with the totality of social evil and social sin.[5]

Jesus' solidarity with the human race reveals a twofold purpose for his death. The energy of his suffering on the cross had two purposes for our benefit: first, to remove any debt to sin that we may have incurred;

second and more positively, to provide a great impetus for the human family to keep moving in a positive evolutionary loving direction. He died on the cross in obedience to his gospel message of God's unconditional love for humanity. He died in solidarity with a selfish humanity that was bent on diminishing itself. And he died to turn that diminishment into grace for our evolutionary development.

For Teilhard, the cross is the symbol "not merely of the dark, regressive side of the universe," but "the symbol of progress and victory." It is Christ on the cross "who bears and supports the weight of the world in evolution." For Teilhard, Christ's death is his triumphal act asserting that love, not selfishness, is the true basis for human society. Love, all-embracing love, is the life-force of the Body of Christ.[6]

Teilhard believed that everyone, not merely community officials and leaders, had opportunities to make a positive difference in their communities, no matter how large or small that contribution might be. He felt that we all had the responsibility to do what we could to further the evolutionary growth of God's project. Teilhard writes,

> Charity does more than call on us to bind up wounds: it urges us to build a better world here below, and to be in the forefront of every attack launched to forward the growth of mankind....And personal salvation is important not so much because it will bring about our own beatification as because it makes us effect in ourselves the salvation of the world.[7]

Teilhard believed that the power of love would ultimately prove to be stronger than the love of power. It would be love, not selfishness, that would transform the world.

SPIRITUAL EXERCISE: PERVASIVENESS OF SOCIAL SIN

What are the social sins of which you are most conscious? Racism? Sexism? Greed? Domination? Other prejudices? The culture of violence and war? Human trafficking? Do you think we as the human community have improved in any of these areas?

A Fresh Look

If we want to explore a theology of love, let us consider with Teilhard at how love pervades the Scriptures. We may be surprised.

John the Evangelist is explicitly clear on the subject of the divine nature. He says very directly and without qualification, "God is love, and those who abide in love abide in God, and God abides in them" (1 John 4:16).

St. Paul says the greatest force in the world is love, and love is eternal (see 1 Cor 13).

At the Last Supper, Jesus gave his apostles his personal commandment to "love one another. Just as I have loved you" (John 13:34). Jesus is transcending the Ten Commandments, many of which are lists of things *not* to do. Instead, Jesus is focusing on positive actions of love, such as understanding, forgiveness, patience, caring, and so on.

We are tempted to think that the Hebrew God of the Old Testament is mainly a judge and punisher, but consider how the Mosaic Law summarizes our relationship to God and to each other. *The only verb used is* love.

Love God with your whole mind, heart, will, and strength.

Love your neighbor (that is, everyone else) as yourself.[8]

Notice, God does not ask for worship, praise, gratitude, obedience, fasting, sacrifice, sorrow for sin, and so on. God asks only for love. Why else would God make the action of loving central to worship and daily life, if God's divine nature was not Love?

So God must be in love with us. Jesus explicitly says so in his prayer to the Father: "The glory that you have given me I have given them, so that they may be one, as we are one, I in them and you in me, that they may become completely one, so that the world may know that you have sent me *and have loved them even as you have loved me*" (John 17:22–23, authors' emphasis).

Notice, too, God asks that I love my neighbor as if my neighbor was me, my own self, and a part of my very mind, heart, and body. Why else would God have us practicing love of neighbor throughout our life, if not to prepare us to mature in our ability to love and become all-embracing in that love?

SPIRITUAL EXERCISE:
IS GOD'S PROJECT ALL ABOUT LOVE?

Were you surprised at how much of the Scriptures are based on us loving God and loving each other—and on how much God loves us?

God Loves Creation

Late at night, Jesus went to meet Nicodemus, a deeply spiritual man with an open mind, who ultimately became one of Jesus' disciples. On this first encounter, Jesus was trying to explain to Nicodemus the loving nature of God. God so loved creation, Jesus told him, that he gave creation his only Son (John 3:16). Jesus was telling Nicodemus that God loves all of creation, including our environment, not just human beings. God loved the world to such a degree that he sent his Son to tell the world about the universality and all-encompassing nature of divine love.[9]

Jesus told Nicodemus that he must be reborn by the divine Spirit in order for him to enter into this new mentality, which includes the realization that God is not focused on sin, ritual, worship, and sacrifice, but on love. God makes no exceptions in the extent of the embrace of divine love. God's love is all-embracing. That divine loving embrace encompasses all of nature as well as every single human person. Love leaves out no one and nothing.[10]

In this encounter with Nicodemus, Jesus is making four points: God wants us to know that (1) God loves us unconditionally; (2) God wants our love more than anything else; (3) God wants us to love one another as well as all creation; and (4) God wants us to love ourselves.

These four wishes of God form the basis of our theology and morality of being "born again." The ultimate goal of theology and morality, where God's nature is Love, is total union or oneness. "That they may all be one. As you, Father, are in me and I am in you, may they also be in us...so that they may be one, as we are one [in each other]."[11]

SPIRITUAL EXERCISE: A VISIT WITH NICODEMUS

Read the third chapter of John's Gospel. Do you agree that the four points listed above are the message Jesus wants to leave with Nicodemus to ponder?

God as Relationship

Given that God is Love and there are three Divine Persons in God, God must be a relationship. St. Augustine sensed this in the fourth century. In his treatise on the Holy Trinity, he likened the Father to a Lover, the Son to a Beloved, and the Holy Spirit to the love that flowed between the Father and the Son. Thus, the Holy Spirit, in our language, becomes the Third Person (of the Trinity) that emerges as their relationship-love.[12]

The Qualities of Love[13]

Some of the more obvious qualities of love include the following:
Love is primarily relational, that is, it wants to form relationships. Love wants to share whatever it has; it wants to connect with others. It uses the forces of Attraction and Connection inherent in all things and creatures to make connections and form unions.[14] Even the religious hermit, in addition to relating to God, must live in relation to his surroundings, local animals and insects as well as the forces of nature and the weather.

Love is creative, that is, it wants to bring into being things that never were. It wants to create a future that is more loving. In creating new things and new relationships, love complexifies life and pushes us to higher levels of consciousness. Teilhard describes this four-stage law as "a certain *evolutionary pressure*," which is "the ultimate mainspring of all vital movement."[15] Love completes the law of Attraction-Connection-Complexity-Consciousness.[16]

Love must continually evolve. Love cannot remain static. This means that unless loving relationships continue to grow and mature in their ability to love and become more and more all-embracing, they tend to stagnate and may even become toxic. In this way, the law of Attraction-Connection-Complexity-Consciousness continues to cycle toward ever-higher levels of consciousness.[17]

Love is outwardly self-expressive, that is, it wants to express itself *outside itself in tangible ways.* Love wants to show itself in actions as well as in words. In this way, the law of Attraction-Connection-Complexity-Consciousness also spreads horizontally outward.[18]

SPIRITUAL EXERCISE:
OTHER IMPORTANT QUALITIES OF LOVE?

Does the above list of four qualities of love cover all the important points about love? As an additional challenge: How can you relate those four qualities to the Law of Attraction-Connection-Complexity-Consciousness?

As Qualities of God

From the scriptural writings of John the Evangelist and St. Paul, we can see that God manifests each of these four qualities of love:[19]

God is primarily relational. The Trinity itself—Father, Son, and Holy Spirit—is a relationship. As a relational being, God wants to establish relationships with the human family, both individually and collectively. God created humans as relational beings.[20] While the human mind can conceive of an individual person as a separate being, there is no such thing in the real world as an "individual," there are only people in relation with each other and with all of nature. We are all inextricably intertwined with each other, with nature, and with God in Christ. Just as God as Trinity is relational, so we are relational.[21]

God is creative. As Love, God cannot not create. God had to create the universe. That act of creation was not completed in six divine days, as the Book of Genesis suggests, but is still ongoing, since the universe God created is an evolving universe. It requires constant relating to, constant tending and blessing, constant nurturing.[22] Thus, God never for a moment ceases creating, never ceases bestowing existence on every element of creation, and never ceases for a moment loving creation with unconditional love. In human terms, God never rests. These processes of ongoing creation is what we have been calling God's plan. We are in partnership with God. With God, we are many teams and ultimately one team, working to complete the divine project.

God must continually evolve. This idea may sound heretical to some, but just think about it for a moment. We encounter a God who is a Trinity of persons and whose nature is Love. Because God, as Trinity, is a relationship and is continually creating relationships with the evolving universe and with the human family, these relationships must somehow be "changing" God. A loving, relating God cannot be an aloof God, an untouchable, immovable Being. God is involved in relating to us in Christ. As the human family matures, both God and we must somehow be changed by the relationship(s).[23] If it is a divine law that Union Differentiates, somehow God, in forming a union with us — a covenant of love — must reveal more of who God is and how God loves. We human beings are certainly changed by our individual and collective relationships to God; we become more and more "differentiated."[24]

Those who hold a static and unchanging worldview need a God who is already totally transcendent and unchangeably absolute oneness, truth, goodness, and beauty. Once we acknowledge that God, whose name is Love, is continually creating an evolving universe and relating to it personally, we look at God in a very different way. God never loses anything of essential God-ness. God wants our love, and God is asking to form relationships with us, individually and collectively. It cannot be that only we human beings are affected by those relationships while God remains untouched and unaffected.[25]

God is self-expressive. Any creative artist can only express outwardly what is inside his or her mind, heart, and imagination. God must create, and anything created by the mind and heart of God must be a self-expression of God. If God is by nature Love, then any outward expression of God must be an expression of the divine nature. The object created must be somehow like God, that is, capable of love; capable of relationship; capable of being creative; capable of bringing new beings (Third Selves) and new things (artistic, technological, scientific, etc.) into existence; capable of maturing and evolving intellectually, emotionally, and spiritually; and capable of self-expression.[26]

SPIRITUAL EXERCISE: FOUR QUALITIES

How does this description of the four qualities of a God who is Love challenge your personal image of God? Do you find some of these four qualities easier to accept, and others more difficult?

St. Ignatius's *Spiritual Exercises*

As a Jesuit, Teilhard made an annual retreat every year. During that retreat he worked his way through the process that formed the spiritual source of every Jesuit's spiritual life, its founder's book, *The Spiritual Exercises*. Its culminating spiritual exercise was called in Latin *Contemplatio ad Amorem*. It might be a good way to end this chapter on Teilhard's view of love.

Often, the Latin title of the *Contemplatio* was translated into English as "A Contemplation for Attaining Divine Love," which could be misinterpreted as "Getting God to Love You." Actually, a better translation would be "Contemplation for Learning How to Love the Way God Loves."

Ignatius begins the *Contemplatio* by stating two important spiritual truths about the nature of love:

> The first is that love ought to manifest itself more by deeds than words.[27]
>
> The second is that love consists in mutual communication between the two persons. That is, the one who loves, gives and communicates to the beloved what he or she has, or a part of what one has or can have; and the beloved in return does the same to the lover. Thus, if one has knowledge, one gives it to the other who does not; and similarly in regards to honors and riches. Each shares with the other.[28]

Remember that these two truths are truths about God and God's way of loving. These describe some of the ways God shows love.

If we human beings were to practice only these two truths about love—showing our love in action, not merely in words, and sharing our minds and hearts with each other—it would transform our lives and the lives of people around us. For example, for many years, Ralph let his wife, Melissa, get out of bed early to prepare coffee. One day, he told her, "You stay in bed and I'll prepare the coffee." This small act of love he continued to perform for the rest of their lives. In practicing the second truth, Ralph and Melissa, when they got in bed at night, took turns giving examples of what they were thankful for that happened that day. When Ralph or Melissa mentioned something unusual, the other might ask why they were grateful for that happening. In sharing their reasons, they were revealing something of their mind and heart to each other.

In the body of this spiritual exercise, the *Contemplatio*, Ignatius points out four developmental stages in learning to love the way God loves.

In the first stage, *giving gifts*, God gives tangible objects to us. These include physical life, family, friends, animals, plants, trees, flowers, and all of nature. Thus, love is manifested more by deeds than words. As we learn to give tangible gifts to others, such as providing food and clothing to the hungry and homeless, we are practicing this first stage of loving.

In the second stage, *personal presence*, God remains at our side along with the gifts given. God doesn't mail the gifts to us; God brings them directly, especially through members or cells in Christ's Body. People, animals, plants, and the rest of nature are parts of the Body of Christ, so when one of these people or creatures brings us some small gift, like Ralph bringing a cup of coffee each morning to Melissa, it is Christ's personal presence.

In the third stage, *cooperative interaction*, God keeps acting through those gifts with us and for us. This reflects Ignatius's second spiritual truth; that love consists in mutual communication, giving, and communicating. People who have dogs as pets frequently describe the joy of being with their dog, whether the pet is sitting at their side, walking beside them, or showing signs of affection. The pet's presence and interaction is very evident.

In the fourth stage, *mutual indwelling*, the most evolved form of loving, God shares the divine Self (the ultimate gift) with us. In this way, God enables us (God and me) to act as one, I in God and God in me. Ralph and Melissa's sharing their moments of thanksgiving is a kind of mutual indwelling hinted at here.

Perhaps, the most obvious example of the four stages of loving that Jesus used was the gift of the Eucharist. The Eucharist is freely given to us (*giving gifts*), the gift itself is Christ's *personal presence*, Christ keeps acting in us and upon us through the Eucharist (*cooperative interaction*), and he makes his home in our hearts (*mutual indwelling*).

To give an example of the four stages of loving at a very human level, suppose I discover that my nephew has developed an interest in playing chess and has joined the chess club at school. At the first stage (*giving gifts*), I might buy a chess set and mail it to him. If I were to love him at the second stage (*personal presence*), I would deliver the gift to him personally. If I wanted to express the third stage of love (*cooperative interaction*), I might play a few games of chess with him. If I wanted to show love at stage four (*mutual indwelling*), I might teach him a number of the strategies I had personally developed after playing chess for many years, thus sharing something of my inner life with him.

In practicing God's way of loving where such four-stage love is needed the most—among the poor, the sick, the homeless, the handicapped, the disenfranchised, the undocumented, the addicted, and the criminal—it becomes more difficult. For example, Patricia and Louis often buy fun gifts for the homeless in Tampa, such as sunglasses, baseball caps, tee shirts, and jackets (stage one, *giving gifts*). However, instead of delivering them personally to the homeless (stage two, *personal presence*), we give our gifts to two of the women at church who bake breakfast for a group of homeless every Saturday morning. These two gracious women deliver our gifts. They operate at stage two with their personal presence.

As far as we can tell, however, no one from our church community is expressing love for the homeless at the two highest stages. If they were, it would mean (for stage three, *cooperative interaction*) that they would sit at breakfast with the men and women there as they eat and try on the baseball caps, sunglasses, and shirts, admiring them and enjoying their delight. Loving the homeless at stage four (*mutual indwelling*) would involve somehow sharing life with them, perhaps agreeing to live with the homeless under the Interstate highway bridges for a week or longer, or taking one or more of them home to live with you.

SPIRITUAL EXERCISE: FOUR STAGES OF LOVING

Can you find examples of expressions in the ways you show love to different people at each of these four levels? Are there some people you love only at the first stage? At the first two stages? Are there even a few to whom you show how you love them using all four stages?

God Welcomes Us at Any Stage of Love

If we have not matured in our loving to reach the third and fourth stages of loving the way God loves, God still welcomes us unconditionally at whatever stage we have reached. That is the essence of *agape* love. It is all-accepting and all-embracing.

Jesus asks us to "Be perfect, therefore, as your heavenly Father is perfect" (Matt 5:48). However, the Aramaic words Jesus used here may also be translated as "all-accepting" or "all-embracing." Either of those translations fits the scriptural context of this saying more naturally than "perfect." While it is clearly impossible for us human beings to be "perfect as God is perfect," we can certainly mature and improve in our ability to be more and more accepting and all-embracing.

In John's Gospel, after his resurrection at the shore of Lake Tiberias, Jesus prepares breakfast for his forlorn and discouraged disciples. After the meal, Jesus takes Peter aside and asks him (according to the Greek, but not in English translations): "Peter, do you love me *with agape love* [that is, unconditional love]?" Peter, being the truthful man that he is, answers honestly, "Lord, you know I love you *as a friend and brother* [that is, with filial love]." Peter acknowledges that he does not yet possess *agape* love for his master, since during the Lord's passion, Peter betrayed him. Jesus asks him again, "Peter, do you love me *with agape love?*" Once again, Peter can acknowledge only that he is merely at the level of love of a friend or brother.

Finally, in the third exchange, Jesus asks a different question, saying, "Peter, do you love me *as a friend* [that is, with filial love]?" Peter can truthfully answer, "You know that I love you *as a friend.*"

Jesus is willing to accept our love at whatever level we can give it to him.

In the next few sentences, Jesus tells Peter that he will eventually grow into *agape* love for Jesus, and that Peter will show *agape* love by giving his life for Jesus and his followers.

If the only love we can give to Christ and to God at present is less than unconditional *agape* love, God is ready to accept us at that level.

At whatever level of love we are capable of offering at present, God will give us the Holy Spirit, the Spirit of Love, so that in time, we will mature in love and be able to offer God *agape* love.

Teilhard dreams of the day when all of humanity will be able to live with one another in *agape* love. That day will mark the culminating fulfillment of God's plan and the accomplishment of God's project.

SPIRITUAL EXERCISE: LEVELS OF LOVE

We typically relate to most of the people we encounter each day in the workplace, in our neighborhoods, or at church as mere acquaintances. Can you name people you relate to in true friendship? Are there any you relate to with *agape* love, that is, unconditionally, as with the love that parents often show toward their children?

CHAPTER 13

Omega Love

TEILHARD'S EXPLORATION of love took him all the way to the end of time. He named the successful completion of God's project the Omega Point.[1] St. Paul called it the *Pleroma*.[2] For both of them, it would represent the fullest maturation or development of the universe—particularly, of human beings.[3] The fullest maturation of humanity would represent maximum complexity and maximum consciousness, many billions of minds and hearts consciously thinking and loving as one being. In other words, these billions of minds would have cooperated, collaborated, and conspired to help create what they would realize as one new transcendent being. For Christians, this transcendent being that humans helped create would be the cosmic Christ in all his fullness.

At the Omega Point, all self-reflectively conscious beings would realize at least three things:

- They have been living in a sea of divine love (the Divine Milieu) since the universe began and all through its evolutionary history.[4]
- This sea of love (the Divine Milieu) is, in fact, a person, a Divine Person.[5]
- This Divine Person has been attracting them to this state of consciousness since the first moment of creation.[6]

At Omega, continual and mutual explosions of unconditional love would be operating in each person in accordance with each one's capacity or spiritual maturity. People would be able to embrace all persons and things to the limit of their ability. Each element in the universe would be filled with reciprocal love, giving and receiving love.

179

Each new union formed by each new relationship in Omega would have "differentiated" its members, enabling them to become more and more all-embracing toward more and more of creation. In the end, there would be a paroxysm[7] of love, all consciously happening within the Divine Person.[8] There would be no limit to how many other hearts one human heart could hold.

Teilhard does not eliminate people of other religions from this eternal love fest. Nevertheless, he points out that Christians have a special role to play in God's plan. As a Roman Catholic priest, Teilhard would say that the revelation of this plan has been given to the Christian community. For him, Christians have the responsibility to help fulfill God's plan. In Teilhard's perspective, this fulfillment—the Omega Point or *Pleroma*—will happen in and through the universal Body of Christ. He believes that God's plan will converge, culminate, and integrate in one divine cosmic being.

How can Omega Point or *Pleroma* be described to a reader? Your human body and mind may serve as a metaphor for this culminating moment.

Scientists are studying the human biome. They are analyzing all the different species of microbiotic creatures that live in your human body, each with its own DNA, not yours. They estimate that the cells of those other creatures in your body outnumber cells with your DNA by ten-to-one.[9] Right now, each of those visitor cells, as well as your own cells, are aware only of their own existence, purpose, and needs. Similarly, at this moment in God's plan, human beings, although we, in fact, live in the universal divine being, still think of ourselves as individuals making our own way through life.

Once again, using your human body as a metaphor, imagine that each of those trillions of cells in your body developed self-reflective consciousness, just like a human being. Each cell would come to realize that it is also living and participating in your bodily life. To those microscopic cells, you would seem like an immense being. They would come to realize that they "live and move and have their being" in you, that they, in some sense, were living your human life.

We might imagine such a bacterium in, say, Charlie's body that has come to fullest consciousness saying, "Wow, I'm living the life of a human person! I'm not just a bacterium in Charlie's colon, I am sharing Charlie's life, helping him stay healthy. He knows me and loves me. And I can know and love all the other microbes that share life with me in Charlie's body."

So, in the Parousia (or what Teilhard called Omega), each of us would come to realize that we are also living and participating in a divine bodily life. To us tiny human beings, the divine body seems an immense being. We would come to realize palpably that we "live and move and have our being" in this universal being. We would know and experience that we were participating in that divine life. More importantly, we would come to realize that we are unconditionally loved by that universal person.

Note that the human body metaphor is not totally accurate. For unlike the human body where individual cells die and are disposed of by the human body, in the cosmic Body of Christ, no individual being—certainly no conscious being—is ever lost or discarded by the cosmic Body. This difference is a clear article of faith as expressed in the Nicene Creed as the Communion of Saints. In Christ, no one ever dies.

We might imagine a Christian that has come to fullest consciousness saying, "Wow, I'm living the life of a Divine Person! I'm not just a human being walking on Earth. I am sharing Christ's life, helping him evolve toward Omega. Christ loves me unconditionally, and I am learning to love more and more people unconditionally."

It may occur to some to ask this question: What happens *after* Omega? That question contains a number of questions within it, including the following: Will there be a kind of chronological time after Omega or will there just be God's time? How can this fantastic love fest be stopped? Won't everyone want to know everyone else at deeper and deeper levels and how each contributed to God's plan? Won't each person in Christ's Body want to thank every other person for all the loving things they did while on Earth?

Unfortunately, Teilhard never addressed these questions. His primary purpose was to show that evolution had to reach a culmination point, Omega.

Yet we in the twenty-first century have not yet reached Omega. And we still do not fully realize we are at this moment living in a divine cosmic Body. What does Teilhard suggest will help us get there? What new dimensions of our spirituality do we need to develop? What kind of loving do we need to learn?

Teilhard never named the special kind of loving that would finally propel us into Omega. So, we have given it the name "Omega love."

Teilhard seems to have been capable of experiencing a sense of Omega love since his childhood. He was truly blessed. He received this ability as a divine gift, or grace.[10] He claimed he experienced this love throughout his life. In his book *The Divine Milieu*, he described it as passionately loving God and, simultaneously, passionately loving the world. He often described feeling it as a kind of divine fire.

> The world gradually caught fire for me, burst into flames...
> this happened all *during* my life and *as a result of* my whole
> life, until it formed a great luminous mass, lit from within
> that surrounded me...the diaphany of the divine at the heart
> of a glowing universe...able to insinuate itself everywhere...
> a power to penetrate all things...and so amorize the cosmic
> Milieu.[11]

Teilhard's prayer was that all of us would be able to see the world and God as he saw them.

SPIRITUAL EXERCISE: ENOUGH ENERGY

Can you see why there had to be some kind of Omega love with enough energy to propel us into Omega? Why don't the kinds of love we usually experience have enough energy to bring about Omega? Review the three awareness requirements for Omega at the beginning of this chapter.

Developing Omega Love

Teilhard wants us to develop this Omega love by staying aware of what the completion of God's project will look like and feel like.

The first thing he would want you to remember is that everything in the universe is *still in process*. For him, nothing in the universe is fixed or complete *yet*. Currently, nothing has yet reached its fullest maturation or completeness, not even heaven or the kingdom of God; certainly, not the universe. For example, scientists tell us that a new star is formed and being born somewhere in the universe about every three minutes. The bottom line is that in an evolutionary world, everything is still in process.[12]

To describe the ongoing evolutionary nature of things, Teilhard uses the suffix *-genesis*. Genesis describes something being created, gestating, birthing, becoming, developing, maturing, and so on. Thus, to characterize a universe still in process, Teilhard uses the term *cosmogenesis*. To characterize our living planet still in process, he uses *biogenesis*. To denote humanity in process, he uses *anthropogenesis*.

For Teilhard, Christ too—the universal or cosmic Christ—is also in process; he calls it *Christogenesis*. The universal Christ will reach its fullest maturity, complexity, and consciousness at Omega. Until then, the cosmic Christ continues to develop in Christogenesis.[13]

If you prefer to use St. Paul's *Pleroma* as the fulfillment of Christ, then Teilhard's term *pleromization* describes the process that will get us there.

For Teilhard, each of these maturing processes—anthropogenesis, cosmogenesis, Christogenesis—will eventually integrate into one grand process as they approach Omega—or *Pleroma*—when Christ will be all in all.

From Teilhard's writings about Omega, anthropogenesis, and Christogenesis, we can identify three spiritual practices that may help us to develop a sense of Omega love. We might label the three as follows:

- Loving the Heart of Christ
- Loving the Eucharist
- Loving Evolution Itself

Each of these three spiritual practices will be further developed in subsequent pages. But for the moment:

Loving the Heart of Christ describes an evolutionary form of devotion to the Sacred Heart of Jesus developed by Teilhard. It reminds us that reaching Omega presents an interpersonal challenge. In it, each of us needs to learn to embrace lovingly an ever-wider range of people, beliefs, and ideas—even when it may seem almost impossible.

Loving the Eucharist also describes an evolutionary form of traditional devotion to the Eucharist developed by Teilhard. He reminds us that Christ in his cosmic Body on the altar is, as it were, a "new" Christ each day. And we are being transformed through the Eucharist more and more into his life and his Heart each day, as he longs for and approaches Omega, beckoned there by the loving Creator waiting, inviting, and attracting us.

Loving Evolution Itself is a totally new kind of loving first described by Teilhard. He reminds us that cosmogenesis as a process is still very active. Creation—and therefore evolution—continues to happen during each moment, each day, each year, each century. Loving the evolutionary process also involves loving and longing for ever-increasing complexity and consciousness, and always longing for more union.

Let's look at each one of these spiritual practices in more detail.

1. Loving the Heart of Christ

Teilhard's ideas about evolution and Omega love were deeply influenced by his devotion to the Sacred Heart of Jesus. His mother had been extremely devoted to the Sacred Heart and introduced this spiritual practice to her son at an early age. Reflecting on the image of the Sacred Heart throughout childhood helped Teilhard develop and enrich his understanding of God and Christ.[14]

In Teilhard's thought, the Sacred Heart of Jesus eventually became the Heart of the risen Christ. When he looked at paintings of the Sacred Heart, he was no longer seeing the heart of Jesus of Nazareth but the heart of the universal Christ. Then, as his thought developed further, the Sacred Heart became a vision of Christ radiating love from *within* the center of the universe. The Sacred Heart was now not only the Heart of the risen Christ but also the Heart at the Center of Evolving Creation. This is the vision of Christ Teilhard asks us to enter into if we want to understand and experience Omega love.[15]

The story is told of Teilhard as a young man in his early thirties looking at an image of the Sacred Heart in an empty church.[16] As he studied the image, he wondered how an artist might represent the fullest humanity of Jesus without making the picture look too individualistic. He was mentally trying to figure out how such an expanding image might be drawn.

As he stood there gazing at the image, he was overtaken by a kind of mystical experience. The contours of the picture before him began to dissolve and expand in the folds of Christ's robe and glow of his head. The image kept expanding and expanding beyond the borders of the picture frame, beyond the walls of the church. It kept reaching further and further outward. It seemed to him that Christ and the world became indistinguishable. The vibrations of Christ's heart's radiance seemed to extend to the farthest reaches of the universe. Yet, in his vision, the individual objects maintained their individual identity. Teilhard said he could distinguish each of them. Each person and thing was somehow transformed, but none of them ever disappeared or dissolved. Finally, Teilhard's gaze was brought back to the source of their transformation, the face and heart of Christ himself.[17]

Teilhard never forgot the vision he saw that day in church. As a result, he was able to rescue devotion to the Sacred Heart from a kind of sentimentality and quasi-superstition it had slipped into over the years,[18] and reenvision it. He took the traditional devotion and integrated it into his powerful vision of the universe. In this way, he developed a mature and evolutionary devotion to the Sacred Heart.[19]

Scattered throughout his essay "The Heart of Matter," Teilhard described the Sacred Heart with various images, for example, how it gave him "a sense of the solidity of Christ…the immersion of the divine in the corporeal…a glowing core of fire…able to insinuate itself everywhere…to make love of the cosmic milieu." The Sacred Heart of Christ became for him "the alchemical vessel in which fiery transformation happens."

As Teilhard's theological vision evolved, the Sacred Heart continued to be a focal point for him. In his luminous metaphor of the Sacred Heart of Christ, Teilhard describes that Heart as the *within* of the universe. This *within*—the Sacred Heart—is the loving, compassionate consciousness of the universe that has been all-embracing since the first moment of creation.

For Teilhard, the Sacred Heart at the center of the universe reveals the *within*—the innermost being—of God the Creator. Teilhard firmly believed that the nature of God is universal, unconditional love. He came to realize that to have the experience of divine consciousness was the deepest "within" any human consciousness could attain. It would be to know the heart of God. It would be to know Omega love.

Just as God's innermost being is love, so our innermost being is love as well, for we are created in the image and likeness of God.

The challenge of Teilhard's spirituality for us is to allow our innermost being to become activated by the Spirit, and for us to learn how to guide and direct our love energy that awaits there. As we become more and more conscious of our innermost being, we are attracted more and more toward the innermost being of God.

Our human ability to think and watch ourselves think marks a major stage in awareness of our immense human "within," as Teilhard might put it. As individuals, we can learn to grow in awareness of *the within of all humanity* as we delve into literature and art (novels, biographies, plays, film, history, painting, architecture, etc.), study science, and enter into relationships and teams.

Just as we say that evolution progresses through complexity and consciousness, we could also say that evolution is moving us toward an ever-deepening, ever-richer *within*.

In the human person, for the first time in evolutionary history, consciousness became aware of its own operating system. For the first time, we could watch ourselves think, watch ourselves be attracted to others, watch ourselves have an insight, watch ourselves get angry. We became aware of our own *within*. We could also recognize the *within* of others—the inner life of other human beings, even the inner life of animals, especially our pets. This moment of reflective self-awareness was a great leap forward, an immense evolutionary event. One might say it was as significant an event as the first great leap in evolution, the formation of the first atom.

Images of the Sacred Heart typically show a perpetual flame arising from its center.[20] Fire symbolizes the burning away of our selfishness so that our basic goodness, our true nature *as love*, can shine through. The fire in the heart of God is the same fire that burns in us. That is the interior vision Teilhard wants us to develop in order to begin to grasp Omega love. That love will give us the ability to acknowledge divinity within ourselves and see our true purpose on Earth as helping achieve God's fullest vision for creation. Each of us is challenged to live each day as if we were an instrument of God's work in the world.

An early church writer declared that "our God is a consuming fire" (Heb 12:29). In this vision, divine fire becomes a purifying force that burns away our selfishness. It is the call to us who are currently centered in self to de-center and re-center our self in the Heart of Christ. Thus, we let Christ's burning heart become the fiery center of ourselves. For St. Paul, Christ becomes the source of our self-esteem (2 Cor 10:17–18).

In Christ, we do not lose our self or our self-esteem. Rather, we find it, enhanced and enriched, because we are living in Christ. Our primary spiritual practice is to turn our personal energy into compassion for others. Thus, compassion becomes a visibly productive part of our newfound self-esteem.

The prayer of St. Margaret Mary Alacoque states the connection well:

> O divine fire…consume me and I will not resist.…Your lively flames make those live who die in them.…I adore you most Sacred Heart of Jesus. Inflame my heart with the divine love with which your own is all on fire.[21]

For St. Margaret Mary, fire, which is typically associated with hell, became the fire of divine love. For Teilhard, the Sacred Heart became a divine pledge that the universe of matter will not end by fire but be reborn in it. For him, at the heart of matter was a lovingly beating world-heart, the burning heart of God. It was a heart on fire. God was manifesting divine love from and within the heart of matter.[22]

Thomas Berry, in formulating his idea of the *New Story* of creation, was much indebted to Teilhard's insights about the Heart of Christ. Thomas Berry was wont to say to his students, "You become aware that the Heart of Christ is a heart that has been beating in and through 13.7 billion years of the universe unfolding."[23] You begin to realize that we human beings connected to that Heart are literally the cells and vessels through which this Heart continues to beat into the future. We are responsible for guiding forward the energies of love.

SPIRITUAL EXERCISE:
THE *WITHIN* OF CHRIST'S HEART

Using your own imagination, try to recreate Teilhard's vision of the Sacred Heart that he saw in the painting in the church. Ask for the grace to see the breadth and depth of the *within* of Christ's Heart.

SPIRITUAL EXERCISE:
HOW MANY HEARTS CAN A HEART HOLD?

Start naming the "hearts" that your heart holds. Count them, individually. Begin with those who are currently alive on Earth. Don't forget the hearts your heart holds of those who have died. Whose hearts is God asking you to begin holding? Some to whom you are naturally attracted? Others who are not very attractive? How many hearts can your heart hold?

---

2. Loving the Eucharist

Teilhard's eucharistic understanding[24] and his evolutionary devotion to the Heart of Christ are two complementary spiritual forces of Omega love. The Heart of Christ is a force reaching *outward*, lovingly embracing and including more and more people and the world into its wide embrace, while the Eucharist is a force drawing everything *inward*, bringing people and the world closer and closer together in love. The Heart of Christ reaches *outward*. The Eucharist gathers *inward* and "assimilates to itself humanity and the entire universe."[25]

Teilhard stressed the importance and centrality of the Eucharist, but he did not put in writing important elements of his personal eucharistic spiritual life, so that we could follow his example.[26] He takes for granted that we will find our own way in this process. What he offers are his insights about the Eucharist and what it means to us today, living in an evolutionary world.

In the past, for most centuries of Christian history, no one knew that the universe—including Earth—was evolving. They believed that we lived on a relatively unchanging, but cyclical Earth that was the center of the cosmos. Earth's seasons changed, but continued in their eternal cycle. Life from one year to the next was much the same. People spent their lives avoiding sin and doing good, waiting for the day they would be called to heaven. Because nothing on Earth really changed, the eucharistic host the faithful received at the liturgy was unchanging too; it was always the body and blood of Jesus of Nazareth.

The startling awareness that we live in an evolutionary universe has forced us to rethink everything. We need to rethink the purpose of human life on Earth. We also need to rethink everything we thought we knew about Christ's incarnation, death, and resurrection. Teilhard realized we must rethink everything we believed about our human purpose and Christ's purpose. We need to reground and reenvision everything within an evolutionary purpose. To find a place to begin this rethinking, Teilhard turned to St. Paul.

Teilhard suggested that St. Paul was the first to recognize an evolutionary process happening to Christ, although Paul lacked the vocabulary to characterize it. He gave us a sense that the Body of Christ was growing and developing. Paul realized that the risen Lord was no longer just Jesus of Nazareth, but he had been transfigured; he had become a new being. In letters to his church assemblies, Paul wrote very little about Jesus of Nazareth, but rather was focused on telling them about the only Christ he knew, the Body of the risen Lord that was continually increasing in numbers and holiness. In Paul's letters, you can count on your fingers the number of times he writes about Jesus of Nazareth. In contrast, you will find over 150 references to *Christ, Christ Jesus,* or *Jesus Christ.* As Christ was continually assimilating new members to his universal Body, that Body was not staying the same; it was growing and maturing (see Eph 4:10–13).

Teilhard reflected on Paul's insight about the growing and maturing Body of Christ and realized its evolutionary implications. To emphasize the maturing nature of this process, Teilhard called it Christogenesis. It was a term to describe the evolutionary process (God's plan or strategy) for the universal Body of Christ, toward its final fulfillment in Omega (God's project). The universal Body of Christ in its human cells and members was growing, changing, and maturing day by day. Christ's Body was maturing and ripening as the human race grew and matured.

Teilhard's question was, How did this evolving process of the cosmic Body of Christ affect the eucharistic Body of Christ? While the church fathers were intent on asserting the two natures in Christ, human nature and divine nature, Paul was implying the existence of two more natures for Christ, a cosmic nature and a eucharistic nature.

When we receive holy communion today, are we still receiving no more than Jesus of Nazareth, the Jesus that lived over two-thousand years ago?[27] Or is Christ's body on today's altar *the evolving Body of the Christ who lives today?*

Which body would Christ today want us to be receiving?

Teilhard was convinced that St. Paul taught that each believer formed a part of Christ's Body, and so in holy communion, we received today's Body of Christ, the body in which we are currently living in and hope to keep on living in forever. In other words, when people in Paul's Christian communities received the Eucharist, they believed they were receiving each other as well as the living Christ, in whom we all live and move and have our being.[28]

St. John Chrysostom (344–407) reaffirmed Paul's belief, that Christ and his Body are inseparable. Chrysostom here was referring to the people of God, those who followed his way, the collective Body of believers, not the institutional church as a corporate hierarchical entity. This suggests that wherever Christ was, there was also his collective Body (his followers). Wherever his Body was, there was the eucharistic Body of Christ. Chrysostom wrote,

> Just as the head and the body constitute a single human being, so Christ and the Church [the Ecclesia] constitute a single whole....For this reason, through the Eucharist, Christ united himself intimately with us, he blended his body with ours like leaven, so that we should become one single entity, as the body is joined to the head.[29]

For Teilhard, the Body of Christ expresses the integration of all matter and spirit in creation. The Body of Christ contains the entire evolving universe that continues to change and grow and develop each day. As we continue to evolve, the Body of Christ continues to evolve. Just as our human bodies are the same, yet slightly different each day, so the Body of Christ is the same yet different each day as all of its members continue to act and interact.

If the Christ on the altar today is the evolving Body of Christ, then each day it is the same Christ on the altar, yet each day it is somehow a new Christ. Each day the Body of Christ is becoming more and more complete as well as more and more conscious of itself. That is what Teilhard could see on the altar.

Teilhard considered the entire created universe to be the eucharistic host.[30] No one before Teilhard, except for St. Paul, had ever conceived this cosmic notion of the Eucharist, saying that the Eucharist contains the entire created universe.

According to St. Paul, Christ "is the one who holds the whole building together, and makes it grow into a sacred temple in the Lord. In union with him you too are being built together with all the others into a place where God lives through his Spirit" (Eph 2:21–22 GNT). *"The church is Christ's body, the completion of him who himself completes all things everywhere"* (Eph 1:23 GNT). Paul realized that all the living things on Earth were groaning for their fulfillment in Christ (Rom 8:18–30). So the totality of the Body of Christ—even in the Eucharist—must contain all living things. They too must be part of Christ's fulfillment, his *Pleroma*.

The Eucharist has this wonderful power, so that each time people receive the Eucharist, Paul told them, they were becoming more and more assimilated into Christ's Body. In this regard, Teilhard's major realization is that *the Eucharist is daily transforming the cosmos into the Body of Christ*. Here's how Teilhard puts it: "So the sacramental host of bread [on the altar] is continually being encircled more closely by another infinitely larger host, which is nothing less than the universe itself. *The universe itself is the final and the real host into which Christ gradually descends [at mass each day] until his time is fulfilled.*"[31]

Everything that is being transformed into his universal Body is then also in his eucharistic Body.[32]

Teilhard's eucharistic vision offers us more than just a picture of Christ. It is a vision in which all human striving, whether scientific or moral—whether aimed at personal fulfillment, material advance, or sheer excellence of performance—is cosmically eucharistic. All our human effort and striving to grow and build the Earth is building the Body of Christ.

Once you realize that Christ is trying to bring all human beings to the awareness—the consciousness—that they are part of God's great evolutionary project, you realize that all your work in life makes a contribution to the evolving Body of Christ. Everything that is happening on Earth—whatever you say and do for Christ—is destined to help transform Earth and the universe consciously into Christ.

For Teilhard, the bread lifted up in the Offering at Mass symbolizes all the human effort being spent on Earth this day—all the *positive* contributions made by men and women—to build the Body of Christ, helping it take one more step toward its fulfillment—toward Omega.[33] It is up to us as the members of Christ's Body on Earth to cooperate with God's Plan in achieving this fulfillment. God's desiring the Christ to be fulfilled is what we feel as divine grace.[34] Grace in this context describes the loving inspiration we receive from God to make a positive difference in our world.

For Teilhard, the crushed grapes that make up the wine *symbolize all the suffering and diminishments each human being on Earth this day will have to endure.*[35] Some people will be harmed and crippled in accidents today, some will lose their jobs, some will get sick, and some will have to stop going to work and stay home with a sick child. Many on Earth will go hungry today; some will be rejected, some will be lonely, and some will try their best and fail. In thousands of ways, people all over the Earth today will be hurt and crushed. They will suffer and be diminished by that suffering.

It was then that Teilhard realized that this entire cosmic reality that he was consecrating when he celebrated Mass is what God consecrates every day. Just as the Holy Spirit transubstantiates the eucharistic bread and wine at Mass, so the same Spirit transforms all the bread of human effort[36] and all the wine of human suffering into the Body and Blood of God's divine Son. And God does it every day—in fact, at every moment of every day.

The words of consecration that Jesus taught his disciples to remember him by at the Last Supper were essentially the same words of consecration that God the Creator spoke at the beginning of creation, at the Big Bang. "This is my Eternal Word, my beloved Son. This is and forever will be his body and blood."

"He was in the world, and the world came into being through him; yet the world did not know him" (John 1:10).[37] But we know him; we have felt him.

"From his fullness we have all received, grace upon grace." We have known him. We have felt him (see John 1:1–18 or 1:1–5, 9–14).

SPIRITUAL EXERCISE: A GRAIN OF WHEAT

When you look at the raised host, begin to see yourself as a grain in that piece of bread being transformed more and more completely into the great Body of Christ. When you look into the cup of wine, begin to see yourself as a drop swimming in that wine, being transformed more and more completely into the great Body of Christ.

SPIRITUAL EXERCISE: A TRUE COMMUNION

As you receive Holy Communion, make it a true communion. Bring into your heart all your loved ones and those you know and care about—including your enemies—so that they can be blessed by the power of Christ. So, during communion time, bring into your heart someone who is lonely, someone who is grieving, someone who is depressed or discouraged, and someone who has been rejected. Take them into your heart and bless them.

---

3. Loving Evolution Itself

There is no question that during the past million years the human race has come a long way. We have evolved beyond the cavemen of the Stone Age, the tribes of the Iron Age, the factories of the Industrial Revolution, the computers of the Information Age, and we are now into the robots of our Space Age.

No one questions today that we enjoy unprecedented evolution in communication, transportation, medicine, education, and continual improvements in a host of other areas. Relationships on Earth have grown much more complex, but we are only slowly learning to live together in peace and cooperation in families, communities, nations, and the world.

Gratefully, there have always been pioneers and explorers willing to try something new, or to create something that never existed before their time, or to give us a new perspective on reality. Often in their efforts they fail, but often they succeed. Think of Thomas Edison in communications, the Wright brothers in flight, Einstein in physics, and so on. Teilhard in spirituality also belongs on this list. For their daring, we benefit from their discoveries, creations, and inventions. They are the creators of human evolution.

There are three basic responses to the efforts of these courageous and enterprising makers of evolution.

The first and most general response is an *appreciation of evolution*. Appreciators clearly show approval, admiration, and gratitude for advances being made. They gratefully welcome any evolutionary steps that others make. They encourage and applaud new advancement.

The second response is that of an *entitlement to evolution*. Entitled people are seldom grateful for the efforts of others, but rather take them for granted. They expect improvement and often demand it. They see it as the responsibility of others to keep making advancements that they can utilize for their own pleasure or profit. They have no desire themselves to "make a difference."

The third response is the *love of evolution*. This is the response of those willing to try anything for the betterment of humanity. It is symbolized by former President Jimmy Carter, who at the age of ninety, suffering from multiple cancer, still worked each day. He was heard to say, "My faith demands—and this is not optional—that I do whatever I can, wherever I am, whenever I can, for as long as I can with whatever I have, to try to make a difference."

In other words, when we love someone, we want the best for them. We want to see them prosper. We want them to be the best they can be. We want to make a difference in their lives. So too in the case of evolution, we want to see humanity and our planet go forward. We want to be part of it and to contribute to it. We want it to be the best it can be. We want to make a difference. As Teilhard put it, "I love the universe that surrounds me too dearly not to have confidence in it."[38]

Loving evolution, as an idea or spiritual practice, would have been "meaningless" a century ago. Teilhard insists this is a new kind of loving, characteristic of Omega love.

"The love of evolution is not a mere extension of love of God to one further object. It corresponds to a radical reinterpretation (one might almost say it emerges from a recasting) of the notion of charity."[39]

From a religious perspective, Teilhard suggests that in this radically new kind of loving, we no longer are focused principally on "saving individual souls." Rather, we use all our energy and the forces of nature to "urge on the complete and total operation of the cosmic forces in which the universal Christ is born and fulfilled in each one of us."[40]

For Teilhard, *loving evolution* becomes a unique force for helping carry out God's plan for creation. Loving evolution itself has become for him the only concrete expression of loving capable of achieving God's project, that is, of reaching Omega.[41]

Instead of the twofold commandment to love God and love our neighbor, the evolutionary commandment for Teilhard becomes, "Thou shalt love God in and through the genesis of the universe and of mankind."[42]

This new command offers an "unparalleled field of application and power" in that Omega love opens up vistas to explore and apply in transforming the world. It is a kind of loving that recharges itself and is always seeking to make things new and to give all things a dynamic energy.[43] "Love God in and through the universe in evolution." This is the constructive rule of action: to love God by loving every human being and all creatures on Earth into "forever."[44]

This perspective offers a new vision of the universe. Before now, we took our home planet and solar system for granted. We assumed that it was there for us and would always be there. It was a given. We assumed that it would continue forever providing for all our needs for our grandchildren and their grandchildren, no matter how greedy or wasteful we became. We simply consumed or used whatever we wanted, and trusted that Earth would never run out of resources or that our consumption of resources would somehow never endanger the planet. But we were wrong.

Now that we know differently, namely, that everything is evolving in Christ toward a future with God, we want evolution to keep developing toward that goal. We want consciously to be a part of that development. Keeping our planet—our common home—healthy is a crucial element in the evolutionary process.[45]

This way of thinking is very new. It offers a reverential way of relating to creation. For Teilhard, this new vision of the universe "calls for a new form of worship and a new form of action."[46] New methods of prayer and new forms of ministry are needed.

This new vision calls for us to love the universe into its fullness. We do this not merely by thinking about it or reflecting on the idea of cosmogenesis, but by making cosmogenesis (the mature development of the universe) a central point of our prayer life and a focus of our action. Teilhard asks us to love the universe—at least our small part of it—into its future success. Teilhard wants us to love the universe so much that, as Jimmy Carter said in effect, we are willing to try anything for God.

"Here we have the inner turning point, and a particularly sharp one it is, to which the general development of history has now brought us."[47] The bottom line is that we need to be more than welcoming and appreciative of advances in evolution at all levels. We need to help create and support these advances. We need to become today's trailblazers.

For Teilhard, the most important kinds of evolution toward Omega love that need to happen are growth and development in the noosphere, that is, in the mind and heart of humanity. Currently, our biggest needs are not technological advances in information, communication, and transportation, but advances that are crucial to workings of the mind and heart of humanity. These include fields like education, parenting, healthcare, friendship and teamwork, philanthropy, international relations, ecology and the environment, as well as care for the poor, the forgotten, and the marginalized. We have made marvelous improvement in information technology. What we need is significant improvement in mind-and-heart technology.

Some philanthropic groups recognize that areas like education, healthcare, and ecology are crucial for maintaining and maturing the noosphere. They devote their resources in these areas. Missing are significant advances in *ways of loving.*

We are living in an evolving universe created by a loving God. Teilhard calls it an "amorized universe." As we learn to love in more evolutionary ways, especially as one human family, it will become a universe "stimulated, *activated,* to the limit of its vital powers."[48]

There are many other kinds of spiritual energy, such as the energy spent in suffering[49] or in the basic cares of daily life. Love is the more intense form of spiritual energy that is capable of transforming all the other kinds of spiritual energy and converging them into unity.[50]

Love alone in the world can help us to release the full potentialities of our action.[51] The Divine Milieu of love in which the universe—and each of us—lives and moves is also a cosmic person, the universal Christ.

For Teilhard, we are called in love to participate with the universal Body of Christ in helping achieve Omega. We are called to love the cosmos so much that we help turn it into a living structure that is "inflexibly lovable and loving…a supreme *Someone.*"[52] *Someone,* and no longer something, is being born in the universe. Cosmogenesis is, at the same time, Christogenesis.

In the past, it was enough simply to believe and to serve. We now find that it is becoming "not only possible but *imperative* literally to *love* evolution."[53]

SPIRITUAL EXERCISE: HOW CAN WE HELP?

- Offer encouragement and support to those who are trying to make a difference. Do it as clearly as you can, by word and deed, and through your financial generosity.
- Support specifically those fields of endeavor that can most powerfully promote evolution in the noosphere.

This includes family life, community concern, education, healthcare, and the environment.

- Just as in protecting and preserving the physical health of the planet each of us can do our part in reducing our personal "carbon footprint" and cleaning up the atmosphere, so too, each of us can do our part in cleaning up the health of the mind and heart of the planet. No one can deny that the promotion of gratuitous violence, sexuality, greed, bullying, prejudice, racism, and murder in the media reflects a pollutant of our collective mind and heart. The task is not only to fight against noospheric pollution, but also support those who are helping to build up the human family.

- Follow the example of former President Jimmy Carter. If there is something you can do to build up love, compassion, friendship, teamwork, health, laughter, and joy in the world, do it. Or align yourself with others who can help you accomplish it.

SPIRITUAL EXERCISE: FUNDAMENTAL CHOICES

St. Francis of Assisi prayed, "Make me an instrument of your peace." Formulate your own fundamental choices in words such as, "I choose to be an instrument of God's love in the world," " I choose to be a instrument of healing in the world," "I choose to be an instrument of wisdom in the world," or "I choose to make a positive difference with my life."

Many Kinds of Love

AMERICANS HAVE ONLY one word for snow, but it is said that Eskimos have at least a dozen different words. They need these words to distinguish among the many different kinds of snow they must deal with in daily life—slushy snow, dry snow, powdery snow, crusted snow, icy snow, new snow, falling snow, wind-driven snow, and so on.

Americans have only one word for love, when in fact they may be referring to various kinds of love: "I love my mother. I love jogging. I love strawberry ice cream. I love my teacher. I love my dog. I love God. I love Agatha Christie mysteries. I love my work. I love babies. I love living by the lake. I love my friend. I love my teammates. I love America. I love to help people. I love shopping." And so on. Each is a different kind of love. So we probably need a dozen or more verbs to cover each specific situation where we use the verb *love*.

The ancient Greeks had at least seven different words to express seven different ways of loving.[1]

1. *Storge* (family love). This describes the affectionate love that parents have toward their children and children toward parents, as well as the love between siblings. This kind of affectionate love may be shown among all extended family members such as grandparents, aunts, uncles, cousins, and even in-laws. Family members may also show other kinds of love. Husbands and wives may become best friends (*philia*), as may two siblings. Some parents feel an unconditional love (*agape*) toward their children, especially when they are very young.

2. *Philia* (friendship love). "To the Ancients, friendship seemed the happiest and most fully human of all loves; the crown of life and the school of virtue."[2] Almost every great ancient author, Greek and Roman, wrote about friendship. Friendship bonds were well-documented among monks and others in religious life throughout the centuries.[3] Friendship love is open to everyone.

3. *Eros* (passionate love). *Eros* is what people usually refer to as romantic love or "being in love." *Eros* can occur without sexual activity. In fact, *eros* includes many other things besides sexuality. *Eros* manifests a kind of chemical attraction or biological impulse that causes people to "fall in love" and want to be together. *Eros* is exciting, magnetizing, and preoccupying. Many couples today come together because of erotic feelings, but when the intensity of these feelings wane, usually after a few years, they believe that "love" has gone out of their relationship. Our Western cultural focus is on love as a romantic relationship, where we hope to find all the different loves wrapped into a single person or soul mate. In the Near East, friendship, especially among men, is considered the most important form of love.

4. *Ludus* (playful love). This is the love that delights in things, like dancing, making music, going camping, riding the rollercoaster, playing with animals, shopping, going golfing, playing games together, and the like. We call children who enjoy playing together "playmates."

5. *Pragma* (abiding love or longstanding love). This is the deep mature closeness and understanding that develops between long-married couples. They know one another's quirks, weaknesses, and failings and continually forgive them—or don't even notice them. They know one another's likes and dislikes and accept them. *Pragma* is about making compromises to help the relationship work over time. This love shows patience and tolerance. Affectionate love (*storge*) is also a part of *pragma*, so is *philia*, including *ludus*. "The psychoanalyst Erich Fromm said that we expend too much energy on 'falling in love' and need to learn more how to 'stand in love.'"[4]

Pragma is precisely about standing in love, making the effort to give love rather than just receive it. The Greeks would encourage us to bring more *pragma* into our relationships.

6. *Philautia* (healthy self-love). The idea is that if you like yourself, respect yourself, value yourself, and feel secure in yourself, you will have plenty of love to give to others. The Buddha called this love "self-compassion." Aristotle said, "All friendly feelings for others are an extension of a man's feelings for himself." *Philautia* tells us to abandon our obsession with trying to be perfect or expecting perfection in others. Don't expect your partner to offer you all the varieties of love all of the time.

7. *Agape* (unconditional love). This love is seen as something beyond the other six more natural and human forms of love. *Agape* love is a reflection of the all-embracing, all-encompassing love of God. To love everyone and everything with *agape* love is to love the way God loves, and to love everything that God loves.

The message from the Greeks is to nurture love in its many forms and explore into its many sources. Don't look exclusively for *eros*, but develop *philia* by spending more time with friends, or explore *ludus* by reading the comics every day.

It is important to remember that Teilhard comes at love from a very different perspective. He never wrote a treatise describing the various forms of love. His insightful focus is always on love as an energy source. For him, each of the many different forms of loving is a source of energy. So whatever kind of love you are experiencing at the moment, as long as its expression is healthy and good, it is capable of helping bring about the continual improvement of the human race in helping build the kingdom of God. All forms of love have a positive evolutionary potential. God's purpose and vision has always been to produce a universe overflowing with love. That's what Teilhard would have you remember. All healthy love is a source of energy for evolution.

Notes

Epigraph (p. v)

1. *Toward the Future*, trans. René Hague (New York: Harcourt Brace Jovanovich, 1975), 86–87.

Foreword

1. Pierre Teilhard de Chardin, *Human Energy*, trans. J. M. Cohen (New York: Harcourt Brace Jovanovich, 1969), 23.
2. Teilhard de Chardin, *Human Energy*, 72.
3. Thomas M. King, SJ, *Teilhard's Mysticism of Knowing* (New York: Seabury, 1981), 104–5.
4. Pierre Teilhard de Chardin, *Christianity and Evolution*, trans. René Hague (New York: Harcourt Brace Jovanovich, 1971), 227.

Introduction

1. We are calling the fulfillment of God's final vision for creation *God's project*, Teilhard called it the *Omega Point*, based on the scriptural image that Christ was both the Alpha and Omega of creation (see Rev 1:8; 22:13). Alpha, the first letter of the Greek alphabet, symbolizes that Christ's presence and love filled creation from the beginning. Omega, the final letter of the Greek alphabet, symbolizes that Christ in all his fullness will manifest the completion of God's creative project. St. Paul called the fulfillment of God's project the *Pleroma*, a Greek term for "complete fulfillment" (see Col 1:19; 2:9; Eph 3:19; 4:13).

Chapter 1: Teilhard's Perspective on Love

1. To be fair, in 1969, Teilhard's French publishers did assemble a small white clothbound gift book titled *On Love* (English translation) with excerpts on the theme from his various writings. However, most material for this small, slim volume are excerpts from essays in a Teilhard collection called *Human Energy*. Teilhard regards love as a supreme form of human energy.

2. "The Spirit of the Earth," in *Pierre Teilhard de Chardin: Human Energy*, trans. J. M. Cohen (New York: Harcourt Brace Jovanovich, 1969), 32.

3. Ibid., 34.

4. Ibid., 33.

5. *Pierre Teilhard de Chardin: Christianity and Evolution*, trans. René Hague (New York: Harcourt Brace Jovanovich, 1971), 182.

6. Teilhard frequently quotes St. Paul in Col 1:17: "In him all things hold together." Paul also says in Acts 17:28, "In him we live and move and have our being."

7. *Christianity and Evolution*, 178–79. Teilhard also describes this ongoing evolutionary process as cosmogenesis (180); for Christians and for Teilhard, *cosmogenesis* is also *Christogenesis*, the fulfillment of all things in Christ (181). For a colorful description of Isaiah's vision of the fulfillment of God's plan for Earth, see Isaiah 65:17–25.

8. See especially Jesus' Sermon on the Mount (Matt 5—7).

9. See *Christianity and Evolution*, 160. For Teilhard, God acts "evolutively," that is, *from within*, by stimulation and enrichment.

10. This divine command of mutual love among human beings is rooted in Hebrew Scriptures and reaffirmed in Christian Scriptures. See, for example, Deut 6:5; Lev 19:18; Matt 22:36–40. However, Teilhard points out that this "connecting, grounded in the scriptures," requires a shift from a traditional metaphysics based on *esse* (being) to a metaphysics based on *unire* (uniting or connecting). See *Christianity and Evolution*, 178. This is not an insignificant switch, for it affects the basis of all our theological and moral thinking.

11. The culminating moment in the 30-day retreat of the *Spiritual Exercises* of St. Ignatius of Loyola is what Ignatius called the *Contemplatio ad Amorem*. Some have translated this Latin title ambiguously as "Contemplation for Attaining Divine Love," which could be

misunderstood as a way of getting God to love you. A clearer expression of Ignatius's intent in this contemplative experience might be "Learning to Love the Way God Loves."

12. *Christianity and Evolution*, 184.

13. *Pierre Teilhard de Chardin: Activation of Energy* , trans. René Hague (New York: Harper & Row, 1970), 379, 390.

14. Matthew Kelly, ed., *Beautiful Mercy: Experiencing God's Unconditional Love so We Can Share It with Others* (Erlanger, KY: Dynamic Catholic Institute, 2015), 5–6.

15. *The Future of Man: Pierre Teilhard de Chardin*, trans. Norman Denny (New York: Harper & Row, 1964), 245. Unfortunately, translations of Teilhard's writings into English were made before the common use of inclusive language, for example, "people" or "human beings" instead of "man" or "men."

16. Ibid.

17. For Teilhard, the universality of Attraction and Connection are natural laws that affect everything in the universe from the first moment of creation. See, for example, *Activation of Energy*, 379, 390.

18. Ilia Delio, ed., "Evolution and the Rise of the Secular God," in *From Teilhard to Omega: Co-creating an Unfinished Universe* (Maryknoll, NY: Orbis Books, 2014), 49.

19. See *Christianity and Evolution*, 22, 23, 26.

20. *Human Energy*, 145. *Activation of Energy*, 18.

21. *Christianity and Evolution*, 157–58.

22. See Augustine's *De Trinitate*, bk. 8, chap. 7.

23. See Hosea 6:6. "For I desire steadfast love and not sacrifice, the knowledge of God rather than burnt offerings." See also Teilhard in *Future of Man*, 244–45. "Only union *through* love and *in* love…can physically possess the property of not merely differentiating but also personalizing the elements which comprise it."

24. Scottish inventor James Watt (1736–1819) is credited with being the first to use fire to create steam in order to drive the steam engines that powered factories and locomotives.

25. *Human Energy*, 33–34.

26. Ibid., 158.

27. *Activation of Energy*, 375.

28. For Teilhard, from now on, spirituality is not focused on the individual "monad" but on the "dyad," or the relationship. See "The Evolution of Chastity," in *Pierre Teilhard de Chardin: Toward the*

Future, trans. René Hague (New York: Harcourt Brace Jovanovich, 1975), 71.

Chapter 2: God's Love Project

1. *Future of Man*, 94.
2. *Toward the Future*, 23.
3. "The Sense of Man," in *Toward the Future*, 23 (emphasis added). What Teilhard envisions and describes in what we are labeling "God's project" is an enrichment or development of St. Paul's theology of the "Body of Christ" and the Church's theology of the Mystical Body of Christ. In this regard, Teilhard also explores other terms to describe God's project, for example, "the immense organism we are constructing." In this context, he also invents new words such as *Christogenesis* and *cosmogenesis*. In using "genesis" in these terms, he wants to emphasize that the divine project or process is an actual and practical "work in [evolutionary] progress," rather than a mere theological concept or spiritual vision.
4. This was a fundamental insight about love from St. Ignatius of Loyola, expressed in his *Spiritual Exercises*, §230.
5. See Hosea 6:6: "For I desire steadfast love and not sacrifice, the knowledge of God rather than burnt offerings."
6. *Future of Man*, 290.
7. Ibid., 99. This is what Teilhard called the "principle of ascension and synthesis."
8. Paul Hawken, *Blessed Unrest: How the Largest Movement in the World Came into Being and Why No One Saw It Coming* (New York: Viking, 2007); and Arjuna Ardagh, *The Translucent Revolution: How People Just Like You Are Waking Up and Changing the World* (New York: New World Library, 2005).
9. For a development of the Omega Point, see Robert Faricy, *Teilhard de Chardin's Theology of the Christian in the World* (New York: Sheed & Ward, 1967), 67–72. For a development of Paul's *Pleroma* from Teilhard's perspective, see idem, 122–29.
10. See Louis M. Savary, "Expanding Teilhard's 'Complexity-Consciousness' Law," *Teilhard Studies* 68 (Spring 2014).

11. *Teilhard de Chardin: The Phenomenon of Man*, trans. Bernard Wall (New York: Harper & Row, 1959), 264.

12. "Two Principles and a Corollary," in *Toward the Future*, 159.

13. Echoing the medieval philosopher Nicolas of Cusa, Teilhard writes, "Driven by the forces of love, the fragments of the world seek each other so that the world may come into being." *The Phenomenon of Man*, 264–65. Love accounts for the "convergence of the universe upon itself" (265).

14. See Louis M. Savary and Patricia H. Berne, *Kything: The Art of Spiritual Presence* (New York: Paulist Press, 1988).

Chapter 3: Love as Energy

1. *Pierre Teilhard de Chardin: Human Energy*, trans. J. M. Cohen (New York: Harcourt Brace Jovanovich, 1969), 33. "The most telling and profound way of describing the evolution of the universe would undoubtedly be to trace the evolution of love."

2. Ibid., 38.

3. Ibid., 33. "In its essence [love] is the attraction exercised on each unit of consciousness by the centre of the universe in course of taking shape."

4. Ibid., 32. "Love is the most universal, the most tremendous and the most mysterious of the cosmic forces." And, "In its most primitive forms, when life was scarcely individualized, love is hard to distinguish from molecular forces."

5. Coretta Scott King, *My Life with Martin Luther King, Jr.* (New York: Holt, Reinhart & Winston, 1969; Avon edition), 117.

6. Theodosius Dobzhansky, "Nothing Makes Sense Except in the Light of Evolution," *American Biology Teacher* 35 (1973): 125–29.

7. Francis S. Collins, *The Language of God: A Scientist Presents Evidence for Belief* (New York: Free Press, 2006).

8. Kazuo Murakami, *The Divine Code of Life: Awaken Your Genius and Discover Hidden Talents* (Hillsboro, OR: Beyond Words Publications, 2006).

9. *Human Energy*, 129.

10. In 1949, with a grant from the Lilly Foundation, Sorokin founded the Harvard Research Center for Creative Altruism. After

retiring, Sorokin devoted his energies to its promotion. Unfortunately, for lack of funding, his center was short-lived. In 1950, Sorokin's book *Altruistic Love: A Study of American "Good Neighbors" and Christian Saints* appeared. In 1954, his book *The Ways and Power of Love: Types, Factors, and Techniques of Moral Transformation* was published. Copies of his books are likely to be found only in some older university libraries.

11. *Human Energy*, 126.

12. "The Sense of Man," in *Toward the Future*, 15.

13. "Principle and Foundation," Ignatius of Loyola, *Spiritual Exercises*, §23.

14. Before the discovery of evolution and the realization that God had created an evolutionary universe, Teilhard observed, most religions promoted escape from the world as a primary spiritual orientation, rather than involvement in the world's progress. In Teilhard's words, up until now those religious traditions have been "primarily concerned to provide every man with an individual line of escape." *Activation of Energy*, 240.

15. *Activation of Energy*, 240.

16. Although the word *salvation* occurs throughout the scriptures, it has often been given the very limited meaning of "being saved" (i.e., "Your sins are forgiven") or more often "attaining eternal life" or "getting to heaven." The Aramaic word Jesus would have used for "salvation" has a much richer connotation, as expressed by "the fullness of life."

17. Louis M. Savary, *The New Spiritual Exercises in the Spirit of Pierre Teilhard de Chardin* (New York: Paulist Press, 2010), 47.

18. See *Christianity and Evolution*, 222–24, where Teilhard also recognizes the love of *dilectio* (Latin for love based on attraction to the other), and describes it as "the most 'activating' of spiritual attractions."

19. Teilhard talks about this maturing process as a "collective drive toward 'fuller being.'" And he sees in the quickening evolution of the noosphere a "unanimous and concerted drive to reach, all together, some higher stage of life." *Christianity and Evolution*, 215.

20. For Teilhard, this "sense of species" (the human race thinking and feeling together) must happen on a "higher plane." *Christianity and Evolution*, 215. In a similar vein, Albert Einstein observed, "We

cannot solve our problems with the same level of thinking that created them." Thus, the need to reach a "higher plane" of consciousness.

21. Teilhard discusses the pattern of involution in "Two Principles and a Corollary," in *Toward the Future*, 150–53.

22. For an extended treatment of the noosphere, the "thinking envelope" surrounding Earth, see Teilhard's *Man's Place in Nature*, trans. René Hague (New York: Harper & Row, 1966), chapters 4 and 5. Also "The Formation of the Noosphere," in *The Future of Man*, trans. Norman Denny (New York: Harper & Row, 1964), 161–94.

23. "Two Principles," in *Toward the Future*, 155n. Teilhard's exact words here, typical of his "involutional" writing style, are that the cosmos is in a "process of total, multi-centric re-involution upon itself."

24. "The Evolution of Chastity," in *Toward the Future*, 86.

25. Although Teilhard never lived to experience the vast potentials of the Internet and the array of communication satellites orbiting Earth, he predicted the role they would serve: "the creation of a true nervous system for humanity; the elaboration of a common consciousness." See Teilhard's *The Vision of the Past*, trans. J. M. Cohen (New York: Harper & Row, 1966), 59–60.

26. Teilhard calls "noogenesis" the gradual maturing process of humanity specifically in its ability to use the noosphere wisely.

27. See *Christianity and Evolution*, 224.

28. This is a principle taken from Ignatius's *Spiritual Exercises* (§230) on its final, crowning exercise, The Contemplation for Attaining Love, whose purpose is learning to love the way God loves. Teilhard would have made this spiritual exercise over fifty times in his life.

Chapter 4: Relationships Are Real Beings

1. Sociology is the social science that formally recognizes the reality, identity, and personality of human groups. French philosopher Auguste Comte (1798–1857) was one of the first to define this new way of looking at society in its groupings. By the late nineteenth century, sociology had become a familiar academic program in universities that scientifically studies the behavior of social groups.

2. Frederick Perls, *Gestalt Therapy Verbatim* (Lafayette, CA: Real People Press, 1969), 4.

3. There are, of course, other possible, quite negative ways of perceiving relationships. In certain unhealthy intimate relationships, it is possible for partners to lose their identity and sense of self. In some cases, people entering a relationship can be diminished rather than enhanced. This may be the case in codependent relationships or where one or both partners are chemically addicted, schizophrenic, sociopathic, narcissistic, severely emotionally wounded, or extremely immature. We have chosen not to focus on such emotionally destructive relational problems as they remain outside the scope of this book.

4. Pierre Teilhard de Chardin, "Human Energy," an essay in *Human Energy*, trans. J. M. Cohen (New York: Harcourt Brace Jovanovich, 1969), 144.

5. Ibid.

6. Ibid.

7. Andrew A. Rooney, Foreword, in Bob Elliott and Ray Goulding, *The Bob and Ray Show* (New York: Athaneum, 1983), vii.

Chapter 5: "Union Differentiates"

1. Christopher M. Bache, *The Living Classroom: Teaching and Collective Consciousness* (Albany: State University of New York Press, 2008).

2. An explanation of "union differentiates," a common expression for Teilhard, something that appeared to be self-evident to him, can be found in many of his writings. As a start, I suggest Teilhard's *The Human Phenomenon* and a book of essays called *Human Energy*. Note that Teilhard's book *Le phénomènon humain* was originally translated into English in 1959 by Bernard Wall and titled *The Phenomenon of Man*. A well-received 2003 translation by Sarah Appleton-Weber with the gender-inclusive title *The Human Phenomenon* was published in the United Kingdom by Sussex Academic Press.

3. The emergent property principle applies at all levels of connection or union. Table salt has the emergent properties of being a seasoning for food as well as a preservative for food. Neither of the

chemicals—sodium or chlorine—has those properties; neither can lay claim to possess them.

4. These youngsters were students from the Patel Conservatory in Tampa, Florida.

5. Teilhard conceived many neologisms, like "union differentiates," concepts of processes and events happening that no one had yet coined words for. Among dozens, consider biosphere, noosphere, involution, anthropogenesis, cosmogenesis, Christogenesis, and Omega Point.

6. The concept of adultery has been reduced in our own day to having sexual intercourse with someone else's spouse. But the root meaning of adultery is an act that intends to break up a sacred union, a relationship blessed by God. Thus, a jealous mother-in-law may commit adultery by spreading gossip with the intention of breaking up a marriage between her son and daughter-in-law or between her daughter and son-in-law. In the Hebrew Scriptures, at times certain tribes were referred to as an "adulterous nation" or an "adulterous generation." This did not mean that those people were having frequent public sexual orgies, but rather that they had intentionally violated their sacred relationship with their God and were worshipping other gods. In other words, they were breaking apart a sacred union.

7. John Macmurray, *Persons in Relation* (London: Faber & Faber, 1961), 44–63. We will meet Macmurray again in the chapter on Parent-Child Relationships.

8. See, e.g., Abraham Maslow's Hierarchy of Needs, http://www.simplypsychology.org/maslow.html.

9. *Activation of Energy*, 377.

10. Ibid.

11. For an extended treatment of suffering and energy, see Savary and Berne, *Teilhard de Chardin Seven Stages of Suffering* (Mahwah, NJ: Paulist Press, 2015).

12. See his essay "Christianity in the World," in *Science and Christ*, trans. René Hague (New York: Harper & Row, 1965), 98–112.

13. Ibid.

14. Pope Francis's encyclical *Laudato Si: On Care of Our Common Home* (June 2015) focuses on how contemporary financial systems and environmental practices are negatively affecting the world's poorer people.

Chapter 6: A Higher Way for Committed Partners

1. Among those who brought Teilhard's ideas into the deliberations of Vatican II included Fathers Henri de Lubac, Jean Danielou, Yves Congar, Walter Kasper, and John Courtney Murray.

2. As early as 1936, Teilhard began developing his understanding of sexuality and his realization that the mutual love of the spouses must be "structurally essential" in the church's understanding of marriage and of the love of God. See his "Sketch of a Personalistic Universe," in *Human Energy*, especially 72ff.

3. *Catechism of the Catholic Church*, §§2362–63.

4. This essay was published in a later collection of Teilhard's essays, called *Toward the Future* (New York: Harcourt Brace Jovanovich, 1975), 60–87. It is interesting to note that, while most of Teilhard's essays were collected and published by Harper & Row in seven or eight volumes all before the mid-1960s, this essay and a number of others seem to have been left behind. They were collected and published, not by Harper, but by Harcourt, and then only in the mid-1970s.

5. "The Evolution of Chastity," in *Toward the Future*, 60.

6. Ibid.

7. Ibid., 63.

8. Ibid. Teilhard observed an irony in Scripture. While God, in the Book of Genesis, created men and women to join together and become fruitful in marriage—never mentioning chastity as a way of life—John in the Book of Revelation gives primacy of place near God's throne to those "who have not defiled themselves with women" (Rev 14:4). This attitude of sexuality as sinful is based on certain unspoken assumptions, and those assumptions are based on a traditional attitude toward the world. Throughout the history of humanity before the nineteenth century, Christians assumed they lived in a world that was basically unchanging and pervaded by sin and evil, sexuality being a preeminent source of both sin and evil. For them, this Earth merely served as a difficult and challenging testing ground for human beings to qualify for eternal life, with sexual temptations listed among the most difficult to resist.

9. *Toward the Future*, 61.

10. *Human Energy*, 34–5.

11. For a very contemporary viewpoint for singles on the distinction between chastity and mere abstinence from sexual activity, see Arleen Spenceley, *Chastity Is for Lovers: Single, Happy and (Still) a Virgin* (South Bend, IN: Ave Maria Press, 2015).

12. For those consecrated religious who choose to be a Bride of Christ, a favorite scriptural book is the Song of Songs (or the Song of Solomon), the story of two lovers yearning for each other, each desiring intimacy with the other.

13. In teaching the way that God loves, Teilhard, like Ignatius Loyola, the founder of the Jesuits, emphasizes that "love ought to manifest itself more by deeds than by words" (*Spiritual Exercises*, §230).

14. *Human Energy*, 35. Teilhard's emphasis.

15. Faricy, *Teilhard de Chardin's Theology*, 183.

16. Teilhard develops this idea of creative union in his essay "My Universe," in *Science and Christ*, 81–85.

17. For the many examples of couples used in this book, I am deeply indebted to Cornelia Jessey and Irving Sussman's *Spiritual Partners: Profiles in Creative Marriage* (New York: Crossroads, 1982), 4.

18. Charles Forbes and René de Montalembert, *Haigiography of Saint Elizabeth of Hungary*, 1839.

19. *Toward the Future*, 65.

20. Ibid., 66.

21. Faricy, *Teilhard de Chardin's Theology*, 184.

22. Jessey and Sussman, *Spiritual Partners*, 54.

23. *Toward the Future*, 68.

24. Jessey and Sussman, *Spiritual Partners*, 54.

Chapter 7: More Fully Human

1. See, e.g., *Christianity and Evolution*, 186, 205–6, 224–25.

2. "The Evolution of Chastity," in *Toward the Future* (New York: Harcourt Brace Jovanovich, 1975), 68.

3. Jessey and Sussman, *Spiritual Partners*, 88.

4. Throughout the text, we capitalize the words Attraction, Connection, Complexity, and Consciousness when they refer to one of the stages of Teilhard's evolutionary Law of Attraction-Connection-Complexity-Consciousness.

5. Jessey and Sussman, *Spiritual Partners*, 90; and Raissa Maritain, *We Have Been Friends Together* (New York: Longmans, Green and Co., 1942), 25.

6. *Toward the Future*, 69.

7. *Toward the Future*, 70.

8. Ibid.

9. Jessey and Sussman, *Spiritual Partners*, 55.

10. Ibid., 12–13.

11. Ibid., 83.

12. Ibid., 95; and Raissa Maritain, *Raissa's Journal: Presented by Jacques Maritain* (Albany, NY: Magi Books, 1974), 400.

13. *Toward the Future*, 70.

14. Ibid.

15. Before the Second Vatican Council in the 1960s, the church had consistently affirmed that the sole purpose of marriage was the procreation of children. Given that sole purpose, moral theologians argued, every act of sexual intercourse in marriage had to be open to procreation. Because of this stipulation, the use of any means that would artificially prevent conception became a violation of the solitary sacred purpose of marriage.

16. As a Roman Catholic priest, whenever Teilhard uses the word "Church," he is referring to the institution, the Roman Catholic Church.

17. *Toward the Future*, 71.

18. Ibid.

19. Jonathan Luxmoore, "Papal Letters Raise Issues around Clerical Friendships with Women," *National Catholic Reporter*, March 11–24, 2016, 10, 12. In mid-February 2016, the BBC ran a television documentary, "The Secret Letters of Pope John Paul II," written and narrated by a Catholic journalist Edward Stourton. Quotations in the text are from Stourton, except for the exact quotation from the pope's letter. Stourton had access to three decades of the pope's letters to Anna Teresa Tymieniecka in the Vatican Library, but had no access to her letters to him. She entrusted over seven hundred of them to Poland's Cultural Ministry, and its library refused to release them.

20. Wanda Poltawska wrote the book titled *Retreats in Beskidy*.

21. Jonathan Luxmoore, "Papal Letters Raise Issues," 10, 12.

22. Carl Jung, psychiatrist and depth psychologist and a contemporary of Teilhard, was very strong on the need for both men and women

to develop the major traditional qualities of the feminine psyche as well as those of the masculine psyche, if they wished to develop personal wholeness. Jung's description of the full human person is likely what Teilhard envisioned. For a fuller development of this concept, see Ann Belford Ulanov, *The Feminine: In Jungian Psychology and Christian Theology* (Evanston, IL: Northwestern University Press, 1971).

23. This notion will be treated more fully in the following chapter.

24. *Toward the Future*, 72.

25. Ibid.

26. Ibid., 73.

27. What human physiology tells us is that more than half of a person's physical body weight—Jesus' body included—is accounted for by thousands of different species of bacteria and viruses, each with their own DNA, most of which enjoy a symbiotic life with us and our own personal cells.

28. *Toward the Future*, 78.

29. Although the Roman Catholic Church did not acknowledge "mutual love of the spouses" as a primary purpose of sexual expression in marriage until Vatican II in the 1960s, Teilhard had been promoting the idea of sex as a means of "spiritual fulfillment of husband and wife" many years before. See, e.g., *Christianity and Evolution*, 144.

30. See, e.g., *Christianity and Evolution*, 183, 222; *Science and Christ*, 154, 157, 180, 182, 200; *Activation of Energy*, 264, 267, 333, 371.

31. *Toward the Future*, 77.

32. Ibid., 75.

33. Ibid.

34. Ibid., 76.

35. Ibid., 78.

36. Ibid., 80.

37. Ibid.

Chapter 8: Invisible Partners

1. "Everything in the universe is made by union and generation by the coming together of elements that seek out one another." *Writings in Time of War*, 192.

2. *Toward the Future*, 70.

3. Ibid. Teilhard's poem dedicated to the feminine principle so fascinated Teilhard's fellow Jesuit Henri de Lubac that in 1971, de Lubac wrote a book, now difficult to find, called *Eternal Feminine: A Study of the Text of Teilhard de Chardin*. You may read the poem itself in a Teilhard collection titled *Writings in Time of War (1916–1919)* (New York: Harper & Row, 1968).

4. *Toward the Future*, 70.

5. *Teilhard and Jung: Complementary Approaches to Spirituality* (lecture by Simon Cowell, London, April 12, 1997). According to Cowell, Dutch parapsychologist Dr. Michael Pobers told Teilhard's biographer Claude Cuenot of a conversation he had had with Teilhard over dinner in New York in late 1952. Pobers writes, "I was greatly impressed by his extensive knowledge and deep understanding of Jungian theory, in particular the notions of the archetype and the collective unconscious."

6. Rev. Franklin E. Vilas, "Teilhard and Jung: A Cosmic and Psychic Convergence," *Teilhard Studies* (Spring 2008): 1.

7. Although Carl Jung was writing during Teilhard's life, his psychological insights into the dynamics of unconscious masculine and feminine energies did not become popular until the 1960s, well after Teilhard's death.

8. Mircea Eliade, *Shamanism* (Princeton, NJ: Princeton University Press, 1964), 72.

9. Nicholas Berdyaev, *The Destiny of Man* (New York: Harper Torchbooks, 1960), 61–62.

10. *Toward the Future*, 70–72.

11. If Teilhard had had an opportunity to apply Jungian psychology to his evolutionary spirituality, he would have been excited to learn how invisible partners and the energy resources they provide could be taught to people.

12. This is the kind of complete human person Teilhard envisioned. For a fuller development of this concept, see Ann Belford Ulanov, *The Feminine: In Jungian Psychology and Christian Theology* (Evanston, IL: Northwestern University Press, 1971). See also John Sanford, *The Invisible Partners: How the Male and Female in Each of Us Affects Our Relationships* (New York: Paulist Press, 1980).

13. Jung's work later became popularized in books such as John

Gray's *Men Are from Mars, Women Are from Venus* (New York: Harper Collins, 1992).

14. Jung calls these various energies "archetypes." An archetype is a bundle of related unconscious energies; to each bundle of energies Jung gives a name, such as "Mother," "Companion," "Solitary," etc. For Jung, these energies reside in an area of the mind he called the "collective unconscious," in contrast to the "personal unconscious." The personal unconscious holds those energies, talents, abilities, and experiences unique to each person. In contrast, the collective unconscious holds all those energies that are common to everyone and shared collectively by everyone. Because they affect everyone, archetypes in the collective unconscious are very powerful forces; they influence individuals and communities in very powerful ways. Teilhard would have described Jung's masculine and feminine archetypes as spiritual energy resources, much as Teilhard saw love and union as spiritual energies.

15. In his essay "The Eternal Feminine," Teilhard explicitly mentions the first two feminine archetypes, the Mother and Companion (for the latter archetype, Teilhard prefers the name "Bride"). Much of Teilhard's poem is about the archetype of the Wise Woman or Wisdom (Jung's "Medium") and there is a section devoted to the archetype of the Virgin (Jung's "Solitary"). See *Writings in Times of War*, 192–95.

16. In classical Jungian terminology, these four feminine energies (or archetypes) are called *Mother, Hetaira, Amazon,* and *Medium.* See Ulanov, *The Feminine*, 193–211.

17. Jessey and Sussman, *Spiritual Partners*, 55.

18. I have chosen to use the four archetypal masculine energies (or archetypes) as listed by Toni Wolff, a close personal associate of Jung himself, to complement the four feminine energies. See Toni Wolff, *Structural Forms of the Feminine Psyche*, trans. Paul Watzlawik (privately printed for the C. G. Jung Institute, Zurich, July 1956). They are Youth (*Puer Aeternus*, Eternal Youth), Hero, Father/Counselor, and Sage. More recently in the men's movement of the 1990s in various books, writers Robert Moore and Robert Bly list the four major masculine archetypes as Lover, Warrior, King, and Magician. Unfortunately, Teilhard does not explore these masculine archetypes, since he is specifically focused on how the feminine archetypes are the main source of creativity and the flow of energy in a man.

Chapter 9: Parent-Child Relationships

1. *Science and Christ* (New York: Harper & Row, 1965), 159.

2. Ibid.

3. For Teilhard, this collective transformation will happen not only in humanity's collective "brain," but "it is in the direction and in the form of a single 'heart' that we must look for our picture of a super-mankind." See ibid., 160.

4. *Science and Christ*, 200.

5. Ibid.

6. John Macmurray, *Persons in Relation* (London: Faber & Faber, 1961). Most of the ideas here attributed to Macmurray in this chapter may be found in his chapter 2, "Mother and Child," 44–63. Teilhard would have approved of this new definition, had he lived to read Macmurray's books.

7. John Macmurray, *The Self as Agent* (London: Faber & Faber, 1961). He also revisits his argument throughout his companion book, *Persons in Relation*.

8. Teilhard develops his philosophy of action in his essay "Action and Activation," in *Science and Christ*, 174–86. He discusses our human nature's "capacity to desire and act" (174) and our "capacities and aspirations for understanding and creating" (175). Along this line, Teilhard often speaks of a natural "zest for action." See, for example, *Christianity and Evolution*, 224.

9. Macmurray, *Persons in Relation*, 17.

10. This is a paraphrase of Teilhard's thought, for example, as found in *Science and Christ*, 158–59, and elsewhere.

11. *Science and Christ*, 201.

12. In a report given to his fellow Jesuits during a study week in 1947, Teilhard encourages them to participate in such research. See "The Religious Value of Research," in *Science and Christ*, 199–205. Only much later, in the documents of Vatican II, is the entire church, including priests and religious, encouraged to engage in advanced research. For a good example of "conspiration" in the document on *The Church in the Modern World, Gaudium et Spes*, we read, "May the faithful, therefore, live in very close union with the other men of their time and may they strive to understand perfectly their way of thinking and judging, as expressed in their culture. Let them blend new sciences

and theories and the understanding of the most recent discoveries with Christian morality and the teaching of Christian doctrine, so that their religious culture and morality may keep pace with scientific knowledge and with the constantly progressing technology. Thus they will be able to interpret and evaluate all things in a truly Christian spirit" (§64).

13. *Vision of the Past*, 60.

14. Teilhard's concern would be not to confuse the philosophies of "individualism" with "personalism." For him, individualism encourages each human unit to "believe itself justified in setting itself up as a center for its own self" (*Science and Christ*, 139). In contrast, in personalism, human units "are seeking one another...striving for unity... [and] essential affinities" (142).

15. Macmurray, *Persons in Relation*, 46–50. Many of Macmurray's ideas are presented on the following pages. Teilhard would totally agree with Macmurray in defining the human being as person. See, e.g., *Activation of Energy*, 286, 325.

16. Macmurray defines an instinct as "a specific adaptation to environment which does not require to be learned." See Macmurray, *Persons in Relation*, 48. For human infants, most adaptations to environment must be taught or learned by trial and error. They are not instinctual. Teilhard would prefer to express the distinction differently: between animals who are prereflective and human beings who are reflective and, more specifically, self-reflective. Teilhard defines reflective as "the state of a consciousness which has become capable of seeing and foreseeing oneself." *Activation of Energy*, 316n.

17. *Science and Christ*, 154.

18. All these influential interactions are expression of the evolutionary law identified by Teilhard that "union differentiates." Another way of stating this law is to say that "union creates," that is, only within relationships is the uniqueness and fullness of each person created.

19. Attachment theory in psychology originated with the seminal work of John Bowlby. See M. D. S. Ainsworth, "The Development of Infant-Mother Attachment," in *Review of Child Development Research*, ed. B. Cardwell and H. Ricciuti (Chicago: University of Chicago Press, 1973), 3:1–94; and John Bowlby, *Attachment and Loss*, vol. 3: *Loss* (New York: Basic Books, 1969).

20. Teilhard does not discuss the development of the human infant in any of his writings, since his focus is much more generic.

Yet the material in this chapter fits well with his evolutionary laws of Attraction-Connection-Complexity-Consciousness and Union Differentiates.

21. Yudhijit Bhattacharjee, "The First Year," *National Geographic* (January 2015): 76.

22. Ibid.

23. Ibid., 76–77.

24. See Anthony Biglan, Brian R. Flay, Dennis D. Embry, and Irwin N. Sandler, "Nurturing Environments for Promoting Human Well-being," http://www.ncbi.nlm.nih.gov/pmc/articles/PMC 3621015/.

25. Anthony Biglan, Ted K. Taylor, "Why Have We Been More Successful in Reducing Tobacco Use than Violent Crime?" *American Journal of Community Psychology* 28, no. 3 (June 2000): 269–302; Anthony Biglan, *Direct Written Testimony in the Case of the U.S.A. vs. Phillip Morris et al* (Washington, DC: U.S. Department of Justice, 2004), see https://www.justice.gov/sites/default/files/civil/legacy/2014/09/11/20050103%20Biglan_Written_Direct_and_%20Demonstratives_0.pdf.

26. Yudhijit Bhattacharjee, "The First Year," *National Geographic* (January 2015): 58–77. The following stories and quotations were reported in the same article.

27. Teilhard might say that the human infant needs to participate in a direct human dyad to be able to learn any noosphere skills, such as language. Only later in life can a youngster recognize the "person" on the television screen or in a telephone voice, in order to be influenced by the dyadic interaction that might occur in these media.

Chapter 10: Love and Friendship

1. "Love Makes the World Go 'Round" was written in 1961 by Bob Merrill. It served as the theme song for the Broadway musical *Carnival*.

2. Hermann Buhl, *Lonely Challenge*, trans. Hugh Merrik (New York: Dutton, 1956), 292.

3. For his early letters, see Teilhard's *The Making of a Mind: Letters from a Soldier-Priest*, trans. René Hague (New York: Harper &

Row, 1979). For some letters from his later years, see Thomas M. King and Mary Wood Gilbert, eds., *The Letters of Teilhard de Chardin and Lucille Swan* (Washington, DC: Georgetown University Press, 1993).

4. Martin Buber, *I and Thou*, 2nd ed. (New York: Scribner, 1958), 3.

5. Quoted by Michael Leach in "What Organ Sees the Invisible?" in his weekly column "Soul Seeing," *National Catholic Reporter*, November 5, 2013.

6. Arthur Sheehan, *Peter Maurin: Gay Believer* (Garden City, NY: Hanover House, 1959), 91–93.

7. Although Teilhard never enunciated this fifth aspect of friendship, it is merely another expression of the law of Attraction-Connection-Complexity-Consciousness recycling upon itself. Thus, in this process, friends keep finding new levels of Attraction, which lead to deeper Connections, and so on.

8. "The Spirit of the Earth," an essay in *Human Energy*, trans. J. M. Cohen (New York: Harcourt Brace Jovanovich, 1969), 30.

9. A psychologist might categorize a grown-up that continues to believe and act in ways that say, "I am the center of the world," as having a narcissistic personality disorder.

10. David Brooks, "The Moral Bucket List," *New York Times*, op-ed page, April 11, 2015.

11. Teilhard often wrote of having a "zest for life." A Teilhard scholar, Ursula King, developed this theme in a charming essay, "The Zest for Life: A Contemporary Exploration of a Generative Theme in Teilhard's Work," in *From Teilhard to Omega: Co-creating an Unfinished Universe*, ed. Ilia Delio (Maryknoll, NY: Orbis Books, 2014), 184–202.

12. In an essay written just a few years before his death, "A Sequel to the Problem of Human Origins: The Plurality of Inhabited Worlds" (*Christianity and Evolution*, 229–36), Teilhard discusses the high probability of having at least one "human race" (self-reflective species) evolving per galaxy among billions of galaxies. Although we have not yet established the fact of such a species existing, Teilhard feels we must develop a theology that is "open to...the possibility...of their existence and their presence" (234).

13. *Human Energy*, 31.

Chapter 11: Love in Teams

1. Four and a half years of Teilhard's letters from the front lines of World War I are collected in a book, *Pierre Teilhard de Chardin, The Making of a Mind: Letters from a Soldier-Priest (1914–1919)*, trans. René Hague (New York: Harper & Row, 1971).

2. Ibid., 61, 71–73, 81–82, 104–5, 157.

3. Teilhard, in later writings, described this process as de-centering and re-centering.

4. Teilhard de Chardin, *The Heart of Matter*, trans. René Hague (London: Collins, 1978), 176.

5. The essay is titled "On Looking at a Cyclotron," in Teilhard's *Activation of Energy*, trans. René Hague (New York: Harcourt Brace Jovanovich, 1970), 347–57.

6. Ibid., 350. What he called "a phenomenon of 'second sight.'"

7. Ibid., 350–51.

8. Ibid., 351.

9. Ibid., 356.

10. Earlier, he describes what he means by the "ultra-human." When "our most firmly established categories are taken to a certain degree of intensity and concentration, they tend to synthesize into some completely new psychic reality whose nature is as yet unexplored." Ibid., 351.

11. Ibid., 352.

12. Ibid., 352–53.

13. Ibid., 353.

14. Ibid.

15. Ibid., 354.

16. Ibid., 356 (authors' emphasis).

17. Brian Swimme, "Teilhard de Chardin: An Inquiry into Group and Organizational Presence," *California Institute of Integral Studies* PARP 7005-01 (Fall 2011). See http://www.awakeningtobeing.com/.

18. Ibid.

19. See *Human Energy*, 144.

20. Teilhard, *The Activation of Energy*, trans. René Hague (New York: Harcourt, 1976), 30.

21. Ibid., 35–36.

22. Ibid., 357.

Chapter 12: A Theology of Love

1. Teilhard discusses some ideas on this theme in his unpublished 1947 essay "Suggestions for a New Theology," in *Christianity and Evolution*, 173–86. In this essay, he also assures us that "my ideas have matured" rather than his previous "provisional or incompletely worked out observations on this subject" (173).

2. The biblical material of Mosaic Law, as recounted by the Deuteronomic (D) editors of the Hebrew Scriptures, can be found principally in the Books of Numbers and Deuteronomy.

3. Teilhard notes this continuity of preoccupation with sin in a number of places. An excellent example is in "The Evolution of Chastity," *Toward the Future*, 63–64.

4. See *Christianity and Evolution*, 195. "In the case of a system which is in process of organization, it is absolutely inevitable that local disorders appear during the process."

5. While Teilhard acknowledges that Christ died "as the Lamb bearing the sins of the world," he chooses to emphasize Christ's death as "a positive element of reconstruction or re-creation" (*Christianity and Evolution*, 145). Putting together the two reasons for Christ's redemptive/evolutive death on the Cross, Teilhard describes it as "A baptism in which purification becomes a subordinate element in the total divine act of raising up the world" (146).

6. *The Divine Milieu*, 102–4. See also *Christianity and Evolution*, 225, 162.

7. "Christianity in the World," in *Science and Christ*, trans. René Hague (New York: Harper & Row, 1965), 123.

8. See Deut 6:5; 10:12–13, 20–21; 11:1.

9. See *Christianity and Evolution*, 224. Teilhard suggests that "the modern Christian" sees "the entire process of evolution as ultimately and strictly *loving and lovable*" (Teilhard's emphasis).

10. "Indeed, God did not send the Son into the world [creation] to condemn the world [creation], but in order that the world [creation] might be saved through him" (John 3:17).

11. See John 17:11–23, where Jesus repeats multiple times his prayer for the oneness of all.

12. See Augustine's *De Trinitate*, book 8, chap. 7, where he develops metaphors to describe the Trinity of divine persons. One such

relational metaphor is Father as Lover, Son as Beloved, and Holy Spirit as the Love that flows between them and outward. Although Teilhard seldom refers to the Holy Spirit, he does reflect Augustine's love metaphor when he explicitly describes Christ as the "Son-Object-of-Love." See *Christianity and Evolution*, 181.

13. We have found Teilhard's later essays, most unpublished in his day, reprinted in the last half of *Christianity and Evolution*, to be most helpful in shaping this chapter.

14. *Christianity and Evolution*, 222, where Teilhard identifies both "molecular and atomic *attractions*" and, in human beings, "consciousness in the form of *attractions*" (Teilhard's emphasis).

15. Ibid., 194n.

16. Ibid., 204.

17. Teilhard frequently describes this evolutionary love process as "anthropogenesis," the ever-fuller development of the human family. See, for example, ibid., 161 and 175, where he describes "an innate, tumultuous upsurge of cosmic and humanist aspirations."

18. Teilhard sometimes describes this drive as "man's zest for action." See ibid., 224–25.

19. Ibid., 208, where God's Plan is "to renew the atmosphere of the universe and to 'amorize' evolution."

20. "Then God said, 'Let us make humankind in our image, according to our likeness'" (Gen 1:26).

21. See Teilhard's descriptions of the Trinity, the historic Christ, and Revelation in ibid., 157–60.

22. See ibid., 160n, where Teilhard says, "God never acts except evolutively," and 179.

23. See ibid., 178–79. Remember that in static-world theology, metaphysics was traditionally based on the concept of *esse* (being). For a world evolving in love, Teilhard insists, metaphysics must be based on the concept of *unire* (union, or Connection). Only through Attraction and Connection can growth in Complexity and Consciousness occur.

24. By the law that Union Differentiates. The dynamics of this law were discussed in chapter 4.

25. See *Christianity and Evolution*, 179. Scripturally, the cosmic Christ (who is divine) is constantly being "differentiated" (or "built up") by the actions and interactions of the beings that belong to that cosmic body. See 1 Pet 2:5; Col 2:7; Eph 2:22; 4:6. In *Christianity and*

Evolution, 227, Teilhard envisions the goal of God's project, or Paul's *pleroma* (see Eph 4:13; Col 2:10), as "the mutual completion of the world and God."

26. While animals and plants may not be capable of intellectual or spiritual activity, they are self-expressive in their own ways.

27. *Spiritual Exercises of St. Ignatius*, trans., George E. Ganss, SJ (St. Louis, MO: Institute of Jesuit Sources, 1992), §230. Teilhard would have "made" the Spiritual Exercises annually during his entire Jesuit life, thus, at least fifty-five times! So this expression of "love as action" would have permeated his spirituality. See the entire essay, "The Contingence of the Universe and Man's Zest for Survival," in *Christianity and Evolution*, 221ff.

28. *Spiritual Exercises of St. Ignatius*, §231. This mutual sharing of mind and heart among human beings is what continually moves the evolutionary process forward. For Teilhard, this second truth describes the energy behind the evolution of the noosphere.

Chapter 13: Omega Love

1. For Teilhard, the Omega Point represents the "spiritual peak" and complete fulfillment of creation. If you asked Teilhard for a definition, he would say that Omega represents "the complex unit in which the organic sum of the reflective elements of the World become irreversible within a transcendent Super-ego" (*Heart of Matter*, 39).

2. For St. Paul, the *Pleroma* will occur when Christ is all in all. See Col 1:15–20; 2:9–10; Eph 1:9, 23; 4:13.

3. Teilhard called the long process of the evolution of humanity *anthropogenesis*. See, for example, *Activation of Energy*, 168, 210, 328. Anthropogenesis is a process of "collective reflection that is beginning to grow vertically in the noosphere…[toward a] hitherto hidden pole of a unification both organic and mental" (328).

4. This is a major theme in his spirituality book, *The Divine Milieu*.

5. For Teilhard, "Christ is Identical with Omega." That is the title of a section of his essay called "My Universe," in *Science and Christ*, 54–56. His footnotes on page 54 offer an exhaustive list of scriptural references from St. Paul's writing in this regard. See also *Activation of Energy*, 381.

6. "The grandest and most necessary attribute we can ascribe to him [Christ] is that of exerting a supreme physical influence on every cosmic reality without exception" (*Science and Christ*, 56–57). For Teilhard, Christ is the Attractor, the Evolver, and the universal Center of all. See *Science and Christ*, 170; and *Heart of Matter*, 54–55.

7. *Paroxysm* is defined as "a sudden attack or violent expression of a particular emotion or activity." Teilhard felt this was an appropriate descriptor for the passionate burst of love and activity involved in the loving unions and final Union in Christ that would characterize Omega.

8. In other places, he describes the Omega moment as "an explosion of dazzling flashes" and "a general global conflagration" of mutual love. See *Heart of Matter*, 50.

9. The human biome refers to the aggregate of microorganisms that live in the human body, mostly in the digestive system, but also on the surface and in deep layers of our skin. Because we currently know very little about the biome, the United States National Institutes of Health instituted the Human Microbiome Project (HMP), with the goal of identifying and characterizing the microbiota in human beings, both healthy and sick. Some additional evolutionary facts about the human biome in the fossil record may be found in "Gut Reaction" by Adam Hadhazy in *Discover Magazine*, September 2015, 66–69. Republished as "Uncovering Our Ancestral Microbiomes," February 2016. See http://discovermagazine.com/2015/sept/18-gut-reaction.

10. Teilhard's mystical gift—seeing the universe in all its multiplicity existing in a united whole bound together by divine love—is not unique. Versions of it have been noted in the mystics of many different religions. A number of American writers around the turn of the twentieth century were exploring and researching these special experiences, including Robert M. Bucke's *Cosmic Consciousness* (1901) and William James, *The Varieties of Religious Experience* (1902). It is exemplified in the poem *Leaves of Grass* (1852) by Walt Whitman. Teilhard's difference was that he wanted to find a way to invite everyone into this experience.

11. *Heart of Matter*, 15–16, 44, 47.

12. Teilhard refers to "an inflexible law of a Universe in which nothing is produced or appears except *by way of birth*" (*Heart of Matter*, 54).

13. Ibid.

14. See ibid., 41.

15. Teilhard describes this process in vivid detail in ibid., 40–44.

16. Actually, the account is told in the form of a short story Teilhard wrote of a man having a vision. It seems safe to assume the man in the story was Teilhard himself.

17. See Robert Speaight, *The Life of Teilhard de Chardin* (New York: Harper & Row, 1967), 79. You may read the entire account in full detail in the appendix to Teilhard's essay "The Heart of Matter" in the collection called *The Heart of Matter*, 61–67.

18. *Heart of Matter*, 43.

19. "What…attracted him to the Sacred Heart was its symbolic power and its superhuman appeal—the discovery 'in you of an element even more determinate, more circumscribed, than your humanity as a whole.' The Sacred Heart…was for Teilhard a means of devotional escape from whatever was 'too narrow, too precise, and too limited' in the traditional image of Christ" (Speaight, *Teilhard De Chardin: A Biography* [London: Collins, 1967], 128).

20. "…a fire with the power to penetrate all things" (*Heart of Matter*, 47).

21. *The Letters of St. Margaret Mary Alacoque: Apostle of the Sacred Heart*, trans. Fr. Clarence A. Herbst (1954; repr., Charlotte, NC: Tan Books, 1997).

22. *Heart of Matter*, 15.

23. Thomas Berry, *The Christian Future and the Fate of the Earth*, ed. Mary Evelyn Tucker and John Grim (Maryknoll, NY: Orbis Books, 2009). Thomas Berry was explicit in placing his vision in the lineage of the cosmic Christ, found in St. John's Gospel, the writings of St. Paul, Thomas Aquinas, and Teilhard. Yet even while placing his vision in this Christian lineage, Berry understood that "Cosmic Person" was a shared religious concept, differentiated to be sure in each religion, but nonetheless present in the religions of the world.

24. The principal eucharistic passages in Teilhard's writings are the following: "The Mass on the World" (1923); section II-c of "My Universe" (1924); section III-2 of *The Divine Milieu* (1927); section III-7 of "Introduction to Christianity" (1944).

25. "Christ can reach Omega only by assimilating into himself all that surrounds him. That includes us and the entire universe. That is why we eat the communion bread—to be assimilated into him" (E. Benz, *Evolution and Christian Hope*, trans. H. Frank [Garden City, NY: Doubleday, 1966], 225). This same idea is developed in a number of

places. See, for example, Henry de Lubac, *The Religion of Teilhard de Chardin*, trans. R. Hague (New York, Image Books, 1968); or Georges Crespy, *La pensée théologique de Teilhard de Chardin* (Paris: Universitaires, 1961), 85n12.

26. Teilhard's "Mass on the World" is perhaps the clearest example of his eucharistic devotion. The text of this mass is easily accessed by googling "Teilhard's Mass on the World."

27. The church fathers affirmed that all the events that happened to the historical Body of Christ are reflected in the sacramental body on the altar. Therefore, for them, the incarnation is reflected in the Eucharist on the altar, so is the nativity, so is the public life of Jesus, his passion, death, and resurrection, and the Christ in glory at the right hand of the Father. For example, it is said that St. Augustine and St. Athanasius both liked to envision in the consecrated host the baby Jesus in the manger at the nativity. For Augustine, every mass was a celebration of Christmas. Other fathers (see Justin Martyr, *Apol.* I, 66; Irenaeus, *Adv. Haereses*, V, 2) describe the eucharistic consecration at mass as the descent of the Word of God on the altar through an *overshadowing* by the Holy Spirit. Notice that word *overshadowing*. It was by the overshadowing of the Holy Spirit that the Word of God formed for himself a body in the womb of the Blessed Virgin. They saw the same kind of overshadowing happening in the Eucharist on the altar.

28. Both St. Augustine and St. Leo the Great identified the growing Body of Christ with the Eucharist. Augustine wrote, "The many of us are one bread and one body."

29. John Chrysostom, *Homilies on the Epistles to the Corinthians* 24.1–2 (PG 61:199–201).

30. As he describes it in his essay "My Universe," in *Science and Christ*, 65. See also *Christianity and Evolution*, 73.

31. See the essay "My Universe," in *Heart of Matter*, 201ff.

32. See *Science and Christ*, 65–66. Teilhard finds a strong basis for this in St. Paul: "Through [the Son] God was pleased to reconcile to himself all things, whether on earth or in heaven, by making peace through the blood of his cross" (Col 1:20).

33. As the priest offering the bread says, "The bread we offer you [is the] fruit of the earth and *work of human hands*, it will become for us the bread of life."

34. *Science and Christ*, 57.

35. As the priest offering the wine at mass says, "We have this

wine to offer, fruit of the vine and work of human hands. It will become our spiritual drink."

36. As the priest offering the bread at mass says, "The bread we offer you: fruit of the earth and work of human hands, it will become for us the bread of life."

37. "In the beginning was the Word, and the Word was with God, and the Word was God. He was in the beginning with God. All things came into being through him, and without him not one thing came into being" (John 1:1–3).

38. "My Universe," in *Science and Christ*, 41.

39. *Christianity and Evolution*, 184.

40. Ibid., 184.

41. Or in Teilhard's own words, "…carrying to its term the effort of planetary self-arrangement on which depends the cosmic success of mankind." See "My Universe," in *Science and Christ*, 41.

42. *Christianity and Evolution*, 184.

43. Ibid., 184. In this way, we unite with Christ, we communicate (or super-communicate) "with him (without fusion or confusion — for as love unites its terms, so it differentiates and personalizes them) through all the height, the breadth, the depths and the multiplicity of the organic powers of space and time."

44. *Activation of Energy*, 266.

45. Caring for our common home is the central theme of Pope Francis's encyclical *Laudato Si: On Care for Our Common Home*, 2015. It is the first encyclical in papal history on ecology and the environment.

46. *Activation of Energy*, 41.

47. Ibid., 267. We are in "a remarkable and specifically favored phase of a movement whose crucial step, at a given moment, consists in becoming conscious of—and taking responsibility for—itself" (268).

48. Ibid., 266.

49. See Louis M. Savary and Patricia H. Berne, *Teilhard de Chardin Seven Stages of Suffering* (New York: Paulist Press, 2015).

50. "…as one might expect in a universe built on the plane of union and by the forces of union" (*Christianity and Evolution*, 186).

51. *Activation of Energy*, 266.

52. Ibid., 266.

53. *Christianity and Evolution*, 184.

Appendix: Many Kinds of Love

1. For a fuller development, see Roman Krznaric, *How Should We Live? Great Ideas from the Past for Everyday Life* (Katonah, NY: BlueBridge, 2011).

2. C. S. Lewis, *The Four Loves* (New York: Harcourt Brace, 1960), 87.

3. For a development of forms of friendship among Christian consecrated religious through the twelfth century, see Adele M. Fiske, "The Survival and Development of the Ancient Concept of Friendship in the Early Middle Ages" (unpub. diss., New York: Fordham University, 1955).

4. See www.yesmagazine.org/happiness/the-ancient-greeks-6-words-for-love-and-why-knowing-them-can-change-your-life.

Index

Friendship, 41–42, 45, 51, 53, 84, 94, 99, 135–48, 149, 200, 221n7

God: Attraction, 10–11; and chastity, 74–76, 79, 80, 83, 91–92, 97; Connection, 27–28, 61; and conspiration, 121; Creator, 4–5, 192; and energy, 22, 24; and evolution, 88, 143, 194–95; and feminine, 99–100, 103; forgiveness, 166; as love 24, 26, 128, 142–43, 163–64; 169–78, 185–86, 187, 194–95, 201; as lover 166–68; love energy of 6–7, 9, 66; Omega Point, 180, 181; purification, 81
God's project, 14–21, 23, 29, 30, 38, 64–65, 67, 77, 95, 96, 98, 118, 154, 179, 182, 189, 191, 203n1 (introduction), 206n3, 224n25. *See also* love: divine; kingdom of God; Omega Point

Holy Trinity, 11, 41, 171, 172–73, 223n12

Ignatius Loyola, St., 41. See also *Spiritual Exercises*
Involution, 34–36, 209n21, 211n5

Jesus Christ, 189
John, St. (Evangelist), 6, 26, 65, 100, 163, 169, 172, 177, 227
John Paul II, Pope (Karol Wojtyla), 89, 91, 111; friendship with Anna Teresa

Tymieniecka, 89–90
Joyce, James, and Nora Joyce, 8, 20, 106, 111

Kingdom of God, 15, 30, 63, 76, 77, 182, 201

Love: as cosmic force, 3, 194, 207n4; of creation, 4, 65, 170, 173; as creative, 6, 65, 77, 171; divine, 6, 14, 26, 34, 135, 170, 174, 179, 187; as driving force of evolution, 5, 11–13, 24–26, 38, 149, 201; as energy, 4, 11, 17, 31, 97, 98, 187; human, 3, 64, 73, 74, 78, 94, 128, 135; law of, 5, 19–20, 26, 34–35, 38; learning to, 5, 7, 28, 140, 163, 175, 181; mutual, 72, 94, 204n10, 212n2, 215n29, 226n8; and natural laws, 8, 65; as nature of God, 6, 170, 185; and the physical body, 74; purification of, 81–82; qualities of, 26, 171–72; and religion, 5, 28, 35, 66, 79, 180, 226n10; sexual, 72; and supreme marriage, 75–76, 78–80; unconditional, 5–7, 9, 18, 65, 126, 128, 163, 168, 173, 177, 179, 181, 185, 199, 201; ways of loving, 199–201. *See also* agape; charity; chastity; creation; friendship; God's project; John, St.; Paul, St.

Macmurray, John, 61, 120–21, 122–23, 125, 218nn15–16

Index

Maritain, Jacques, and Raissa
    Maritain, 84, 85, 87, 91, 97, 107
Marriage: chastity, 73, 78–80,
    97, 212n8; and evolution,
    71–72, 91, 94; and feminine,
    86, 87–88; fully human,
    84; individualist, 43–44;
    mutual, 99, 145, 212n2,
    215n29; procreation, 214n15;
    romantic, 42; supreme, 75–76,
    78–80; Third Self, 45, 46–48
Maurin, Peter. *See* Day, Dorothy
Murakami, Kazuo, 24, 36

Omega Point, 14, 15, 18, 179–80,
    203n1 (introduction), 225n1

Paul, St., 12, 14, 18, 26, 142, 169,
    172, 179, 180, 188–90, 203n1
    (introduction), 206n3, 225n2,
    228n32
Pleroma. *See* Omega Point

Relationships: Attraction and
    Connection, 20, 27; energy,
    106, 138; evolution, 12, 31, 36,
    37, 38, 61, 219n18; God, 171–
    73; higher, 145; individualist
    perspective, 42–43, 44; inner
    union, 99, 102; love, 26, 28,
    54, 82–83, 84; negative, 210n3
    (chapter 4); parent-child,
    117–34; as real beings, 39–52;
    romantic perspective, 42; self-
    development, 91; spirituality,
    13, 30, 92; Third Self, 44–48,
    49–50, 54, 85, 86, 90, 139,
    145, 150, 152; youth
    energy, 115

Religion, 4, 17, 100, 164,
    208n14, 227n3

Salvation, 27, 29–30, 32, 38, 61,
    62, 63, 165, 168, 208n16
Second Vatican Council, 72,
    87, 88, 212, 214n15, 215n29,
    218n12
Sin, 99, 170; emphasis on
    avoiding, 16, 28, 63, 95; in
    Jewish-Christian tradition,
    164–66, 212n8; sorrow for, 81
Spiritual Exercises, 27, 30, 174–
    76, 204n11, 206n4, 209n28,
    213n13
Spirituality: energy, 22–23,
    216n11; evolution, 5, 18,
    27, 62–63, 88, 109, 193;
    individual, 20, 27–30, 32, 38,
    43; infancy, 119; innermost
    being, 185; relationship,
    13, 20, 49–50, 52, 205n28;
    science, 60; traditional, 62,
    91–92, 96

Teilhard de Chardin, Pierre: and
    anthropogenesis, 183, 211n5,
    224n17, 225n3; and Carl
    Jung, 100–103, 113, 214n22,
    216n7, 216n13, 217n14; and
    Christogenesis, 183, 189, 196,
    204n7, 206n3, 211n5; and the
    Church, 71, 72, 88, 142, 143,
    214n16; and the cyclotron,
    152–54, 155, 156, 157; and
    the Divine Milieu, 179, 196;
    Divine Milieu, The (writing),
    182, 225n4; and the
    Eucharist, 183, 188–92,

233